AF556096

First Published, 2016

ISBN 978-93-83723-10-2

Published by
LG PUBLISHERS DISTRIBUTORS
49, Gali No. 14, Pratap Nagar
Mayur Vihar Phase I, Delhi 110 091
Tel : 011 2279 5641 email: lgpdist@gmail.com

Printed at
Sapra Brothers, Delhi 110 092

Contents

List of Boxes, Figures, Maps and Tables

Preface

The British annexed Punjab in 1849 and introduced many institutional and structural changes in the economy of the region.

The most remarkable change was introduced in the land system; the earlier Mughal/Sikh system of land revenue in the form of share of crops was replaced by the fixed cash rent system. These changes destabilised the old village community and the village cottage industry gradually disappeared. The traditional Jajmani/Sepi system was gradually replaced by cash exchange between the artisans and farmers. The disintegration of cottage industries compelled the former artisans to become agricultural labourers. Further, the number of this class was swelled by the peasants who became landless owing to the cash rent system in agriculture. The colonial period documents show that in Punjab from the late 19th century onwards a class of landless agricultural labourers emerged and grew rapidly. These developments created two types of agricultural labourers; casual agricultural labourers who were hired on a daily basis, and permanent farm servants who were hired for the whole year. The pattern of employment and wages of these labourers differed considerably in different regions of Punjab. The majority of these agricultural labourers were from the scheduled castes and other lower castes who were earlier doing skilled artisan work. The vast non-uniformity prevailed in their nomenclature, pattern of employment and wages within a state. In the post-green revolution period, the agricultural labour markets in Punjab changed completely. The prevalence of the traditional 'patron-client' relationships in agricultural labour markets came to an end. In place of that earlier system, a new class of cash wage agricultural labourers emerged and became dominant.

Of the two types of agricultural labourers existing in Punjab, economists have studied the impact of the green revolution on the employment, wages and working conditions of casual agricultural labourers. The permanent farm servants have been largely neglected and have been studied only as a by product of work on casual labour.

The significance of the permanent farm servants in the commercial agriculture especially on the big farms has been accepted all over the world. In Punjab, the permanent farm servants are hired by big farmers for responsible farm operations like spraying of chemicals on crops, etc. But no one has tried to study the practice of the hiring of permanent farm servants and other working conditions in Punjab.

This present book which is the revised version of my Ph.D. thesis has incorporated the growth, emergence, working conditions and wages of the local and migrant permanent farm servants in Punjab. Finally, the relevant policy implications were given to strengthen the skills of permanent farm servants along with the various social welfare and protection policies for this class of agricultural labourers.

Varinder Sharma

Acknowledgements

This book is a revised version of my Ph.D. thesis. I am thankful to Prof. H.S. Shergill and Prof. J.S. Brar who supervised my thesis meticulously and encouraged me to revise it to publish in a book form.

From the beginning of my research on the permanent farm servants in Punjab upto the completion of this book, I have many memories in mind. At several seminars and lectures I discussed this issue of farm labour with Prof. (late) G.S. Bhalla, Prof. Randhir Singh, Prof. M.K. Khurana, Prof. S.S. Gill and Prof. Ranjit Singh Ghuman, they all gave me useful suggestions and guidance. During the periods of stress and strain, Prof. Lakhwinder Singh, Prof. Ronki Ram, Prof. Sukhwinder Singh, Prof. Manjit Singh and Prof. Gurmail Singh gave me moral support and useful insights of the farm labourers' problems in Punjab.

My special thanks are to Dr. Pramod Kumar, Director, Institute for Development and Communication (IDC), Chandigarh, who not only allowed me to work on this theme while working full time in the IDC, but also actively encouraged me to publish it in book form.

I also acknowledge the leaders of farm workers' unions, farm labourers and farmers who spared time for interviews even during their resting hours. The villagers of surveyed villages provided me even shelter and food during field surveys. I am indebted to them.

The help of the library staff of Panjab University, Chandigarh, Punjabi University, Patiala, Jawaharlal Nehru

University, New Delhi is specially acknowledged. The archive section of the World Bank, Washington, ILO, Geneva and National Archives, New Delhi provided me the rare documents on permanent farm servants and deserve special thanks.

The library staff of the IDC, Chandigarh is also acknowledged.

I am also grateful to my friends, colleagues and family members who encouraged me to complete this book.

Varinder Sharma

1

Introduction

The green revolution agricultural technology resulted in far-reaching changes in production, productivity, working conditions, farm incomes and income distribution in rural Punjab. The production relations in the agricultural sector also underwent considerable change under the impact of new technology and the commercialization of agriculture unleashed by it. Traditionally, the division of labour in the villages of Punjab was caste-based. The menials from the lower castes generally worked as agricultural labourers for the land owners. The land owners used to pay wages to the labourers for this work in kind. The landowners and landless were mutually dependent on each other. Such traditional 'patron-client', relationships, between farmers and farm labour almost disappeared with the coming of the green revolution. The class of cash wage agricultural labourers emerged at a fast rate with the development of commercial agriculture. The various perks which were earlier provided to the agricultural labourers disappeared and cash payment for labour work became the rule. The use of hired labour, relatively to family labour, also increased at a rapid rate. As a result, the number of male agricultural labourers working on farms in Punjab grew almost fourfold, from 3.19 lakh in 1961 to 11.04 lakh in 2001.[1] The hired labourers constituted only 17.8 per cent of all male agricultural workers (cultivators plus agricultural labourers) in 1961 but rose to 39 per cent by 2001.[2]

With the rise of this new agricultural labour class, the question of their wage rate and working conditions emerged as an important issue for policy makers and researchers. However, most of the studies conducted by scholars on agricultural labour in Punjab are almost exclusively on the wage rates and employment of casual agricultural labourers. The question of wage rate and working conditions of permanent agricultural labourers or attached farm servants has been virtually ignored by scholars. This is surprising as permanent farm servants constituted almost one-third of hired agricultural labour used on Punjab farms at the beginning of the green revolution, and even now about one-fourth of hired labour used in Punjab agriculture is of permanent farm servants. The green revolution technology not only increased the demand for hired labour, but also changed the composition of hired labour used on Punjab farms. The standardization of many farm operations with the spread of the green revolution technology increased the demand for daily wage labourers. On the other hand, the tractorization of Punjab agriculture and spread of power operated tubewells increased the demand of the skilled permanent farm servants. On the whole the demand for daily wage labour (casual labour) increased relatively more than that of permanent farm servants and, as a result, the proportion of permanent farm servants labour in total hired labour used on Punjab farms decreased from one-third in the early 1970s, to one-fourth by the middle of the first decade of the 21st century.[3] So the green revolution not only increased agricultural productivity, but also resulted in a significant change in the labour structure on Punjab farms. The demand for hired farm workers grew at a faster rate than the pool of local rural labourers. As a result of this demand-supply gap in the agricultural labour market, a large influx of migrant agricultural labour from eastern India occurred in Punjab since the beginning of the green revolution. The estimates of the number of migrant labourers in Punjab agriculture (in 2007); vary from 4.21 lakh in the lean period and 8.42 lakh in the peak season [Sidhu et al., 2007].[4] Although the migrant agricultural labourers typically work as casual labourers in the peak season, but some of them have also started working as permanent farm servants on a full year contract.[5]

From their very emergence in the last decades of the 19th

century the modern agricultural labourers in Punjab have taken two distinct forms or types: the casual labourer who works on a daily cash wage basis, and the permanent farm servant who works on a full year contract, mostly in cash but sometimes also in terms of share of the produce. As mentioned earlier, the wage rates and working conditions of permanent farm servants have been somehow ignored by most researchers on agricultural labour in Punjab. On account of that gap in the literature the focus of this book is on permanent farm servants working on Punjab farms. For reference and clarity purposes these two types of hired agricultural labourers working in Punjab agriculture are briefly described:

(i) Casual Labour: The casual labour is hired either on a daily cash wage or to do a definite piece of work for a fixed amount of cash. In the case of this type of labour, neither is the labourer under any obligation or binding to work for the same employer next day, nor is the farmer bound to provide him with work every day. Most of these casual labourers are hired to do peak season, standardized and routine farm operations. These casual labourers probably come nearest to the Marxist concept of 'Free Wage' labour. Being a daily wager a casual labourer has minimal little interest and commitment to production and productivity of the farm.

(ii) Permanent Farm Servants: The permanent farm servants are hired on a yearly basis and work on the farm throughout the year on a regular basis. There are two types of contract on which permanent farm servants are hired: the cash wage contract and the share wage contract. In the former the permanent farm servant gets a fixed cash amount for the whole year's work, and in the latter he gets a share in the produce of the farm, after the deduction of cost of material inputs. In the pre-green revolution days, the share wage-based permanent farm servant was the dominant type, but this type has virtually disappeared under the impact of the green revolution. However, in the cotton belt of Punjab, the share wage contract still prevails, although even there it seems to be on the way out. A permanent farm servant is hired by the farmer for the duration of an agricultural year, i.e. from June to May. The wage rate and terms of contract are partly explicit (even written sometimes), and partly implicit. Normally the permanent farm servants are hired by the big farmers, although some medium and small farmers may also sometimes hire permanent farm servants. The annual wage or share of the permanent farm servant is mutually determined between the farmer and the worker. The permanent farm servants are usually entrusted with the more important agricultural tasks like tractor driving, motor-operated tubewell operations, supervision of casual labour, spray of insecticides/ pesticides on the farms, etc. The permanent farm servants are relatively more committed to the farm; because their regular interaction with employers results in the development of personal relations. The permanent farm servant often eats with the employer and may even live on the farmer's premises. He also gets various pecuniary and non-pecuniary benefits from his employer (farmer). Many permanent farm servants take part of the wages in advance from their employers. Some of them also borrow money from their employers. This results in creating a sort of personal bond between permanent farm servants and their employers.

In the literature on agricultural labour in Punjab one comes across very few studies on employment, wages and working conditions of the attached or permanent farm servants. There can be many reasons for this neglect of permanent farm servants by researchers. The most important seems to be that data on the employment, wages and working conditions of permanent farm servants is not usually available in the secondary sources. In the first and second rural labour enquiry reports during the 1950s, the agricultural labour was divided into casual and attached labour. Some scholars severely criticized such demarcation; as a result of that statistical authorities stopped collecting information on permanent farm servants and casual labour separately. The permanent farm servants are also normally less unionized compared to casual labourers, and on account of that do not arouse the interest of left-oriented researchers. Even their categorization as free agricultural workers, in the Marxist sense, is considered to be problematic by some researchers. Their relations with the farmers are thought to be somewhat feudalistic and bonded labour type. That is why one finds virtually no study on the wages and working conditions of permanent farm servants in Punjab. On the other hand, on the wages and working conditions of casual labourers, there are many studies. This is a serious gap in research in view of the importance of permanent farm servants in Punjab agriculture.

The importance of permanent farm servants in Punjab agriculture is likely to increase in future as most of the peak season operations get mechanized and for other farm operations the technical skill level increases. The skilled operations on the farms can be efficiently performed only by permanent farm servants and cannot be entrusted to daily wage labourers. Keeping in view this gap in the literature, the present study was planned and focused solely on the wages and working conditions of permanent farm servants employed on Punjab farms. In view of the non-availability of secondary data on wages, and working conditions of permanent farm servants, the present book is mainly based on primary data collected by the author himself, though some secondary information is also used. The methodology, data, sample design and location of sample villages in a map have been given in the appendix in Chapter 1. An effort is made to picture the level and pattern of wage rates of permanent farm servants and to find out the main determinants which explain the considerable variations in the wage rate of permanent farm servants observed in real life.

Earlier Studies

There are very few direct and explicit studies on permanent farm servants in India. The focus of most of the studies on farm labour has been on casual agricultural labourers. The permanent farm servants have been studied only along with the casual agricultural labourers and as a minor category. Here we reviewed some of the relevant studies to find out the existing evidence on the wages, employment and working conditions of the permanent farm servants in India and Punjab.

Wages of Permanent Farm Servants

Manabendu Chattopadhay[6] in his study compared the wage rates of casual hired labourers and annual permanent farm servants. He used the Farm Management Studies data for the years: 1954-55 to 1958-59 and 1968-69 to 1970-71. He compared the daily wage rates of casual labourers and permanent farm servants and concluded that yearly earnings and daily wages of permanent farm servants were higher in advanced agriculture states like Punjab, Kerala, Uttar Pradesh and Andhra Pradesh. On the other hand, daily wage rates of casual labourers were higher in less developed agriculture states like Orissa, Assam and West Bengal.

Gurmukh Singh and Nirmal Singh[7] in their study highlighted the impact of the green revolution on the structure, composition and wage structure of permanent hired labourers in different agro-climatic zones of Punjab on the basis of 1974-75 data. They divided Punjab, into six zones, i.e. paddy zone, paddy-maize zone, maize zone, maize groundnut zone, cotton-bajra-maize zone and cotton-bajra zone. Out of the total sample of 225 permanent farm servants, 132 were working as cash wage permanent farm servants, 39 were getting payments in kind, and the remaining 54 worked as sharecroppers or 'siris'. The permanent farm servants under various systems of payments also got perquisites in addition to cash payment and share of crops. Under the cash wage system the average money wage of permanent farm servants was estimated at Rs. 2,494.20 per year; under the kind wage system, the average wage earned came to Rs. 2,523.29. On the average a share wage permanent farm servant earned Rs. 2,523.29. On the average a share wage permanent farm servant earned Rs. 3,412.53, out of which 87.03 per cent was in the form of share of produce and 12.97 per cent as perquisites. In their study they found maximum cash wages (Rs. 2,846.62) in maize-groundnut zone and kind plus cash wages in cotton-bajra zone, kind wages (Rs. 2,560.57) in paddy zone and cash plus kind (Rs. 3,083.25) in the cotton-bajra zone.

Pranab K. Bardhan[8] analysed the wage rates and employment of casual and permanent farm labourers under different demand and productivity conditions. The study was based on NSS data in rural West Bengal. The wage rate of casual labourers was influenced by per capita land cultivated by the household for which the labourer worked, age of the worker, dependents per earner and composite agriculture development index, etc. The regression results indicated that the wage rate was sensitive to demand and productivity conditions. Similarly, it was found that the monthly wage rate of regular farm servants was sensitive to demand factors. It was also observed that the unequal land distribution, severe unemployment, low mobility and lack of alternative opportunities make the employer stronger in fixing the terms of labour contract. The rapid agricultural development increases the demand of attached labour.

Ajit Kumar Ghose[9] in his study discussed how the wage rates are determined in the labour markets of casual and attached labourers. The author highlights that the wage rates of casual labour are determined entirely within the framework of supply and demand. In the peak seasons the employment of casual labourers reaches the full employment level and their wage rate cross the minimum wage level fixed by the government. On the other hand the wage rates of attached labourers are predetermined and depend mainly on the subsistence level specific to a region.

Ashok Rudra[10] in his study discussed the types of farm servants in the villages of West Bengal along with their terms of contract and wage rate. The author differentiated the permanent farm servants from casual labourers on the basis of the tasks performed on the farm. The permanent farm servants perform the more responsible tasks on the farm and in the homes of their employers. The pattern of wage payment of permanent farm servants varied from village to village. Further the author discussed the variations in the wage rates of permanent farm servants within the same village and the factors which explain these variations.

Rakesh Basant[11] in his study divided the agricultural labourers into two categories, i.e. casual labourers and attached/ permanent farm servants. The author highlights that these two types of labourers are different from each other in terms of their contract and working conditions. The casual labourers are generally hired on a daily basis, especially during peak seasons. The casual labourers come from many castes and some of them even own some land. On the other hand, the majority of the permanent farm servants is from the scheduled castes and is landless. The labour of the permanent farm servants is used on farms over the whole year. Further, by using farm management studies data for the years 1954-55, 1967-68, 1968-69 and 1969-70, he compared the daily wage rates of casual agricultural labourers and permanent farm servants for some Indian states. In the case of Punjab, he found the daily wage rate of casual labourers was higher than per day earnings of permanent farm servants.

Gerry Rodgers et al.[12] in their study compared the wage rates and working conditions of casual and permanent labourers for the years 1971 and 1981. The primary survey was conducted in seven villages of north-east Bihar. This region was considered a highly advanced agricultural region during the 1960s. The authors concluded that despite the agricultural development in this region no remarkable change occurred in the institution of permanent farm labour. Moreover, the real wage rates of permanent labourers did not increase, like those of casual labourers from 1971 to 1981.

Neeldari Bhattacharya[13] has highlighted the traditional mode of payments of labour in agriculture during the colonial period (1870 to 1940) in central and south-east Punjab. Both the cash wage system and kind wage system prevailed in Punjab agriculture at that time. In the long run the cash wage system increased significantly, but the real wage increased only marginally.

Utsa Patnaik[14]compared the earnings of the permanent and casual farm labourers in rural areas of Haryana. The annual earnings of the permanent farm servants were higher than those of casual farm labourers. However, the daily wage rate of permanent farm labourer worked out to be lower than the daily wage of casual labourers.

Ranjit Singh Ghuman[15] et al. in their study estimated the wage rate of the attached farm servants in three cultural zones of Punjab, viz. Majha, Malwa and Doaba. The study found that the highest proportion of the attached farm servants (almost 71 per cent), were getting wages over Rs. 20,000 per year in the Doaba region and the smallest proportion (53 per cent) in the Malwa region; the Majha region being in the middle in terms of the highest wage rates.

M.S. Sidhu[16] et al. in their study made an attempt to compare the wage rate of the permanent migrant labourers in four districts of Punjab, viz. Ludhiana, Jalandhar, Amritsar and Sangrur. The overall monthly average wage rate of a permanent migrant labourer in rural areas was found to be Rs. 1,915.46. The maximum wage rate was earned in district Ludhiana, followed by Jalandhar and Sangrur districts. The average wage rate of a local permanent labourer in this study was estimated to be Rs. 1,954.17 per month, which is only slightly (2 per cent) higher than the wage rate of the migrant labourer.

Pattern of Employment of Permanent Farm Servants

Here an attempt is made to survey the relevant studies on demand and employment conditions of permanent farm servants. In traditional agriculture land was cultivated by the family members of the owners or by tenants. Only in certain peak farm operations some outside labour was employed. In the earlier times the 'sharecroppers' were hired as the permanent farm servants. However, nowadays cash wage permanent farm servants along with the casual labourers have become predominant. The old customary practices have changed with the coming of the new agricultural technology since the mid-1960s. The commercialization of agriculture and mechanization of farm operations, particularly extensive use of tractors, has changed the employment scenario in the agriculture of Punjab, Haryana and western UP and resulted in changing the employment and working conditions of farm labour.

Daniel Thorner[17] in his study has suggested that in the early 1950s the rural population of Punjab and Pepsu consisted of: big land owners (*biswedars*), tenants (occupancy and tenants at will) and attached sharecroppers (siris) the permanent farm servants. He has suggested that a class of 'free wage' labourers did not exist in Punjab during the 1950s.

C. Muthiah[18] in his study discussed the importance of the institution of permanent farm servants or pannaiyals. The author discussed the situation of agricultural labour in Thanjaur district of Tamil Nadu. The study found that due to the fertile land and high agriculture productivity the agricultural labour always remained in high demand in this district. Further, the institution of permanent farm servants or pannaiyals always served the needs of both land owners and labourers. The long labour contract gives assurance of continuous labour supply, especially during peak seasons to the landowners and the labourers get assurance of continuous employment. The permanent farm servants get continuous employment for a minimum of 9 months and casual labourers only for 6-7 months. The permanent farm servants get 10 per cent more wages than casual labourers besides free boarding and lodging. The author emphasized that such long-term labour contracts should be encouraged. The destabilization of long-term labour contracts will create shortages of labour in advanced agriculture regions and will create diseconomies to each party, i.e. labourers as well as farmers.

Ashok Rudra[19] in his study has tried to highlight the use of labour on mechanized and non-mechanized farms in Punjab. The mechanized farms save on casual labour compared to the non-mechanized farms, but the intensity of use of permanent farm servants is more or less the same (one permanent farm servant for 26-29 acres on the average) on these two types of farms. The pattern of employment of agricultural labour is affected by the use of tubewells and tractors. The demand for casual labourers has also increased due to the use of new agricultural technology. Introduction of tractors increased the demand for permanent farm servants, but had no impact on the demand for casual labourers. On the other hand, tubewells seem to displace permanent farm servants and create a greater demand for casual labourers. So, the net impact of mechanization on demand for permanent farm servants remains uncertain.

S.S. Acharya[20] examined the impact of HYV (high yielding

varieties) seeds and mechanization on the employment of casual labour and permanent farm servants on the participant and non-participant farms. He defined participant farms as those which cultivated minimum 50 per cent area under HYV seeds, and others which cultivated less than 50 per cent area under HYV seeds divided into non-participant farms. The author found that both on the participant and non-participant farms the use of pump sets increased the demand of casual labour relatively more than of permanent farm servants. On the non-participant farms irrigated with pump sets the share of the casual labour was 16.3 per cent and of permanent farm servants, 6.0 per cent. Similarly, on the participant farms it was 26.4 per cent of casual labourers and 11.8 per cent of permanent farm servants. The tractorised participant farms used 45.3 per cent labour of casual labourers and 32.9 per cent of permanent farm servants. From this study one may conclude that the pump sets increased the demand for casual labourers relatively more. On the other hand, tractorization increased the demand for both casual labourers and permanent farm servants.

Kusum Chopra[21] tried to study the changes in factor inputs, especially the variation in labour input in Punjab agriculture after the use of tractors. Tractorization affected the employment of different types of agricultural labourers. The results indicated that farm operations which came under mechanization affected the labour use. The seed bed preparation is the major work of the tractor and it directly affected the employment of permanent farm servants. Certain seasonal farm operations like cotton picking, vegetable plucking and paddy transplantation, etc., increased the use of female casual labourers. According to Chopra, full time family members' employment increased on all farm categories except the category of 15-30 acres. The demand of male casual labourers increased compared to permanent farm servants after the introduction of new technology and mechanization of agriculture.

Pritam Singh[22] in his study, by using the Farm Management Studies data relating to Punjab for the period of the late 1960s, analysed the use of permanent farm servants on the different size categories of farms. The author found that the labour of permanent farm servants was used to the maximum on the bigger farms having an area more than 15 hectares. The number of farms having an area more than 20 hectares, was just 12 per cent in total sample, but was using 89 per cent of the hired permanent farm servants. The average number of permanent farm servants on such a farm was three. The average number of permanent farm servants hired per farm in the sample as a whole was 1.79. Many medium farms and even some small farms were found hiring permanent farm servants. The author did not find any bondage of permanent farm servants with their employees due to debt, etc.

Shyamal Roy[23] et al. in their study tried to test the hypothesis that tractorization increased the use of casual and regular farm labourers. The increased multiple cropping and reduction in the harvesting and sowing period after tractorization increased the demand of labour. In the new production process the seasonal demand for labourers increased. The land reclamation or area expansion programmes, etc., also resulted in greater demand for labour of both types. The increase in employment of annual farm labourers reflects a demand for skilled workers, particularly those who know tractor driving. The tractor-owning farmers demand more labour than the farmers who are without tractors.

M. Atchi Reddy[24] discussed the growth of permanent farm servants along with the nature of their contract from 1881 to 1921 in Andhra Pradesh. In 1881, out of the total agricultural labourers, 44 per cent were permanent farm servants and 56 per cent daily field labourers. In 1921, the proportion of permanent farm servants marginally increased to 46 per cent. Further, the author elaborated that during the late 19th and 20th century farm servants worked for a particular employer for one year. The contract started generally from June. The farm servant was free to join any other employer after completion of the contract. The skills of the farm servants were given great weight by employers in hiring a permanent farm servant. The permanent farm servants were also given some perks such as food and were mostly paid kind wages.

H.S. Shergill[25] has attempted to infer the influence of three components of new technology, viz. tractor, motor operated tubewells and chemical fertilizers, on the employment of share wage annual farm servants in Punjab. It was observed by the author that the introduction of tractor technology in Punjab agriculture had the most revolutionary impact on the labour hiring practices of Punjab farms. Introduction of tractors alone reduced the chances of traditional share wage annual farm servants being employed by 25 per cent. Increased intensity of the use of fertilizers also contributed significantly to the disappearance of this type of traditional (share type) hired labourer. The change in irrigation technology (increased use of tubewell irrigation) however, did not significantly affect the labour-hiring practice to any significant extent.

Krishna Bharadwaj[26] in her study categorized the farm workers into permanent workers and casual labourers. In the permanent workers she included the permanent farm servants and family labour. The author pointed out that the permanent farm servants are hired on big farms, especially in Punjab and increasing demand of permanent farm labour is even met by employing migrants as permanent farm servants. In Punjab some of the migrant farm workers have started living permanently and work as permanent farm servants. The study did not find any hostile relations between permanent farm servants and their employers.

Sarmistha Pal[27] in her study examined the task-based segmentation between casual labourers and permanent farm labourers. This study is theoretical as well as empirical, and is based on ICRISAT villages-wise data. This study concludes that to reduce the hoarding costs of permanent labour, the permanent labour is used by employers indiscriminately in both non-monitorable and monitorable tasks. The author further found that greater use of regular labour in non-monitorable tasks in paddy crop relatively to cotton. In monitorable tasks in paddy crop greater use of casual labour predominated. In cotton crop the use of casual labour remained high, in both monitorable and non-monitorable tasks.

Working Conditions of Permanent Farm Servants

In agriculture the relationship of the employer and the employee (a farmer and a farm worker) is quite informal and personal because of the limited number of hired workers on each farm. In the rare case of a dispute between the two the mutual problems are solved with the help of village elders. Secondly, since agricultural production depends significantly on nature, the formal rules and regulations to govern the working hours and conditions of labour cannot be of much use. So 'the patron-client' type relationship and implicit contract prevail in rural labour markets of less developed countries. Keeping in view the informal nature of labour contract of permanent farm servants it is necessary to describe the working conditions of permanent farm servants in some detail. The working conditions consist of many facets, more important of which are working hours, employer-employee relationship, non-pecuniary/ pecuniary benefits and nature of the contract (written/ unwritten) etc.

Pranab K. Bardhan[28] explained the relationship of employers (farmers) and employees (farm labourers) in Eastern India. The need of job security of an employee (farm labourer) and the employer's need for a dependable and readily available source of labour supply influenced significantly their mutual relationship. The relationship between the two, therefore, is of mutual dependence and does not reveal 'feudal subordination' of the worker to the farmer. The labour tying arrangements between attached labourers and the farmers are often strengthened by the provision of consumption credit by the farmers to the attached farm labourers.

Pranab Bardhan and Ashok Rudhra[29] discussed the terms of contract and types of attached farm labourers in West Bengal. The study found the following types of attachments in the labour contract: First, fully unattached labourers or daily/casual labourers. Such type of labourer enters into an agreement or contract with a particular employer only for a single day at a time. The next category is of 'fully attached labourer', who has a contract of one year. Thus, a permanent attached labourer has to work for his employer continuously for the whole year.

In the temporary absence of the permanent farm servant, due to illness, etc., a member of his family usually acts as a substitute. Such a labourer gets his payment partially in advance and partially at the end of the year. The study also describes the category of 'semi-attached labourer'. A labourer of this type enters into contract for a shorter period (less than one year), especially during the busy season. He cannot work for any other employer so long as the employing farmer needs his services; otherwise he is free to work for other employers. In the third category, the labourer is not bound even for a shorter period. The relationship is an informal one. The 'semi-attached' labourers usually get daily wages. The study did not find any case of bonded labour in West Bengal. They also found that attached and semi-attached labourers did not participate in the agricultural labourers' trade union movement.

Suman Sarkar[30]argued that apart from a growing body of casual agricultural labourers, there are attached labourers of different types. The terms of these different types of labour contracts vary and their wage rates also vary from village to village. The indebtedness of a labourer to an employer and the economic dependence of the former on the latter in many cases give rise to personalized long-term contracts.

A plethora of studies exists on the wage rate of casual agricultural labourers[31] but very few on the wage rates of permanent farm servants. Those studies on permanent farm servants have been briefly reviewed. The present study on the attached/permanent farm servants is a humble attempt to fill this gap in the literature. We have not reviewed any study on the wage rate of the casual agricultural labourers because our focus is on permanent farm servants. But in the literature we could not locate any study which explains variations in the wage rate of permanent farm servants over time and across villages and regions[32]. On the wages of permanent farm servants we got some scattered information in a few studies like Utsa Patnaik[33] who has compared the daily earnings of casual agricultural labourers and permanent farm servants, in a study which is mainly focused on casual labourers. The issue of temporal and spatial variations in the wage rate of permanent farm servants has remained unexplored mainly because secondary data on wages of permanent farm servants are virtually non-existent. The information on wages of agricultural labour is not published separately for casual and attached/ permanent farm servants. The reason for this seems to be the devastating criticism of this distinction (attached versus casual) made by Raj[34] in connection with the first and second agricultural labour enquiry reports. He was of the view that these two types (casual/attached) were not mutually exclusive catch alls for non-homogeneous groups. Due to this devastating criticism, the statistical authorities dropped the casual/attached classification altogether in subsequent enquiries. The Rural Labour Enquiries of (1963-64) and (1974-75) completely ignored these two types of labourers in Indian agriculture. The wages data given in *Agricultural Wages in India*, apply to casual labour operations. In the NSS (National Sample Survey) 27th Round (1972-73) and 32nd Round (1977-78) Employment and Unemployment survey data have been collected for casual and regular labourers. The data were not considered reliable owing to the confusion among the field staff regarding 'casual' and 'regular' labourers. The minimum wage rate is fixed by the Department of Labour (Punjab) separately for a casual agricultural labourer and permanent farm servant on the basis of the consumer price index applicable to agricultural labourers. The data are not published and not being available in the time series form cannot be used for analysis. Thus, the paucity of secondary data on wages of permanent farm servants hamstring the researchers to make time series and cross section analysis of wage rates of permanent farm servants; as they did in the case of casual farm labourers. That is why almost all studies on wage rates of agricultural labour pertain to casual agricultural labour.

However, much of the thrust of the reviewed studies is confined to estimating the magnitude of the wage differentials within villages or across villages in a particular region. In these studies no attempt has been made to identify the factors which influenced and generated wage differentials within a region among permanent farm servants. The economic theory suggests that wage variations from person to person are mainly because of the differences in skill levels and productivity. The rigorous testing of the economic and non-economic factors which influence the wage differentials among permanent farm servants has been lacking in the past studies. The present book is an attempt to fill this gap in the literature.

The employment contract of permanent farm servants is usually informal and it is not written in the majority of cases. The formal rules and regulations governing employer-employee relations are completely absent from the agricultural sector. From various studies reviewed above it becomes clear that permanent farm servants enjoy various pecuniary and non-pecuniary benefits from their employers (farmers). The permanent farm servants usually get 'consumption loans' free of interest from their employers. There is very little evidence in the literature of any tensions in relations between permanent farm servants and their employers. It has also been observed that permanent farm servants do not normally participate in the agitations launched by casual agricultural labourers. The permanent farm servants are normally hired by big mechanized farms, where they even supervise casual labourers and perform many technical and semi-managerial tasks such as tractor driving and tubewell operation. However, on many medium farms and even on some small farms also permanent farm servants are hired. The importance of the permanent farm servants as an important separate type of labour is accepted in the *Cost of Cultivation Data* used by the Ministry of Agriculture (Government of India) to recommend minimum support prices for wheat, paddy, etc. In the calculation of cost of cultivation of a crop, casual and permanent farm servant hired labour are treated separately. The review of literature given in this chapter clearly reveals the need for a systematic study of wages, employment and working conditions of attached/permanent farm servants in Punjab. These issues related to permanent farm servants have been almost completely neglected by the earlier researchers.

NOTES

1. *Statistical Abstract of Punjab*, 1970, p. 17.
2. *Statistical Abstract of Punjab*, 2008, p. 66.
3. Calculated on the basis of data of *Commission of Agricultural Prices and Costs* (For Various Years), Ministry of Agriculture, Government of India
4. M.S. Sidhu et al.: *A Study on Migrant Agricultural Labour in Punjab*, 2007, pp. 18-20.
5. For more details see, S.S. Johl: "Gains of the Green Revolution How They Have Been Shared in Punjab". *Journal of Development Studies*, Vol. 11, No. 3, 1975, pp. 178-189.
6. Manabendu Chattopadhyay: "Wage Rates of Two Groups of Agricultural Labourers". *Economic and Political Weekly*, Vol. 12, No. 13, 1977, pp. A20-A22.
7. This study discussed the types of annual labour contracts in Punjab along with the wage rates and pattern of payments in different agro-climatic zones. For more details see, Gurmukh Singh and Nirmal Singh: "Patterns of Employment and Wage Structure of Annual Farm Servants in Different Regions of Punjab." *Agricultural Situation in India*, November, 1978, pp. 501-503.
8. The study was based on the micro data relating to West Bengal. See for more details in Pranab K. Bardhan: "Wages and Unemployment in a Poor Agrarian Economy: A Theoretical and Empirical Analysis." *Journal of Political Economy*, Vol. 87, No. 3, 1979, pp. 479-500.
9. The author also estimated the average annual wage income per adult male agricultural labourer for the years 1950-51 and 1956-57. For these years he used the data of Rural Labour Enquiry Reports. He deflated the data on the basis of the price index number for agricultural labourers for the year 1960-61. Further, the study points out region-wise average annual wage income of attached and casual labour. In case of Punjab the average annual wage income of a male casual labourer was estimated at Rs. 240 in 1950-51 and Rs. 318 in 1956-57. For the same years for an attached permanent farm servant it was Rs. 383 in 1950-51 and Rs. 414 in 1956-57. The highest annual wage for both types of labourers was calculated for the state of Assam. The author found the mean difference between these two types of labourers' wage income was not significant even at 10 per cent level. For details see: Ajit Kumar Ghose: "Wages and Employment in Indian

Agriculture". *World Development*, Vol. 8, Nos. 5&6, 1980, pp. 413-428.

10. This study differentiated the permanent farm servants from casual labourers on the basis of skills and tasks which they perform on the farms. The permanent farm servants are similar to family labour in terms of responsible farm operations they perform. The wide variations exist in the wage rates of permanent farm servants even within a village and among the villages. The details on such long-term labour contracts are available in Ashok Rudra: *Extra Economic Constraints on Agricultural Labour: Results of an Intensive Survey in Some Villages Near Santiniketan, West Bengal*, ILO-ARTEP, 1982, pp. 38-45.
11. The findings of Basant contradict the findings of Chattopadhay. In this study the author estimated daily earnings of permanent farm servants are less relatively to casual labourers but findings of Chattopadhay are the reverse of it. For details see Rakesh Basant: "Attached and Casual Labour Wage Rates". *Economic and Political Weekly*, Vol. 19, No. 9, 1984, pp. 390-396.
12. Gerry Rodgers and Janine Rodgers: "Incomes and Work Among the Poor of Rural Bihar, 1971-1981". *Economic and Political Weekly*, Vol. 19, No. 13, 1984, pp. A17-A28.
13. The study brings out the pattern of wage payments, hiring practices and types of menials in colonial Punjab. The descriptive information given in this study on wage rates of agricultural labourers gives us useful information on the types of agricultural labourers and their wage rates. The attempt made by the author to study the change in real wage rates of agricultural labourers over the years cannot be fully relied on because it is difficult to deflate the data on any particular base year owing to non-availability of data on consumer price indices in the colonial era. The colonial period data are too scattered and lack the proper methodology being followed at the time of collection. For details see Neeldari Bhattacharya: "Agricultural Labour and Production, Central and South-East Punjab: 1870-1940"in K.N. Raj (ed): *An Essay on the Commercialization of Indian Agriculture*, 1985, pp. 104-162.
14. This study, on the basis of primary data relating to Haryana, made an attempt to analyse the transformations in agrarian-structure occurring with the green revolution, within the Marxist framework. For more details see, Utsa Patnaik: *Peasant Class Differentiations: A Study in Method with Reference to Haryana*, 1987, pp. 159-198.

15. Ranjit Singh Ghuman et al.: *Status of Local Agricultural Labour in Punjab*, 2007.
16. This study discussed the residential status of agricultural labourers and their wage rates in Punjab along with their prevalence in various districts. For more details see, M.S. Sidhu et al. *A Study of Migrant Agricultural Labour in Punjab*, 2007.
17. This study gives information of the agrarian structure of the Punjab and PEPSU during the pre-green revolution period. See for details, Daniel Thorner: *The Agrarian Prospects in India*, 1955, pp. 7-17.
18. C. Muthiah: "The Agricultural Labour Problem in Thanjavur and the New Agricultural Strategy", *Indian Journal of Agricultural Economics*, Vol. 25, No. 3, 1970, pp. 15-23.
19. This study focused on the use of permanent farm servants and casual labourers working on Punjab farms during the early phase of the green-revolution. According to this study the mechanization of farm operations, especially use of tractors worked in favour of the employment of permanent farm servants. See Ashok Rudra: "Employment Patterns in Large Farms of Punjab". *Economic and Political Weekly*, Vol. 6, No. 26, 1971, pp. A89-A94.
20. S.S. Acharya: "Green Revolution and Farm Employment", *Indian Journal of Agricultural Economics*, Vol. 28, No. 3, 1973, pp. 30-45.
21. The results of this study contradict Rudra's results. This author has tried to show that tractorization in agriculture reduced the demand of permanent farm servants. For details see, Kusum Chopra: "Tractorization and Changes in Factor Inputs: A Case Study of Punjab". *Economic and Political Weekly*, Vol. 9, No. 52, 1974, pp. A119-A127.
22. Pritam Singh: *Some Aspects of Labour Use in Punjab Agriculture: A Study of Ferozepur District (1967-68 to 1969-70)*, unpublished M.Phil. thesis, 1976.
23. This study shows that permanent farm servants who know tractor driving are in greater demand on Punjab farms. See more details Shyamal Roy et al. "Farm Tractorization, Productivity and Labour Employment: A Case Study of Indian Punjab". *Journal of Development Studies*, Vol. 14, No. 2, 1978, pp. 193-209.
24. M. Atchi Reddy: "Labour Relations in Andhra Pradesh Agriculture: 1881-1981." *Indian Journal of Labour Economics*, Vol. 26, No. 3, 1983, pp. 160-187.
25. This study is on the share wage permanent farm servants (siris) relating to Punjab. The author pointed out that mechanization

reduced the demand of 'siris' in agriculture. See details in H.S. Shergill: "Impact of New Technology on the Employment of Share Wage Annual Servants on Punjab Farms". *Indian Journal of Labour Economics*, Vol. 29, No. 4, 1987, pp. 72-81.

26. Krishna Bharadwaj: *Production Conditions in Indian Agriculture: A Study Based on Farm Management Surveys*, 1991, pp. 19-30.
27. Sarmistha Pal: "Task Based Segmentation of Rural Labour Contracts: Theory and Evidence". *Bulletin of Economic Research*, Vol. 51, No. 1, 1999, pp. 67-94.
28. The author discussed the employer-employee relationship within the framework of labour economics. He did not point out any antagonism between permanent farm servants and their employers, see for details, Pranab K. Bardhan: "Interlocking Factor Markets and Agrarian Development: A Review of Issues". *Oxford Economic Papers*, Vol. 32, No. 1, 1980, pp. 82-98.
29. These authors discussed the various types of labour contracts in agriculture and found that annual permanent farm servants are quiet prevalent in West Bengal. Interestingly, they did not find any bonded labour in their study area. For details see, Pranab Bardhan and Ashok Rudra: "Terms and Conditions of Labour Contract in Agriculture: Results of a Survey in West Bengal, 1979." *Oxford Bulletin of Economics and Statistics*, Vol. 43, No. 1, 1981, pp. 89-111.
30. Like, Rudra this author also pointed out in his study that wage rates and terms of contract vary from village to village. See Suman Sarkar: "India's Agricultural Development: An Alternative Path". *Economic and Political Weekly*, Vol. 21, No. 19, 1986, pp. 825-836.
31. The trend in real wage rates of casual labourers has been studied by Pranab Bardhan: "Variations in Agricultural Wages: A Note." *Economic and Political Weekly*, Vol. 8, No. 21, 1973, pp. 947-950. See also, S.S. Johl: "Gains of the Green Revolution: How They Have Been Shared in Punjab." *Journal of Development Studies*, Vol. 11, No. 3, 1975, pp. 178-189 and Sheila Bhalla: "Real Wage Rates of Agricultural Labourers in Punjab; 1961-1977: A Preliminary Analysis". *Economic and Political Weekly*, Vol. 14, No. 26, 1979, pp. A57-A68.
32. This may be due to the non-availability of time series data on wage rates of permanent farm servants.
33. Utsa Patnaik, op.cit.
34. K.N. Raj: "Some Comments on the Second Agricultural Labour Enquiry" in V.K.R.V. Rao (ed.): *Agricultural Labour Enquiry in India*, 1962, pp. 152-169.

2

Emergence and Growth of Permanent Farm Servants in Punjab

In this chapter we discuss the emergence and growth of the agricultural labourers' class in Punjab from the early 20th century to the post-green revolution period. The main focus of our study being on permanent farm servants, therefore, we have also tried to trace the growth of permanent farm servants over this period. The permanent farm servants and daily casual wage labourers are the two main types of hired labour used in Punjab agriculture. We have mainly relied on the secondary data such as census publications, district gazetteers, settlement reports, cost of cultivation reports of the Commission for Agricultural Prices and Costs (Government of India) for tracing the growth of agricultural labourers in Punjab.

Growth of Agricultural Labourers in India: Summary of Various Views

Most scholars are of the view that before the British rule a considerable class of modern type agricultural labourers in rural areas did not exist. Due to the non-availability of hard data on workforce prior to the British rule, scholars mostly make descriptive statements on the traditional village community and the composition of its working population. A traditional village community consisted of agriculturists, artisans and menials or *kamins* doing all sorts of odd jobs. The agriculturists, artisans and menials constituted different castes. The menials provided their services to the agriculturists and in return they were given payments in kind.[1] The payments were predetermined on the basis of the customs of a village.[2] In the Marxist terminology we may say there was division of labour for the production of commodities, but commodities were not sold, rather were consumed without any transaction in monetary terms.[3]

Although, India was conquered and ruled by various invaders like the Arabs, Turks and Mongols, etc; but the economic structure of the village did not change much under their rule.[4] However, under the British rule the traditional village community started disintegrating. The British rule destabilized the village community in two ways. First, the institutional changes introduced into the land system and induction of cash rent in place of kind rent changed the inter-relation between farmers and menials.[5] Secondly, the de-industrialization of the countryside and trade linkage with the outside world also resulted in change in relations among various social groups in the village. The cottage industry of villages could not compete with the imported mill made products. So many workers in these industries became redundant and shifted to agriculture.[6] The creation of private property rights in land resulted in many ruined farmers selling their land and becoming agricultural labourers. Under the British rule these two reasons were generally mentioned by scholars as being responsible for the rise in the class of agricultural labourers in the rural areas. Patel[7] was the first scholar who studied the growth of agricultural labourers in India with the advent of British rule. He explained, "The traditional Indian society was integrated by agriculture and handicrafts, there was no room for the existence of independent and distinct class of agricultural labourers who were hired by cultivators and were paid in cash or kind wages." According to him the class of agricultural labourers emerged during the late 19th century and early 20th centuries in India. Patel's hypothesis became widely accepted by Indian scholars, particularly by those with left leanings. But Dharma Kumar[8] put forward a different view on this issue. She argued that in South India, members of certain castes were already, by and large, agricultural labourers at the onset of British rule. Similarly, Krishnamurthy[9] concluded that Patel did not follow the actual workers' categories given in censuses of the colonial period. For example he added unspecified labourers with the agricultural labourers. The estimates of Patel exaggerated the number of agricultural labourers. The author further pointed out that in the Indian union the proportion of male agricultural labourers increased only marginally from 24.1 per cent to 24.6 per cent between 1901 and 1961. Similarly, George Campbell[10] in one of the best accounts of India during the first half of the 19th century referred to the fact that as "a rule farming was not carried on by hired labour." R.P. Dutt[11] in his book *India Today* noted that in 1842, Sir Thomas Munro (Census Commissioner) reported that there were no landless peasants in India. From all these studies we may conclude that there might be agricultural labourers before the British rule, but the number of cash wage agricultural labourers of the modern type emerged and increased only during the British period.

Emergence of Agricultural Labour Class in Punjab

In the previous section we summarized the different views on the existence and growth of agricultural labourers in India, particularly during the British period. In this section we have tried to elaborate how the different types of agricultural labourers emerged in Punjab over the years from the late 19th century onwards on the basis of information in district gazetteers and census reports. The practice of hiring agricultural labourers was not uniform in all the districts and princely states of colonial Punjab. Near the closing of the 19th century, i.e. during 1883-84 the permanent farm servants were hired in district Jalandhar, but they did not exist in district Gurdaspur.[12] In district Hoshiarpur the cash wage permanent farm servants were hired by rich zamindars of higher castes like Rajputs.[13] At the beginning of the 20th century the existence of cash wage permanent farm servants is reported in district Jalandhar.[14] At around the same time in district Ludhiana two types of permanent farm servants were employed on farms; one was known as *Litia Kama* (Ploughman) and the second type was *Kama Niz* (Private Farm Servant). The first type was especially hired for ploughing and the second for farming or non-farming work.[15] At the beginning of the 20th century in district Amritsar the permanent farm servant was known by the name *Athri*. Even in district Gurdaspur at the beginning of the 20th century the permanent farm servants were hired, though not in the 19th century.[16] In district Ferozepur, only the share wage permanent farm servants (siris) were hired.[17] At the micro level some village studies give us valuable insights into the institution of permanent farm servants. A village study of village Suner gives us detailed castewise composition of the *siris;* twenty three farmers had hired twenty-six *siris*. Three farmers hired more than one *siri* each and the other twenty-one each. These *siris* were attached with their employers through various mechanisms; payment of advance money was one of them.[18] After the end of the colonial period, the institution of permanent farm servants remained intact. In 1947, an *Athri* cash wage permanent farm servant was commonly hired in district Amritsar as it was the practice in the early 19th century.[19]

The wages of the cash wage permanent farm servants were not uniform in all the districts of Punjab. For example, in district Jalandhar a permanent farm servant was given Rs. one or two per month during the year 1883-84; and in 1904 the wage rate remained the same. Besides this a permanent farm servant was given clothes and food as well. In district Ludhiana a *Kama Niz* and *Litia Kama* were given wages of Rs. one or two per month. In many districts they were paid in kind; as in Amritsar a permanent farm servant was given 40 to 60 kacha maund of grains per annum. The share of a *siri* was based on the plough. On one plough land his share was 1/6th, on two plough land his share wage was 1/10th of total agriculture produce.[20] Besides this, the share of the *siri* (share wage permanent farm servant) or wage rate of a cash wage permanent farm servant was based on his skills and length of tenure with one employer.[21] Most of the permanent farm servants were from the lower castes and hired from within a village.

Under the British rule the second type of agricultural labourers that emerged was daily farm labourers or the present day casual agricultural labourers. The daily farm labourers were hired on a daily wage basis for performing various farm operations like sowing, weeding, harvesting and threshing. The daily farm labourers were generally hired by big landlords on irrigated lands and generally belonged to lower castes.[22] The demand for casual labourers was high in the peak harvesting seasons of kharif and rabi crops.[23] The use of casual agricultural labourers was more relative to the permanent farm servants. In district Jalandhar the proportion of casual agricultural labour was 61 per cent and of permanent farm servants 39 per cent in 1904. The wage rate of casual labour varied from village to village and from season to season. The majority of the casual agricultural labourers were paid in kind in the 19th century. For example in 1883-84, in district Jalandhar a daily farm labourer was paid about a seer of grain for one day's work. In district Gurdaspur two seers of grain per day were paid for weeding and reaping. But gradually the system of cash payment replaced the kind payment system and by 1947 almost all the daily casual labourers were being paid cash wage. From the preceding discussion it is pertinent to conclude that like many other parts of India agricultural labourers emerged in Punjab in the late 19th century and the beginning of 20th century as agriculture was gradually commercialized. The agricultural labourers consisted of daily wage labourers and permanent farm servants.

Table 2.1: Caste Composition of Agricultural Labourers in Punjab

Year	*Number of All Male Agricultural Labourers (Lakh)*	*Number of Scheduled Castes Male Agricultural Labourers (Lakh)*	*Proportion of Scheduled Castes in Male Agricultural Labourers (Percent)*
1961	4.83*	3.41*	70.60
1971	7.79	5.50	70.60
1981	10.47	7.54	72.02
1991	13.88	9.72	70.03
2001	11.04	7.46	67.57

Note: (i) *Source*: Census of India (Various Years)
(ii) * 1961 figures are for pre-organized Punjab as it existed in 1961.

Most of the agricultural labourers belonged to lower castes. Even after independence the caste composition of agricultural labourers has not changed much; most of them are still from scheduled castes.[24] This is clearly shown by information given in Table 2.1 in which the number and share of scheduled castes in total agriculture labourers is given. Over the 1961 to 2001 period the number of agricultural labourers in Punjab almost tripled, but the proportion of scheduled castes among them remained almost the same; about 70 per cent. The scheduled castes are a set of many different castes such as Chamar, Chura, Bauria, etc., and the proportion of agricultural labourers coming from these various castes is quite different. The caste-wise composition of agricultural labourers is given in Table 2.2 and

Table 2.2: Proportion of Agricultural Labourers in Total Male Workers in Various Scheduled Castes (1961)

Caste	*Total Number of Male Workers (i)*	*Number of Male Agricultural Labourers (ii)*	*Agricultural Labourers as Proportion of Total Male Workers (Percent) (iii)*	*Share of the Caste in Total Male Scheduled Caste Agricultural Labourers (iv)*
Chamar/Ramdasia	416060	124213	29.85	36.30
Mazhabi	185959	100026	53.79	29.30
Balmiki/Chura/ Bhangi	156857	63455	40.45	18.60
Adharmi	109448	21330	19.49	6.24
Dhanak	37745	10187	26.99	2.98
Dumna/Mahesh/ Doom	23860	4780	20.03	1.40
Bazigar	19730	4161	21.09	1.22
Kabir Panthi/Julaha	24800	3358	13.54	0.98
Bauria/Bawaria	11975	2873	23.99	0.84
Megh	7769	2090	26.90	0.61
Sansi/Manesh	9651	1963	20.34	0.57
Kori/Koli	21210	1034	4.88	0.30
Od	5896	1000	16.96	0.29
Other Castes	15529	1475	-	-
Total Scheduled Caste (Male Workers/ Agricultural Labourers)	1046489	341945	-	-

Source: Special Tables for Scheduled Castes (Census of India, 1961)

shows a very interesting pattern. The three main castes (among the scheduled castes) that make most of the agricultural labourers of Punjab are: *Chamar/Ramdasia, Mazbi* and *Churas*. Out of all the scheduled caste agricultural labourers 84.20 per cent came from these three castes in 1961. So out of all the agricultural labourers in Punjab (scheduled castes plus non-scheduled castes) about 60 per cent belong to these three castes of the scheduled castes.

Growth of Agricultural Labourers in Punjab (1901-1931)

In the previous sections we discussed how the agricultural labourers emerged in colonial Punjab from the specific lower castes. In this section we have made an attempt to analyse how the number of agricultural labourers increased in Punjab in the first quarter of the 20th century. The relative weight of agricultural labourers in total farm workers in Punjab is also compared with other regions of India.

To trace the growth of agricultural labourers in Punjab in the pre-independence period is rather difficult due to various problems with available data. The definitions used for agricultural labourers differ somewhat from census to census, for the 1901 and 1911 census the information is available in terms of population supported and for the census of 1921 and 1931 for working population. In 1941, no census was conducted. So

Table 2.3: Growth of Agricultural Labourers in British Punjab (1901-1931)

Year	*Number of Agricultural Labourers (Million)*	*Proportion of Agricultural Labourers in Agricultural Population (Percent)*	*Remarks*
1901	1.20	8.10	Population Supported
1911	2.40	16.90	Population Supported
1921	0.70	12.90	Working Population
1931	1.00	14.40	Working Population

Original Source: Census of India 1901, 1911, 1921 and 1931
Our Source: Surendra J. Patel: *Agricultural Labourers in Modern India and Pakistan*, Current Book House, Bombay, 1952, p. 29 (Table 4).

we have used census data for the years 1901, 1911, 1921 and 1931 to trace the growth of the agricultural labourers' class in British Punjab. Although the original source of data is various census publications, but we have taken the figures as reported in Tables 2.3 and 2.4 from the well-known study of Surindra J. Patel on *Growth of Agricultural Labourers in India and Pakistan.*

The information given in Table 2.3 suggests that in Punjab during the 1901-1931 period agricultural labourers as a proportion of total workers engaged in agriculture increased from 8.10 per cent in 1901 to 14.40 per cent in 1931. The different basis of figures for 1901, 1911, 1921 and 1931 makes it difficult to make a strict calculation of rate of growth of agricultural labourers over this period. However, quite reliable qualitative conclusions can be drawn. The figures for 1901 and 1911 are comparable and indicate that the number of male agricultural labourers in Punjab doubled in these ten years. Similarly figures for 1921 and 1931 are comparable and indicate about 30 per cent increase in the number of male agricultural labourers in Punjab. On the basis of data given in Table 2.3 one can reasonably conclude that during the first quarter of the 20th century the number of agricultural labourers in Punjab increased

Table 2.4: Proportion of Agricultural Labourers in Total Agricultural Population in Punjab Vis-à-vis Other Regions (1920s)

Province/Region	*Agricultural Labourers as Proportion of Total Agricultural Population (Percent)*
Punjab	14.5
United Provinces	21.8
Bengal	33.0
Central Provinces	52.0
Madras	54.0
Bihar and Orissa	35.0
Assam	25.0
Bombay	57.0

Original Source: Report of the Indian Statutory Commission, 1930.
Our Source: Surendra J. Patel: *Agricultural Labourers in Modern India and Pakistan*, Current Book House, Bombay, 1952, p. 65 (Table 6).

and their proportion in total agricultural workers also went up.

The comparison of proportion of agricultural labourers in total agricultural workers in Punjab with other provinces of British India given in Table 2.4 suggests that the class of agricultural labourers was relatively less developed in Punjab compared to other provinces. The data in Table 2.4 are originally from the Report of the Indian Statutory Commission, 1930, but our source is Surendra J. Patel (1952). It may be seen that among all the provinces of British India the proportion of agricultural labourers in total agricultural workers was the lowest in Punjab (14.50 per cent) and the highest in Bombay Presidency (57 per cent). Both Madras Presidency (54 per cent) and Central Provinces (52 per cent) also show a very high proportion of agricultural labourers in total workers engaged in agriculture.

Notwithstanding the problems with the nature of census data, two qualitative conclusions can be safely drawn on the basis of data given in Tables 2.3 and 2.4:

(*i*) The number and proportion of agricultural labourers in total workers engaged in agriculture increased during the first quarter (1901-1931) of the 20th century.

(*ii*) The class of agricultural labourers was relatively less developed in Punjab compared to other provinces of British India.

Growth of Agricultural Labourers in the Post-Independence Period (1961-2001)

The growth of agricultural labourers in Punjab in the post-independence period is discussed in this section. In the 1951 census information on agricultural labourers was not collected, rather the data are in terms of population dependent on various occupations. From 1961 onwards census data on the number of workers in each of the standard nine industrial categories are available and have been used to trace the growth of agricultural labourers in Punjab. Even in these data there are definitional problems about the female participation in full-time work; so most researchers have been using the number of male agricultural labourers. We have also followed that practice. The information on the number of male agricultural labourers and their proportion in total male workers (cultivators and agricultural labourers) in agriculture for the years 1961, 1971, 1981, 1991 and 2001 is presented in Table 2.5.

Table 2.5: Growth of Agricultural Labourers in Punjab (1961-2001)

Year	*Number of Male* Agricultural Workers (Lakh) (i)*	*Number of All Male Agricultural Labourers (Lakh) (ii)*	*Agricultural Labourers as Proportion of All Male Workers in Agriculture (Percent)*
1961	17.89	3.20	17.41
1971	24.40	7.79	31.93
1981	28.04	10.47	37.34
1991	32.82	13.88	42.29
2001	28.67	11.04	38.51
Growth Rate: (Per Year)			
1961-1991	2.04	5.02	-
Growth Rate: (Per Year)			
1991-2001	(-) 1.36	(-) 2.33	-
Growth Rate (Per year)			
1961-2001	1.19	3.15	-

Source: Census of India for Various Years.
* Agricultural Workers = Cultivatiors + Agriculture Labourers

It can be seen that the number of male agricultural labourers in Punjab more than tripled in four decades (1961 to 2001); from 3.20 lakh in 1961 to 11.04 lakh in 2001. However two different trends are also visible over this period of four decades (1961 to 2001). From 1961 to 1991 the number of male agricultural labourers in Punjab increased continuously at the annual rate of 5.02 percent; but between the 1991-2001 period their number decreased at the rate of 2.33 per cent per year. This latter trend is in line with and is part of the overall downward trend in the total number of male workers engaged in farming (Table 2.5). This downward trend suggests that a new phase in Punjab agriculture has started whereby the population engaged in farming has started decreasing.

A similar pattern is observed in the proportion of male agricultural labourers in total male workers in agriculture. This proportion rose from 17.41 per cent in 1961 to 38.51 per cent in 2001. From 1961 to 1991 this proportion rose continuously from 17.41 per cent to 42.29 per cent; but since 1991 it has started decreasing and was 38.51 per cent in 2001.

The main conclusions of this section are now summed up. From a relatively small proportion of total agricultural workers, the number of agricultural labourers in Punjab increased at quite a fast rate in the post-independence period. By early 1991, as the green revolution matured, about two-fifth (42.29 per cent) of all workers engaged in agriculture were agricultural labourers (casual workers and permanent farm servants). However since 1991 the number and proportion of agricultural labourers in total agricultural workers seems to be decreasing.

Permanent Farm Servants in Punjab Agriculture

In this section we discuss the extent of use of permanent farm servants in Punjab agriculture and in various regions of Punjab in the early 20th century. The census of 1901 gives information on the number of permanent farm servants as well as on daily farm labourers in various districts of British Punjab as well as princely states. That information we have used to estimate the number of permanent farm servants and daily wage labourers in central Punjab that approximately coincides with the present boundaries of Punjab. This information is given in Table 3.6 indicates that at the beginning of the 20th century about one-third of all hired agricultural labourers were permanent farm servants, and the remaining two-third daily wage labourers. The proportion of permanent farm servants in total hired labour in agriculture was also estimated for the three traditional regions of Punjab, i.e. Majha, Doaba and Malwa. The highest proportion of permanent farm servants in total hired labour was in the Doaba region; of the total agricultural labourers half were daily farm labourers and half were permanent farm servants. The Doaba region being well irrigated and a large number of landowners being in the Army and government jobs may be the reason for a higher proportion of permanent farm servants being employed by farmers of this region. The use of permanent farm servants was also high in Malwa region; about one-third of all hired agricultural labourers being permanent farm servants. The big size of holdings in the Malwa region may be the main cause of employment of a larger number of permanent farm servants. In the Majha region the use of the permanent farm servants was the lowest; only 17.16 per cent were permanent farm servants in the total hired agricultural labourers. From the information given in Table 2.6 one may conclude that at the beginning of the 20th century about one-third of hired agricultural labourers in Punjab agriculture were permanent farm servants. There are ample references in the literature suggesting that permanent farm servants were hired both on share wage contract as well as cash wage contract. The share wage contract was more popular in the Malwa region and cash wage contract in the Majha and Doaba region. This share wage contract permanent farm servants are even now found (though in small number), in the Malwa region; about 13 per cent of our sample permanent farm servants from the Malwa region, especially in the cotton zone, were working on a share wage contract in the year 2007-08.

Table 2.6: Permanent Farm Servants in Punjab Agriculture: Beginning of the Twentieth Century (1901)

Region	*Permanent Farm Servants (Male)*		*Daily Farm Labourers (Male)*		*All Agricultural Labourers (Male)*	
	Number	*Proportion*	*Number*	*Proportion*	*Number*	*Proportion*
Central Punjab (Approximately Equivalent to Present Punjab)	14311	32.53	29687	67.47	43998	100.00
Majha	2957	17.16	14272	82.84	17229	100.00
Doaba	7599	50.14	7557	49.86	15156	100.00
Malwa	3755	32.33	7858	67.67	11613	100.00

Source: Census of British India (1901).

Trend in the Use of Permanent Farm Servants in Punjab Agriculture

The long-term trend in the use of permanent farm servants in Punjab agriculture is analysed in this section on the basis of the cost of cultivation data published by the Commission for Agricultural Costs and Prices. The information on the use of permanent farm servants in Punjab agriculture at the beginning of the 1970s and in 2005-06 is given in Table 2.7 and shows that in the early years of the 1970s about one-third of hired labour used in Punjab agriculture was of permanent farm servants; almost the same proportion as at the beginning of the 20th century (Table 2.6). However, by 2005-06 this proportion of permanent farm servants in the total hired labour used in Punjab agriculture declined to about one-fourth.

Table 2.7: Proportion of Permanent Farm Servants Labour Used in Total Hired Labour Used on Punjab Farms (Cost of Cultivation Data)

Year	*Proportion of Permanent Farm Servants Labour in Total Hired Labour Used (Percent)*			
	Wheat	*Paddy*	*Cotton*	*Three Crops Combined*
1974-75	41.75%	20.72%	30.09%	34.32%
2005-06	20.90%	28.23%	24.35%	24.62%
Change in Per cent Points	(-) 20.85	7.51	(-) 7.74	(-) 9.70
Change in Simple Per cent Terms	(-) 49.94	36.25	(-) 19.08	(-) 28.26

Source: Commission for Agricultural Costs and Prices (Various Years Reports), Ministry of Agriculture, Government of India.

On the use of permanent farm servants in commercial modern agriculture there are two views among Indian economists. One view is that such labour contracts will gradually disappear in modern commercial agriculture because of its pre-capitalist nature and non-compatibility with mechanized farming.[25] A number of studies on Indian agriculture have argued in favour of the gradual casualization of agricultural labourers and the disappearance of long-term labour contract of the permanent farm servant type overtime.[26]

But there are others, who have tried to show that long-term labour contract of permanent farm servants type still exists even in modern commercialized agriculture. The institution of permanent farm servants is quite compatible with modern agriculture and exists both in developed as well as underdeveloped regions of India.[27] Some studies have shown that the use of permanent farm servants in the advanced agriculture region of Haryana increased with the green revolution.[28] The various studies relating to Punjab also indicate that even after casualisation of agricultural labour, the permanent farm servants for the year round work are still important for specialized tasks.[29] The use of permanent farm servants in Punjab agriculture in various farm operations especially where there is need of skills (e.g. in ploughing and interculture) increased with the green revolution.[30] Besides these empirical studies various theoretical studies have justified the long-term labour contracts in agriculture on economic grounds. This type of labour contract gives assurance of labour supply to an employer and of employment to a permanent farm servant.[31] Some scholars assert that the permanent farm labour contract creates subjugation of the worker to the employer. The employing farmer not only controls them in the workplace, but also demands loyalty from them in village politics.[32] From this theoretical as well as empirical analysis we may draw the inference that the casualisation of agricultural labourers increased with the commercialization of agriculture. But at the same time the demand for permanent farm servants or long-term labour contract continues for getting the assured labour supply to perform skilled farm operations.

On the basis of the above discussion one may suggest that though the use of permanent farm servants in Punjab agriculture has declined over the green revolution period (from 34.32 per cent in 1974-75 to 24.62 per cent in 2005-06), it is unlikely that permanent farm servants will be completely eliminated from Punjab farms. The casual daily wage labour is only a partial substitute for the permanent farm servant. The daily wage labourers can perform many of the routine functions on the farm (such as harvesting and weeding, etc.), as well as a permanent farm servant performs these. But the daily wage labour cannot be very effectively deployed to perform many skilled tasks on the farm such as tractor driving, power tubewell operation and supervision of daily labourers. Moreover, the daily wage labour is more expensive to use in tasks that are not to be performed continuously, but only intermittently at different times in the day and take only one or two hours each time. In view of the above considerations, it can be said that some amount of permanent farm servant labour will always be used in agriculture whatever the degree of commercialization and mechanization of farming. In any case the big farms will always remain dependent on permanent farm servants.

Relationship Between Farm Size and Employment of Permanent Farm Servants

The permanent farm servants are always used on big farms that do not have sufficient number of family members of their own to operate the farm. In Punjab, however, even medium farms and some of the small farms also employ permanent farm servants. On farm size wise employment of permanent farm servants we have used micro farm wise information for the late 1960s from studies in the Economics of Farm Management conducted by the Economic and Statistical Organization, Punjab. These micro-farm size wise data are arranged and presented in Table 2.8 and show that in the late 1960s about 65 per cent of Punjab farms were employing permanent farm servants. A positive correlation between farm size and use of permanent farm servants is also visible in Table 2.8.

About one-fourth of farms of even less than five hectares were using permanent farm servants. Of course, most of the big farms (10 hectares and above) were using permanent farm servants. The very big farms of twenty hectares and above were employing about three permanent farm servants each. The information in Table 2.8 clearly shows that permanent farm servants will always be used on big farms even in the coming years. Since there are indications that the average size of the farm in Punjab has started increasing since 1991 (due a large number of marginal and small farmers leaving farming), so in

Table 2.8: Employment of Permanent Farm Servants on Punjab Farms: Farm Size Wise Pattern (1967-68 to 1969-70)

Farm Size Class (Hectares)	*Number of Sample Farms*	*Proportion Employing Permanent Farm Servants (Percent)*	*Average Number of Permanent Farm Servants Employed Per Farm*	*Percent Share of Farm Size Class in Total Number of Permanent Farm Servants*
0 - 5	67	25.37	1.06	3.49
5-10	153	55.56	1.23	18.61
10-15	99	81.82	1.57	21.71
15-20	75	82.67	1.95	18.80
20 & Above	56	89.29	3.12	29.10
All	450	65.56	1.79	100.00

Notes: (1) Original Source: *Studies in the Economics of Farm Management (1967-68, 1968-69, 1969-70)*, Economic and Statistical Organization, Punjab (Government of Punjab)
Our Source:
(2) Pritam Singh: *Some Aspects of Labour Use in Punjab Agriculture: A Study of Ferozepur District (1967-68 to 1969-70)*, Unpublished M.Phil. Thesis (1976), Centre for Political Studies, School for Social Sciences, Jawaharlal Nehru University, New Delhi.
(3) Samples for 1967-68, 1968-69 and 1969-70 have been clubbed together in the above table.

future the employment of permanent farm servants may even increase in Punjab agriculture.

To conclude, the modern type of hired agricultural labour emerged in India and Punjab with the advent of British rule that resulted in gradual commercialization of agriculture, decline of the village handicrafts and disappearance of traditional patron-client relations from the rural areas. The number and proportion of agricultural labourers increased in India and Punjab during the British period; at a slower rate in Punjab compared to other regions of India. However, after the green revolution the number and proportion of agricultural labourers increased at a fast rate in Punjab. The permanent farm servants have existed in Punjab agriculture from the very beginning of the 20th century; about one-third of the total hired workers being permanent farm servants. However, under the impact of the green revolution the proportion of permanent farm servants in total hired labour has declined somewhat. But it does not seem that permanent farm servants will totally disappear from Punjab farms. Because for performing many skilled operations and on the big farms permanent farm servants labour cannot be replaced by casual daily labourers.

NOTES

1. In the villages of Punjab; menials were from the lower castes and were working for the agriculturists. Even under the Sikh rule in Punjab the village division of labour remained caste-based. See for more details, Indu Banga: *The Agrarian System of the Sikhs (Late 18th and Early 19th Century)*, 1978, pp. 167-187 and Himadri Banerjee: "Agricultural Labourers of the Punjab During the Second Half of the Nineteenth Century." *The Panjab Past and Present*, Part-I (Serial No. 21), 1977, pp. 96-116.
2. The custom of paying the artisans and menials an allowance of grain taken out before the division of crops between the king's officers and the cultivators was very ancient. See footnote on page 17 in The *Indian Village Community* by Baden Powell, 1972.
3. Karl Marx: *Capital* (Volume I), 1986, p. 49.
4. Karl Marx: "The Future Results of British Rule in India", *Selected Works (Volume-I)*, 1976, pp. 494-495.
5. R.Palme Dutt: *India Today*, 1947, pp. 188-190 and Bhowani Sen: *Evolution of Agrarian Relations in India*, 1962, pp. 174-175.
6. Amiya Kumar Bagchi: "De-Industrialization in India in the Nineteenth Century: Some Theoretical Implications". *Journal of Development Studies*, Vol. 12, No. 2, 1976, pp. 135-164.
7. S.J. Patel: *Agricultural Labourers in Modern India and Pakistan*, 1952, p.9.
8. Dharma Kumar: *Land and Caste in South India: Agricultural Labour in the Madras Presidency During the 19th Century*, 1965, pp. 33-63.
9. J. Krishnamurthy: "The Growth of Agricultural Labour in India: A Note". *Indian Economic and Social History Review*, Vol. 9, No. 3, 1972, pp. 327-332.
10. George Campbell: *Modern India*, 1853, p. 65.
11. R. Palme Dutt:, op.cit., p. 8.
12. *District Gazetteer, Jalandhar*, 1883-84, p. 39.
13. *Report of the Indian Famine Commission (Reply to Inquiries of Commission)*, 1898, pp. 418-431.
14. *District Gazetteer, Jalandhar*, 1904, p. 153.
15. *District Gazetteer, Ludhiana*, 1904, p. 117

16. *District Gazetteers, Gurdaspur*, 1914, p. 129 and *Amritsar*, 1914, pp. 71-102.
17. *District Gazetteer, Ferozepur*, 1915, pp. 148-149.
18. *An Economic Survey of Village Suner (District Ferozepur)*, The Board of Economic Enquiry, 1936, pp. 18-19.
19. *District Gazetteer, Amritsar*, 1947, pp. 150-152.
20. Village Suner, op.cit., p. 18 and *Resurvey of Village Chimna (District Ludhiana)*, ESO (Government of Punjab), 1961, pp. 16-17.
21. In tehsil Moga (District Ferozepur) the annual wage rate of a permanent farm servant was Rs.100 and if he continuously worked with the same employer then his wage was Rs.180 with perks. For more details see, Malcolm Darling: *Wisdom and Waste in the Punjab Village*, 1934, pp. 261-278.
22. *Punjab State Gazetteer, Faridkot State*, 1907, p.35.
23. *District Gazetteer, Gurdaspur*, 1914, p.88 and *Settlement Report, Tehsil Batala*, 1909, p.29.
24. The unique features of agricultural labourers in Punjab are, first very few of them do farming independently. Secondly, a majority of them belong to scheduled castes and are non-Hindus. The non-Hindu landless labourers prefer to do non-farming jobs. Excluding other Indian states, data in Punjab on landless Scheduled Castes agricultural labourers really make sense. For more details see Gail Omvedt: "Capitalist Agriculture and Rural Classes in India". *Economic and Political Weekly*, Vol. 16, No. 52, 1981, pp. A140-A159.
25. Such type of labour relations has been studied by E.B. Harper: "Social Consequences of an 'Unsuccessful' Low Caste Movement" in James Silverberg (ed.), *Social Mobility in the Caste System in India*, 1968, pp. 36-65 and Kathleen Gough: *Rural Society in South East India*, 1981, pp. 36-55.
26. Such long-term labour contracts in agricultural labour markets studied by K. Newaj and Ashok Rudra: "Agrarian Transformation in a District of West Bengal", *Economic and Political Weekly*, Vol. 10, No. 13, 1975, pp. A22-A23, see also A. Vaidyanathan: "Labour Use in Rural India: A Study of Temporal and Spatial Variations". *Economic and Political Weekly*, Vol. 21, No. 52, 1986, pp. A130-A146 and Sarmistha Pal: "An Analysis of Declining Incidence of Regular Labour Contracts in Rural India". *Journal of Development Studies*, Vol. 34, No. 2, 1997, pp. 133-155. Further, the declining long-term labour contracts with the introduction of new production techniques have been discussed by Jean-Philippe Platteau: "A Frame Work for the Analysis of Evolving Patron-Client Ties in Agrarian Economies." *World Development*, Vol. 23, No. 5, 1995,

pp. 705-879 and Anindita Mukherjee and Debraj Ray: "Labour Tying". *Journal of Development Economics*, Vol. 47, No. 2, 1995, pp. 207-239.

27. Clive Bell and T.N. Srinivasan: "Interlinked Transactions in Rural Markets: An Empirical Study of Andhra Pradesh, Bihar and Punjab". *Oxford Bulletin of Economics and Statistics*, Vol. 51, No. 1, 1989, pp. 73-83.
28. Sheila Bhalla: "New Relations of Production in Haryana." *Economic and Political Weekly*, Vol. 11, No. 13, 1976, pp. A23-A30.
29. Shyamal Roy and Melvin G. Blase: "Farm Tractorisation Productivity and Labour Employment: A Case Study of Indian Punjab". *Journal of Development Studies*, Vol. 14, No. 2, 1978, pp. 193-209.
30. Bina Aggarwal: "Agricultural Mechanization and Labour Use: A Disaggregated Approach". *International Labour Review*, Vol. 120, No. 1, 1981, pp. 115-127.
31. Pranab K. Bardhan: *Land, Labour and Rural Poverty*, 1984.
32. The subjection, loyalty and servility in the long-term labour contracts have been widely studied by scholars. The intensification of agriculture production, introduction of new crops and multiple crop rotations increased the demand of permanent farm servants all over the world. The subjection and servility over the permanent farm servants is exercised by their employers through their power to fire the permanent farm servants at any time. The farmers (employers) give them various perks like food, shelter and other amenities which create loyalty among permanent farm servants towards their employers in work and even in village politics which is commonly expected by their employers. For more details see Alan Richard: "The Political Economy of Gutswirtschaft: A Comparative Analysis of East Elbian Germany, Egypt and Chile". *Comparative Studies in Society and History*, Vol. 21, No. 4, 1979, pp. 483-518. Some other scholars also gave the same conclusions on the subjection and servility in long-term labour contracts. For details see Julie Anderson Schaffner: "Rural Labour Legislation and Permanent Agricultural Employment in North Eastern Brazil". *World Development*, Vol. 21, No. 5, 1993, pp. 705-719, ibid, "Attached Farm Labour, Limited Horizons and Servility." *Journal of Development Economics*, Vol. 47, No. 2, 1995, pp. 241-270. The subordination in long-term labour contracts in the cultivation of commercial crops has been studied by Jane L. Collins and Greta R. Krippner: "Permanent Labour Contracts in Agriculture: Flexibility and Subordination in a New Export Crop." *Comparative Studies in Society and History*, Vol. 41, No. 3, 1999, pp. 510-534.

3

Wage Rates of Permanent Farm Servants: Structure and Determinants

In this chapter the structure and determinants of wage rates of the permanent farm servants in Punjab are analysed on the basis of data of a random sample of two hundred and forty permanent farm servants spread over thirty randomly selected villages of Punjab. To begin with some theoretical aspects of wage rate determination are briefly discussed. The profile of sample permanent farm servants and their distribution by wage rates is described in the next section. The empirical procedure used to analyse the determinants of wage rates is briefly explained thereafter. In the next section univariate analysis of factors influencing the wage rate is attempted to gain a preliminary understanding of the role of different factors. The 'Age-Wage' rate relationship is analysed in more detail in the subsequent section. In the last section a multivariate analysis of determinants of the wage rate is done with the help of a number of models.

Some Theoretical Aspects of Wage Rate Determination

In the existing literature many studies are available on the wage rate of casual agricultural labourers [Dhavle, Soni, Bardhan and Bhalla, etc.],[1] but very few studies on the wage rates of permanent farm servants, despite the importance of this type of farm labour in many regions of India such as, the north-western green revolution region [Shyamal and Blase, Aggarwal and Eswaran and Kotwal, etc.].[2]

One of the few studies on the wage rate of the permanent

farm servants that we could locate in the literature is by Kalpana Bardhan[3] who analysed the wage rates across states and also across villages to find out the influence of demand and supply factors on the wage rate. Even this study, however, did not discuss exhaustively the wage rate of permanent farm servants. Similarly, Pranab K. Bardhan[4] pointed out the demand creating factors that affect the wage rates of casual and regular farm workers. Most of the standard theories of agricultural wage determination used by development economists make the standard assumption of a single wage rate for all workers in agriculture.[5] The wage rate of permanent farm servants is sensitive to supply, demand, productivity conditions and human capital variables as is the wage rate in any labour market, albeit conditioned by cultural factors and small size of the village labour markets. In the same village one permanent farm servant may earn much more than another depending on various factors related to his person and his employer. Even Marx has emphasized the role of such factors, *"One man is superior to another physically or mentally and so supplies more labour in the same time, or can labour for a longer time, and labour to serve as a measure must be defined by its duration or intensity, otherwise it ceases to be a standard of measurement...... . Further one worker is married; another not; one has more children than another and so on and so forth. Thus, with an equal output, and hence in equal share in the social consumption fund, one will in fact receive more than another, one will be richer than another and so on"*.[6] The human capital theory lays great emphasis on the role of personal factors and skills in the determination of the wage rate [Becker and Joll et.al.].[7] According to human capital theorists in a competitive labour market individuals will get wages according to their marginal productivity and their productivity is enhanced by investing in human capital. Therefore wages depend on the amount of investment in human capital undertaken.[8] However, human capital is not the only factor influencing the wage rate; the conditions in which work is performed also affect the wage rate. Jobs with less desirable working conditions require compensating wage differentials to attract workers. In a competitive labour market the interaction of aggregate demand

and supply of labour determines the overall average price of skills; and the skills differentials among individuals determine the wage rate difference among individuals, with adjustment for working conditions in individual jobs. In the long run, competition among workers and employers tends to equalize wages for workers with the same level of human capital and skills after providing for differences in working conditions.

The institutional economists have challenged the human capital wage determination theory mainly on account of it being based on the assumption of perfect competition in the product and labour markets. The presence of many imperfections in the product and labour markets like monopoly power in the product market is studied by Weiss,[9] unionization in the labour market by Wachtel[10] and the phenomenon of racial and gender discrimination by Smith[11] are important additional factors which affect the wage rate.

The labour search theory, in contrast, maintains the essence of human capital wage determination theory, while dropping the perfect competition assumption of the simple human capital model. This theory is based on the a priori assumption of dispersion of wage rates for a homogeneous labour even if labour supply and demand are stable for indefinitely long periods, because of incomplete knowledge and costly information.[12]

The disagreements on the assumptions underlying human capital wage determination theory have implications for the empirical estimation of wage functions, but even where agreement exists, difficulties in the application of this theory in empirical work persist. Education is the main variable used to represent the level of human capital, but the quality of education, length and quality of experience and the residential status of the workers are the other important variables which influence wage determination. The dummy variables are often used to capture the impact of such factors, but the inherent difficulty in measuring the human capital remains. That is one of the reasons for the low explanatory power of the human capital variable observed in many empirically estimated wage equations. Owing to such measurement problems some critics even deny the relevance of worker productivity in wage determination. However, most of the researchers now accept that human capital is one of the important factors influencing wage rates across industries and professions as well as within industries and professions.

Permanent Farm Servants: Salient Features

The broad profile of the class of permanent farm servants in Punjab as revealed by the information collected on a random sample of two hundred and forty of them is described in the next few pages with the help of a number of salient features selected to represent their age, caste, contract type, etc. The summary of this information in quantitative form is given in Table 3.1. One feature which does not figure in the table, but must be mentioned is that permanent farm servants in Punjab are all males. In the thirty villages from which we picked our sample, we did not find even a single female permanent farm servant.

Given the fact that there are many females among the casual farm workers, this all male character of permanent farm servants suggests that they perform duties on the farm which female labourers can not do. It may be noted that the mean age of the permanent farm servants (30 years) suggests that most of them must be young or middle-aged. However, there were also some quite old permanent farm servants; the oldest in our sample being 65 years. Some very young persons were also working as permanent farm servants; the youngest in our sample being only 14 years of age. It may also be noted from Table 3.1 that the majority of the permanent farm servants (60 per cent) were married persons; the remaining (40 per cent) being unmarried, and consequently of a younger age. As is well known (See Table 2.1, Chapter 2), most of the agricultural labourers in Punjab come from the scheduled castes social group. This was largely so in the case of our sample as well; two thirds (66 per cent) of the permanent farm servants belonged to scheduled castes. But surprisingly, there was quite a sizeable proportion (one-third) of the permanent farm servants who belonged to non-scheduled castes. It suggests many male members of the artisan castes

Table 3.1: Permanent Farm Servants: Salient Features (Summary Statistics)

S.No.	*Description*	
I.	**Age Profile (Years)**	
	1. Mean age	30
	2. Maximum age	65
	3. Minimum age	14
II.	**Caste Status**	
	1. Scheduled caste	66%
	2. Non-scheduled caste	34%
III.	**Marital Status**	
	1. Married	60%
IV.	**Nature of Wage Contract**	
	1. Fixed cash wage contract	94%
	2. Share wage contract	06%
V.	**Literacy Level**	
	1. Literate	21.3%
VI.	**Technical and Managerial Skills**	
	1. Drives tractor on farms	33.3%
	2. Can handle the electric motor operated tube wells	86.7%
	3. Supervises casual labour on the farms	74.7%
VII.	**Employer's Profile**	
	1. Employers having tractors	88%
	2. Employers having electric motor operated tube wells	92%
VIII.	**Employers with Operated Area More Than or Equal to Ten Acres**	80.7%
IX.	**Credit Dependence on Employers**	
	1. Total advance taken (mean)	Rs. 6,997
	2. Advance taken free of interest (mean)	Rs. 5,817
	3. Advance taken on interest (mean)	Rs. 2,180
X.	**Worked for the Same Employer Previous Year Also**	58%

Source: Primary Survey (2007-08)

(mostly backward castes or other backward castes) and some landless members of the cultivating castes have also joined the ranks of permanent farm servants in Punjab. So far as the nature of wage contract is concerned the sample information given in Table 3.1 reveals that, the fixed cash wage contract has become almost universal now; as many as 94 per cent of the permanent farm servants were hired on cash wage contract. However, even the traditional type of share wage contract (siri) that used to be quite popular in the pre-independence era, still persists in a few cases. Out of our sample of two hundred and forty permanent farm servants, 6 per cent were hired on a share-wage contract even in the first decade of the 21st century. However, it will not be wrong to generalize that permanent farm servants in Punjab agriculture today are almost all fixed cash wage contract workers.

The information on human capital related traits of permanent farm servants revealed quite interesting features. Contrary to the usual impression we find that about one-fifth (21.3 per cent) of the sample permanent farm servants were literate and could read and write; these are the people who joined the ranks of farm workers after dropping out of school after a few years. Of course, the great majority of permanent farm servants (78.7 per cent) was still completely illiterate and had never gone to school. But the lack of formal literacy does not mean that they were not sufficiently trained in the necessary skills needed in the modern mechanized agriculture that prevails in Punjab today. It may be observed that about 86 per cent of permanent farm servants could handle adequately the technical operations involved in operating an electric motor operated tubewell. Furthermore, one-third (33.3 per cent) of the permanent farm servants were actually working as tractor drivers on the farms on which they were employed; an activity that requires not only the technical expertise in handling the tractor, but also the knowledge of tilling and sowing operations. Almost three-fourth (74.7 per cent) of permanent farm servants were also working as some sort of foreman on the farms; they were supervising casual labour on the farms. Given the fact that a considerable amount of casual labour is used in Punjab agriculture, particularly in paddy transplantation and paddy harvesting operations, the supervisory role of permanent farm servant assumes greater importance in the productivity and efficiency of commercialized agriculture that prevails in Punjab today.

The size and type of farms on which permanent farm servants are employed also plays an important role in their life and in shaping their wage profile. It may be observed from the data given in Table 3.1 that most of the permanent farm servants (88 per cent) were employed on tractorized farms and as we have earlier observed, 33 per cent of them were working as tractor drivers. Almost all the farms (92 per cent) hiring permanent farm servants were irrigated with electric motor operated tubewells; and most of these (80.7 per cent) were sufficiently big farms (operated area more than or equal to ten acres). Another interesting aspect related to farmers (employers) of permanent farm servants is the credit linkage between the two. Our sample data revealed that taking a cash advance from the employer is a universal practice in Punjab. Every one of the two hundred and forty sample permanent farm servants has taken some cash advance from the employer at the time of joining the farm. The mean amount of advance taken worked out to Rs. 6,997 (Table 3.1), and most of it (82.7 per cent) was free of interest; probably in the form of advance wage payment. But a small amount (mean Rs. 2,180) was borrowed by permanent farm servants from their employers on interest payment basis as well. The relations between the permanent farm servants and their farmers (employers) did not seem to be under much strain; as 58 per cent of the sample permanent farm servants were found to have renewed their annual wage contract with the same farmer with whom they were working the previous year.

On the basis of the summary data given in Table 3.1 and from the above discussion we may conclude that most of the permanent farm servants in Punjab were relatively young married males belonging to scheduled castes and working on cash wage contract. A significantly visible number of them were also literate, but quite skilled in terms of handling of farm machinery and supervision of casual labour. Most of them were working on big tractorized and tube well irrigated farms, and in a majority of cases they continued to work for the same farmer for more than one year.

Wage Rate Structure of Sample Permanent Farm Servants

In the case of casual agricultural labourers the wage rate received by a worker is usually the same irrespective of his personal qualities, particularly when he is working on a daily wage rate basis. However in the case of permanent farm servants hired on an annual basis wage rates differ considerably from worker to worker depending on a large number of factors the influence of which we have analysed in the next two sections. In this section the structure of wage rates of sample permanent farm servants is described briefly to provide the necessary background for the subsequent analysis of determinants of wage rate. The structure of wage rates of sample permanent farm servants is summarized in Table 3.2 and depicted in graph 3.1.

Table 3.2: Distribution of Permanent Farm Servants by Wage Rate (2007-08)

Wage Rate (Rs. Per Year in Thousand)	*Number of Permanent Farm Servants*	*Proportion of Permanent Farm Servants (Percent)*	*Mean Wage Rate (Rs. Per year)*
5,000-12,000	34	14.2	10,038
12,000-19,000	42	17.5	14,778
19,000-26,000	93	38.8	22,819
26,000-33,000	53	22.0	28,866
33,000-40,000	14	5.8	35,824
40,000 & Above	04	1.7	43,159
All	240	100.00	22,153

(i) Median wage rate = Rs. 22793
(ii) Minimum wage rate = Rs. 6033
(iii) Maximum wage rate = Rs. 45892
(iv) Ratio of maximum to minimum wage rate = 7.61
(v) Coefficient of variation (CV) = 36.01%

Source: Primary Survey (2007-08).

For describing the structure of wage rates we classified the wage rates in six different size categories of Rs. 7,000 interval each. It may be observed from Table 3.2 and graph 3.1 that more than 50 per cent (56.25 per cent to be exact) of the permanent farm servants in our sample were receiving an annual wage between Rs. 12,000-26,000. The mean wage rate amounted to

Graph 3.1: Percentage Distribution of Permanent Farm Servants by Annual Wage Rate (Rs.)

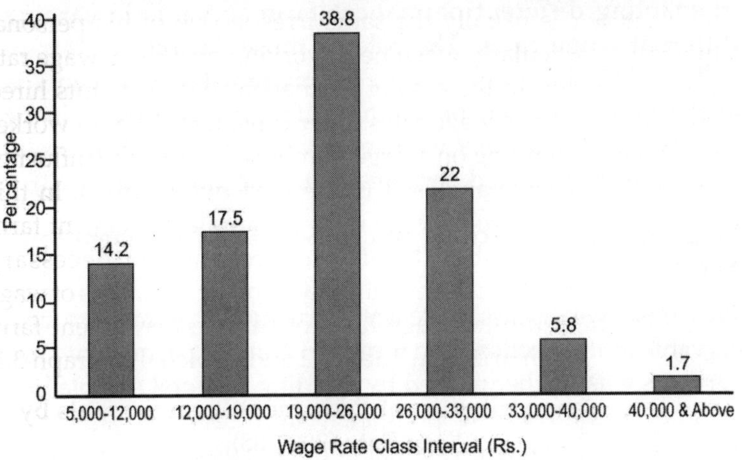

Rs. 22,153 per annum; the median wage rate is also quite near to the mean, being Rs. 22,793 per annum. However, there were some permanent farm servants, 22 per cent of the total, who were receiving an annual wage rate of more than Rs. 26,000 and four of the permanent farm servants in the sample were found to be getting more than Rs. 40,000 per annum. The information in Table 3.2 also reveals that there were many low paid permanent farm servants as well. It may be seen that 32 per cent of sample of permanent farm servants were getting less than Rs. 19,000 per year; more than fourteen per cent of these (32 per cent) were getting less than even Rs. 12,000 per year. So, we observe a quite dispersed wage structure of permanent farm servants in rural Punjab. The difference between the wage of the highest paid permanent farm servant (annual wage Rs. 45,892) and that of the lowest paid (annual wage Rs. 6,033) was indeed very big (Rs. 39,859). The ratio of the maximum to minimum wage rate works out to be 7.61; and the coefficient of variation (CV) was equal to 36.01 per cent and both these figures indicate considerable dispersion in the wage structure of permanent farm servants in rural Punjab. The very large dispersion in the wage rate structure of permanent farm servants suggests that various factors such as age, human capital and skill levels (tractor driving one of them) and other personal attributes determining productivity must play an important role in enabling different permanent farm servants in earning different wage rates. The role of those various factors in influencing the wage rate of permanent farm servants is analysed with the help of a number of regression models in the next two sections. Next we have given the wage structure of skilled and non-skilled permanent farm servants (Table 3.3).

Wage Structure of Skilled and Non-Skilled Permanent Farm Servants

Previously we discussed the wage structure of permanent farm servants in this section. The wage structure of permanent farm servants was further probed by dividing the total sample into 'skilled' and 'unskilled' permanent farm servants. Although there are many categories of skills, but we used tractor driving as the touch stone. So permanent farm servants driving tractors on the farms are called 'skilled' and all the others are called 'unskilled'. The distribution of skilled and non-skilled permanent farm servants in different wage categories is presented in Table 3.3.

From this table it comes out that the skilled permanent farm servants enjoy higher wages relatively to non-skilled. Not even a single skilled permanent farm servant falls in the two lower wage categories of Rs. 5,000 to Rs. 12,000 and Rs. 12,000 to Rs.19000, whereas almost 48 per cent of non-skilled permanent farm servants were getting wages between Rs. 5,000 to Rs. 19,000. Whereas all the skilled permanent farm servants were getting a wage above Rs. 19,000, only about 50 per cent of non-skilled permanent farm servants were getting that much. It may, however, be noted that even some of the unskilled permanent farm servants were getting a quite high wage of Rs. 33,000 or more; may be they have some other attributes or skills for which the farmers are willing to pay a high wage rate. The statistics given at the bottom of Table 3.3 show a large gap in the mean wage rate of skilled and non-skilled permanent farm servants. The mean wage rate of skilled permanent farm servants was 44 per cent higher than that of unskilled permanent farm servants;

Table 3.3: Wage Level and Structure of Skilled and Non-Skilled Permanent Farm Servants

Wage Rate (Rs./ per year in Thousand)	*Skilled*			*Non-skilled*		
	No. of Permanent Farm Servants	*Proportion*	*Mean Wage Rate (Rs./Year)*	*No. of Permanent Farm Servants*	*Proportion*	*Mean Wage Rate (Rs./year)*
5,000-12,000	-	-	-	34	21.25	10,039
12,000-19,000	-	-	-	42	26.25	14,779
19,000-26,000	32	40.00	22,947	61	38.13	22,751
26,000-33,000	34	42.5	28,865	19	11.87	28,867
33,000-40,000	10	12.5	35,926	03	1.87	35,622
40,000 & Above	04	5.00	43,123	01	0.63	43,234
All	80	100	27,896	160	100	19,368
Median wage rate (Rs.)			26,812			20,434
Minimum wage rate (Rs.)			19810			6034
Maximum wage rate (Rs.)			45893			43234
Ratio of maximum to minimum			2.31			7.16
Coefficient of variation (CV)		20.25%		38.48%		

Notes: (i) Source: Primary Survey (2007-08)
(ii) Skilled=Tractor Driver; Non-Skilled = Non-Tractor Driver.

and the median wage 31.21 per cent higher. A large gap also exists in the minimum wage rate of the two types of permanent farm servants. The minimum wage rate of a skilled permanent farm servant is Rs. 19,810, which was even more than the mean wage rate of non-skilled permanent farm servant. However, the difference in the maximum wage rate of skilled and unskilled permanent farm servants was rather small, the maximum wage being Rs. 45,893 in the case of skilled and Rs. 43,234 that of unskilled. Another important difference in the wage structure of skilled and unskilled permanent farm servants is in variation in the wage level. The coefficient of variation in the wage rate of skilled permanent farm servants was 20.25 per cent, compared to 38.48 per cent in that of unskilled permanent farm servants. Similarly, the ratio of maximum to minimum wage was only 2.31 in the case of skilled permanent farm servants, but 7.16 in the case of unskilled permanent farm servants. From the above it may be concluded that non-skilled permanent farm servants are getting on the average lower wages in Punjab than the skilled permanent farm servants. Moreover there is a greater variability in the wage rates of unskilled permanent farm servants than that of skilled permanent farm servants.

Determinants of Wage Rate: Analytical Procedures and Variable Description

In the previous section we have described how the annual wage earned by sample permanent farm servants varied very widely among them; the highest paid earning more than seven times the lowest paid. In this section an attempt is made to explain why some permanent farm servants earn more and some less and what factors account for or explain the wage rate variations among permanent farm servants working on Punjab farms. The role and contribution of different factors in influencing the wage rate of permanent farm servants is analysed with the help of standard ordinary least square (OLS) regression models. Both univariate as well as multivariate regression models are used for this purpose. The qualitative factors, such as caste, influencing the wage rate are included in the form of dummy variable. The dependent variable (the annual mean wage rate) is included in the regression models both in its natural form (rupees per year), as well as in the log form. The main purpose of using the log-form of the dependent variable was that economic variables more often follow the normal distribution, when converted into log form. The explanatory variables used to explain the determination of wage rates were divided into two sets: (i) those related to personal characteristics of permanent farm servants such as age, etc; and (ii) those related to their farm employers and production conditions such as farm size, etc. The wage rate of permanent farm servants is influenced by both sets of factors. In the final regression model both these sets of explanatory variables are mixed to find out the role of different factors in the determination of wage rate of permanent farm servants. We start with a univariate analysis of each factor's influence on wage rate in isolation, under uncontrolled conditions. The advantage of this procedure is that it gives us a preliminary insight into the role of different factors in influencing the wage rate. Subsequently, these explanatory variables are structured in a multiple regression model to find out their net impact (under controlled conditions) on the wage rate. The variables used in the regression model are briefly defined in the following boxes 3.1 and 3.2.

Box 3.1: Definition and Description of Explanatory Variables: Personal Characteristics

Explanatory Variables	*Definition*
Age (Years)	It is a continuous variable.
Experience (years)	For the last how many years a permanent farm servant is working as a permanent farm servant.
D_1 (Dummy):	Permanent farm servant driving tractor on farms = 1; others = 0
D_2 (Dummy):	Knowledge of electric motor operations: Yes = 1; No = 0
D_3 (Dummy):	Permanent farm servant supervises casual labour on farms = 1; others = 0
D4 (Dummy):	Education level of a permanent farm servant: Literate = 1; Illiterate = 0
D5 (Dummy):	Caste : Scheduled caste = 1; other = 0
D6 (Dummy):	Marital status: Married = 1; Unmarried = 0
D7 (Dummy):	Indebted to employer: Yes=1; No = 0

Determinants of Wage Rate: Univariate Analysis

The results of univariate analysis of determinants of wage rate are presented in two sets. In set one [Tables 3.4(A) and 3.4(B)] the role of various personal characteristics of permanent farm servants are analysed and in the second set [Tables 3.5(A) and 3.5(B)] the role of various factors related to the farm on which sample permanent farm servants were working is analysed.

Influence of Personal Characteristics on the Wage Rate

It may be observed from the results presented in Tables 3.4(A) and 3.4(B) that whether we use the natural form of the dependent variable (annual wage in rupees per year) or the log

Box 3.2: Definition and Description of Other Explanatory Variables: Farm Characteristics

Explanatory Variables	*Definition*
Cultivated Area of Employer's Farm	Actual operated area in acres
D_1 (Dummy) :	Size of farm dummy: ≥10 (Acres)=1; Other = 0
D_2 (Dummy) :	Tractor ownership dummy: Owns Tractor=1; Other=0
D_3 (Dummy) :	Electric totor tube well dummy: Owns = 1; Others = 0
D_4 (Dummy) :	Cropping pattern dummy: Wheat- Cotton = 1; Other = 0
Number of permanent farm servants working on the farm	The actual number of the permanent farm servants on the farm excluding the surveyed permanent farm servant.
Family males on the farms	Actual number of adult male members of employer's family working on the farms
D_5 (Dummy):	Continuity of employment dummy: Worked on the same farm last year = 1; Others = 0
D_6 (Dummy):	Type of contract dummy: Cash wage = 1; Share wage = 0
D_7 (Dummy):	Night work dummy: worked on the farm at night also when needed = 1; others = 0

form, the signs of coefficients of different explanatory variables remain the same. Even the statistical significance of the explanatory variables is not changed much, although the level of confidence at which these are significant does change in a few cases. Both the age of the worker and his length of experience (i.e. years of experience) have a positive and statistically significant influence on the wage rate. The older and more experienced workers are found earning more than the younger ones. In both cases the t_{values} are significant at one per cent level. Many earlier studies have also indicated that the wage rate is directly influenced by age and experience [Blaug, Sumner and Frazao, Sahn and Alderman, Blomquist and Koshal et al.][13]

These results, though statistically highly significant, we have to take with some caution on account of two reasons. One is that age and experience are highly positively correlated (r=0.84) and consequently their separate influence is difficult to disentangle in a multiple regression model. In fact only one of these can be legitimately inserted in a multiple regression model. Furthermore, the influence of age and experience on the wage rate and earnings may not be linear as is assumed in the univariate model, the results of which are presented in Tables 3.4(A) and 3.4(B). Both theory as well as common sense suggests that increasing age and experience will have a positive impact on the wage rate of manual workers, such as permanent farm

Table 3.4(A): Influence of Personal Characteristics on Wage Rate-I (N=240)

Explanatory Variables	*Dependent Variable (Y) = Annual Wage Rate (Rs.)* Intercept (α)	*Slope (β)*	t_{Values}	R^2
Age	15288.78	229.84	4.17***	0.10
Experience	19697.96	191.22	3.28***	0.07
Drives Tractor on Farm (D_1): Yes=1, No=0	19367.20	8528.74	7.08***	0.25
Operates Electric Motor on Farm (D_2): Yes = 1, No = 0	13360.62	10223.99	6.06***	0.20
Supervises Casual Labourers (D_3): Yes=1, No=0	13090.10	1224.50	11.15***	0.46
Literacy Level (D_4): Literate= 1, Illiterate = 0	22286.88	-626.38	0.39	0.00
Caste (D_5): Scheduled Caste =1, Others = 0	17962.31	6349.91	4.97***	0.14
Marital Status (D_6): Married=1, Unmarried = 0	17125.82	8379.06	7.33***	0.27
Indebted to Employer (D_7): Yes = 1, No = 0	21625.09	3047.06	1.78*	0.02

Note: t_{values} are significant at : * 10% and *** 1%

Table 3.4(B): Influence of Personal Characteristics on Wage Rate-II (N=240)

Explanatory Variables	*Dependent Variable (Y) = Log of Annual Wage Rate (Rs.)* Intercept (α)	*Slope (β)*	t_{Values}	R^2
Age	9.57	0.01	4.34***	0.11
Experience	9.80	0.01	3.38***	0.07
Drives Tractor on Farms (D_1): Yes=1, No=0	9.79	0.42	6.88***	0.24
Operates Electric Motor on Farms (D_2):Yes = 1, No = 0	9.45	0.57	6.72***	0.23
Supervises Casual Labourers (D_3): Yes = 1, No = 0	9.43	0.68	13.27***	0.54
Literacy Level (D_4): Literate = 1, Illiterate = 0	9.95	-0.07	0.98	0.01
Caste (D_5): Scheduled Caste = 1; Others = 0	9.71	0.33	5.12***	0.15
Marital Status (D_6): Married=1, Unmarried=0	9.65	0.46	8.22***	0.31
Indebted to Employer (D_7): Yes=1, No = 0	9.90	0.19	2.22**	0.03

Note: t_{values} are significant at : **5% & ***1%

servants, only up to a certain age and experience. Once sufficient experience has been attained there may not be any further gain in the wage rate. There may even be a negative impact of age on the wage rate as a farm worker becomes too old to do hard farm work. On account of these complexities the impact of age on the wage rate was analysed in more detail to capture the non-linearities involved and the results of that exercise are presented in Table 3.6.

The univariate results presented in Tables 3.4(A) and 3.4(B) indicate no significant role of formal literacy in the determination of the wage rate of permanent farm servants in Punjab. The coefficient of the literacy dummy variable is not significant even at 10 per cent level, and has the wrong negative sign, implying that formal literacy may even be putting a permanent farm servant at a disadvantage in terms of the wage rate. The folklore also supports this allusion; in rural Punjab it is widely believed that a literate person is no good at doing rough and tough work on the farms. The significant role of professional training and skills in operating modern machinery is clearly revealed by results presented in Tables 3.4(A) and 3.4(B). These are found to exert a significant positive impact on the annual earnings of permanent farm servants. All three variables representing these skills (tractor driving, electric tubewell operation and supervision of casual labour) are found to have a positive and statistically significant (at 1 per cent level in all three cases) impact on the annual wage rate of permanent farm servants; and the impact is quite substantial.

It may be observed from Table 3.4(A) that permanent farm servants driving tractors on farms earned annually Rs. 8,528 more than those not working as tractor drivers. Similarly, the permanent farm servants operating electric motor tubewells earned Rs. 10,223 more, and those supervising casual labour Rs. 1,224 more than those not performing these skilled and supervisory tasks. It may be noted, that in all these cases the explanatory variable is structured as a dummy variable, and consequently the intercept term of the univariate regression equation gives the mean annual earnings of those permanent farm servants who are not performing these tasks, whereas the coefficient of the dummy variable gives the difference (in all the three cases positive) between the earnings of permanent farm servants performing these tasks and the others who are not performing these tasks.

As we have seen earlier (Table 3.1) the great majority of permanent farm servants belong to the scheduled castes social group. We have explored the impact of caste on earnings. The results presented in Tables 3.4(A) and 3.4(B) indicate that permanent farm servants belonging to the scheduled caste social group earn a significantly higher annual wage compared to those who belong to non-scheduled castes. On the face of it this result may seem at odds with the common view and the general impression of scheduled castes being less efficient than non-scheduled castes. There can be many possible explanations of this observed significantly higher mean annual earning of scheduled caste permanent farm servants. One is that farm work is a traditional occupation of the scheduled castes in Punjab and the male children of scheduled castes start working on farms at a very early age and consequently acquire greater experience and expertise in farm work. Secondly, scheduled castes being generally poor are more rough and tough and they are at ease in doing farm work. They are also more submissive and obedient to farm owners, as they are not averse even to do personal and domestic chores for the farmer. On account of these factors farmers may be willing to pay a higher wage to a scheduled caste worker, compared to a non-scheduled caste worker. The non-scheduled caste permanent farm servants are generally males who have failed to acquire a firm footing in their own traditional caste occupation and consequently are likely to be less trained and suited for the tough farm work. Anyhow, the significantly higher wage rate of scheduled caste permanent farm servants, if it persists even in the multivariate regression models, will require considerable more analysis and research for rationalization. The above explanations are only tentative conjectures to account for it.

The last two variables in Tables 3.4(A) and 3.4(B), marital status and indebtedness are also found to have a statistically significant positive impact on the annual earnings of permanent farm servants. It may be noted that both these variables are in the form (0, 1) of dummies and consequently the regression coefficient of the dummy variable indicates that the difference in the annual earnings of married permanent farm servants and non-married ones; and the difference in the annual wage of those under debt to the employer and those free from debt. It may be seen that married permanent farm servants, on the average; earn Rs. 8,379 more than unmarried permanent farm servants. Many plausible explanations can be offered for this significantly high annual wage of married permanent farm servants. Firstly, marital status, age and experience are positively related; married permanent farm servants are on an average older in age and more experienced as well. Given the positive influence of age and experience on the wage rate, it may be partially responsible for the higher observed earning of married permanent farm servants. Secondly, married permanent farm servants being under severe pressure of family consumption needs are supposed to work harder and longer to earn more to meet their family's consumption needs. They are also likely to be more disciplined and responsible for the same reason. The unmarried permanent farm servants being under no such pressure are likely to be more carefree, less hard working and less responsible. On account of these processes married permanent farm servants may be earning significantly more than the unmarried permanent farm servants. On the same lines, the pressure to repay the debt may be making indebted workers more hard working and willing to do all sorts of work, even unpleasant tasks, which permanent farm servants free from debt probably will not be willing to do. On account of the debt pressure, therefore, these indebted workers may be putting in longer hours, performing harder and unpleasant tasks and acting in a more reliable and disciplined manner. These sorts of factors and process may be the plausible explanation of indebted permanent farm servants earning significantly more than the non-indebted permanent farm servants.

Influence of Size and Type of Farm and Production Conditions on the Wage Rate

The analysis of influence of personal characteristics of permanent farm servants on their annual earnings presented in the preceding few pages is followed by an analysis of farm type, farm size and production conditions. The important features of hiring farms that can influence the wage rate of permanent farm servants are size of the farm, degree of mechanization of the farm, cropping pattern, nature of wage contract, time profile of the work to be done and the participation of family members of the employer in farm work. The results of this exercise are presented in Tables 3.5(A) and 3.5(B).

The size of farm variable was tried in two forms: as simple operated area (acres) of the farm and in the form of a dummy variable taking value one for big farms (greater than or equal to ten acres) and zero for small farms (less than ten acres). It may be observed from Tables 3.5(A) and3.5(B) that in both these forms the farm size variable has a positive coefficient that is also statistically significant at 10 per cent level when farm size is taken as a continuous variable, and at 1 per cent when it is structured in the form of a dummy separating big and small farms. On the basis of these results it can be concluded that permanent farm servants employed on big farms get a higher annual wage compared to those working on small and medium farms and the difference in the wage rate of these two groups of permanent farm servants is substantial (Rs. 9,422). Many plausible explanations can be offered for the higher wage of permanent farm servants working on big farms. Of course, big farms being richer comparatively, can afford to pay more to the permanent farm servants hired by them. But, why do they pay more? One reason is that the total amount of work done (per year) by permanent farm servants working on big farms must be more than those working on medium and small farms. Furthermore, the permanent farm servants employed on big farms are more often assigned supervision of casual labour duty; and it is a well known fact that the big farms use casual labour to a larger extent. On the same lines the burden of driving a tractor and operating motor operated tube wells also falls more often on permanent farm servants working on big farms. Another plausible reason is that due to their greater paying capacity and greater need for better permanent farm servants, the big farms are able to pick up the better and more efficient males from the pool of permanent farm servants available in a village. So these more efficient permanent farm servants earn a higher wage rate because of their higher productivity.

The results presented in Tables 3.5(A) and 3.5(B) also indicate that farmers owning tractors pay a significantly higher (Rs. 7,675) annual wage to their permanent farm servants compared to farmers not owning the tractor. Since almost 100 per cent of farms in Punjab now use tractors, so this positive impact of tractor ownership cannot be attributed to the labour productivity enhancing impact of tractors. Because that will be presented in case of all tractor users irrespective of whether the tractor is owned or hired. The more plausible explanation seems to be the positive correlation of tractor ownership and farm size (r=0.24). Both tractor ownership and big farm size being dummy variables, 0.24 is a fairly high correlation between the two. So, it is probably the impact of the big farm size that is being

Table 3.5(A): Wage Rate of Permanent Farm Servants: Influence of Size and Structure of Farms (N=240)

Explanatory Variables	*Dependent Variable (Y) = Annual Wage Rate (Rs.)* Intercept (α)	*Slope (β)*	t_{Values}	R^2
Cultivated Area (Acres)	21091.68	37.38	1.76*	0.02
Big Farm Size (D_1): Operated Area $\geq$ 10 (Acres) = 1; Others=0	14112.41	9422.86	5.62***	0.18
Tractor Ownership with Employer (D_2):Yes=1, No = 0	15399.17	7675.09	4.01***	0.09
Electric Motor Ownership with Employer (D_3): Yes= 1, No = 0	22948.88	-1198.95	0.11	0.00
Cropping Pattern (D_4): Wheat-Cotton = 1, Other = 0	20817.02	5726.73	4.25***	0.09
Number of Permanent Farm Servants Working on the Farms	22200.22	-85.91	0.20	0.00
Number of Adult Male Members of Employers Family Working on the Farms	20692.39	814.61	1.47	0.01
Continuity of Employment with the Employer (D_5):Yes = 1, No = 0	20288.11	3215.76	2.48***	0.04
Type of Contract (D_6): Share Wage = 0, Cash Wage = 1	34123.78	-12734.60	5.00***	0.15
Work in Nightshifts during the Soni Season (D_7): Yes = 1, No= 0	12355.00	10350.27	3.72***	0.09

Note: t_{values} are significant at * 10 % & *** 1%

reflected through tractor ownership due to the univariate nature of the regression models in Tables 3.5(A) and 3.5(B). Anyhow, whether or not tractor ownership has an independent influence on the wage rate will become clear in the next section where we take up the multivariate regression analysis of determinants of the wage rate.

At present three major cropping patterns prevail in Punjab; cotton-wheat rotation is dominant in southern Punjab, maize, paddy and wheat in the foot hills zone, and paddy-wheat in bigger central zone. The influence of the cropping pattern on the annual wage rates of permanent farm servants was explored by structuring it into a dummy variable which takes value one in case of permanent farm servants working in the cotton- wheat zone and value zero for all the others.

It may be seen that the coefficient of this cropping pattern dummy has a positive sign and is significant at one per cent level. This suggests that permanent farm servants in the cotton-wheat cropping pattern zone get on an average a higher annual wage, (Rs. 5,727 more), than those working in the paddy-wheat and paddy, maize and wheat zones. The main reason for the significantly higher wage of permanent farm servants in the cotton-wheat zone seems to be the more extensive amount of work that has to be done by these workers in the cultivation of the cotton crop that takes a longer time to mature and harvest and is also more demanding and even risky because of the many sprayings of pesticides that have to be done to save it from pest attacks. Another reason can be the persistence of share-wage contract in the cotton-wheat zone. The share-wage contract was widely prevalent in Punjab at one time, but has now largely disappeared. But in the cotton-zone it still persists in a few cases. The share-wage contract, on the average, yields a bigger annual wage [see result in Table 3.5(A) and 3.5(B)]. A share-wage contract permanent farm servant gets, on the average, an annual wage that was greater by Rs. 12,734.60 compared to the cash-wage contract permanent farm servants. Why a share-wage contract yields a significantly bigger annual wage to permanent farm servants is a complex question requiring a full-fledged study that cannot be attempted here.

Table 3.5(B): Wage Rate of Permanent Farm Servants: Influence of Size and Structure of Farms (Univariate Analysis) (N=240)

Explanatory Variables	*Dependent Variable (Y) = Log of Annual Wage Rate (Rs.)* Intercept (α)	*Slope (β)*	t_{Values}	R^2
Cultivated Area (Acres)	9.87	0.002	1.97*	0.03
Big Farm Size (D_1): Operated Area ≥ 10 (Acres) = 1, Others=0	9.47	0.54	6.56***	0.23
Tractor Ownership with Employer (D_2):Yes=1, No = 0	9.54	0.44	4.64***	0.13
Electric Motor Ownership with Employer (D_3): Yes= 1, No = 0	9.98	-0.006	0.47	0.00
Cropping Pattern (D_4): Wheat-Cotton = 1, Other = 0	9.86	0.29	3.87***	0.09
Number of Permanent Farm Servants Working on the Farms	9.93	-0.34	0.15	0.00
Number of Adult Male Members of Employers Family Working on the Farms	9.84	0.04	1.47	0.14
Continuity of Employment with the Employer (D_5): Yes = 1, No = 0	9.85	0.15	2.21**	0.03
Type of Contract (D_6): Share Wage = 0, Cash Wage = 1	10.40	-0.50	3.72***	0.09
Work in Nightshifts during the Soni Season (D_7): Yes = 1, No= 0	9.39	0.58	4.11***	0.10

Note: t_{values} are significant at : * 10%, **5% and *** 1%.

The results presented in Tables 3.5(A) and 3.5(B) also indicate the presence or absence of electric motor operated tubewells on a farm does not make any significant impact on the annual wage received by permanent farm servants working on these farms. Similarly, the number of permanent farm servants working on a farm as well on the number of male family members of the farmers working on the farm do not make any significant impact on the wage rate of permanent farm servants. However, whether or not a permanent farm servant has to do night shift work (mainly for irrigating the paddy fields), does make a significant impact on their wage rates. The results suggest that those permanent farm servants who were performing night shift work were getting significantly more (Rs. 10,350 per year) than those not doing night shift work. This is quite understandable because the unpleasantness of the night shift work and also due to the longer hours of work it imposes on the permanent farm servants; because after the night shift he is not given off duty during the day time. A permanent farm servant who works with one employer (farmer) for more than one year also gets more wages [Tables 3.5(A) and 3.5(B)]. One possible reason behind this may be that a permanent farm servant who continuously works with the same farmer (employer) for many years acquires almost complete knowledge of the functioning of that farm, which increases his productivity. Another possible reason can be that only an efficient more productive worker is retained by the employer for more than one year. A farmer (employer), therefore, can rely more on such a tried, tested and efficient worker and that reduces the burden on the employer of running the farm. A farmer will not hesitate to pay more to such a tried, tested and efficient worker.

Non-Linearity in Age-Wage Relationship

In the univariate results presented in Tables 5.4(A) and 5.4(B) we observed that the age of the permanent farm servants has a significant positive influence on the wage rate and so is the case with experience. Age and length of experience are highly positively correlated (r=0.84) and significant at 1 per cent level and both indicate almost the same phenomenon (at least in the case of agricultural labour). Furthermore, we are considering separately specific aspects of experience such as tractor driving, etc; so length of experience as a separate variable was not further analysed. But the role of age as a determinant of the wage rate was further probed for the existence of non-linearity in the relationship of the two. There is ample evidence in the literature on the wage rate determination indicating that the impact of age on earnings is non-linear, particularly in the case of manual workers. Even in the case of white collar jobs it is often found that age impacts earnings in a non-linear manner. To cite a few studies to illustrate this general conclusion found in this literature, we may refer to Sahn and Alderman[14] and Datt[15]. Sahn and Alderman who found that the wage rate of workers in rural areas peaked at the age of 44 years and at 55 years in the urban areas. Up to these ages respectively the age and wage rate were positively related, thereafter the two were related inversely. Similarly, Datt revealed the negative relationship between the wage rate and the age of male casual farm labourers in a few farm operations. It means the age-wage relationship follows an inverted U-shaped curve. To find out whether or not this is true also in the case of our sample permanent farm servants we estimated a regression model in which Age^2 (square) was included as an explanatory variable along with Age. The results of this quadratic model are presented in Table 3.6 and clearly reveal that the "age-wage" relationship in the case of sample permanent farm servants is non-linear.

Table 3.6: Impact of Age on the Wage Rates of Permanent Farm Servants: Exploring the Non-Linearities (N=240)

Explanatory Variables	*Dependent Variable (Y): Annual Wage Rate (Rs.)*	
	Equation – 1 (Dependent Variable in Natural Form)	*Equation – 2 (Dependent Variable in Log Form)*
Age	1776.67	0.09
	(7.16)***	(8.17)***
Age^2	-22.51	-0.001
	(6.36)***	(7.31)***
Intercept	-7995.17	8.26
R^2	0.30	0.35
F_{values}	31.22***	39.51***

Note: (i) Figures inside parentheses are t_{values}.
(ii) F_{values} and t_{values} are significant at *** 1 per cent level.

Graph 3.2: Age-Wage Relationship

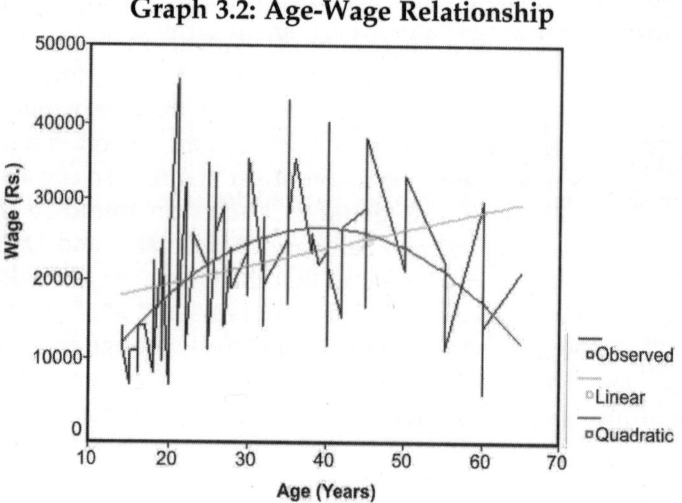

It may be observed that the coefficients of both 'Age' and 'Age'^{2} variables are significant at 1 per cent level for a two-tailed test, but the sign of the 'Age' variable is positive, and that of 'Age^2' variable negative. The negative sign of the 'Age^2' variable indicates that the path followed by the impact of age on wage rates takes an inverted U-shape. The estimated equation-1 in Table 3.6 (in which the wage rate dependent variable is in natural form) was used to trace out the curve showing the relationship between the age and wage rate of sample permanent farm servants. This curve is presented in graph 3.2 and shows clearly the inverted U-shape of the 'Age-Wage' relationship. The visual inspection of this curve suggested that the wage rate of sample permanent farm servants peaked at the age of 39 years and then declined thereafter. Our findings on the age-wage relationship coincide with the findings of Rajaraman[16]. He found the wages of males in the Indian rural labour market became maximum at the age of 40 years. After this age the wages started declining. To confirm this more conclusively, the wage rate of permanent farm servants at ages ten years to seventy years was estimated by using equation-1 (Table 3.6) and these estimated wage rates are reproduced in the appendix 3.1 of this chapter. These estimates confirmed the visual impression and revealed that the highest wage rate was earned by permanent farm servants at the age of 39 years. It means that the wage rate of permanent farm servants keeps increasing with age upto the age of 39, as they gain more experience in farm work and probably also because they gradually become physically sturdier, compared to young age workers. But after attaining the age of 39 years, as a permanent farm servant ages further, his wage rate declines and ultimately, our estimates revealed (given in the appendix) that an aged permanent farm servant (e.g. aged 60 years or above) earns just about half of a permanent farm servant of 39 years. The decline in the wage rate with advancing age after 39 years can be explained in a number of ways. One is that by the age of 39 the experience of farm work reaches the maximum and stops adding to the wage rate as age further advances. Secondly, since farm work involves difficult manual operations, the capacity and stamina to do hard manual work starts declining after the age of 39. Thirdly, by this age the family size and structure of the permanent farm servant becomes more complex and difficult due to the problem of settling of sons and marrying daughters. Consequently he is no longer in a position to devote his full attention and energy to farm work and that makes him a less productive worker and hence the farmers (employers) pay him a lower wage compared to a permanent farm servant at the peak of his working capacity that seems to be reached at the age of 39 years in the case of our sample permanent farm servant.

Determinants of the Wage Rate: Multivariate Analysis

In the preceding section we studied the influence of different factors in determining the wage rate of sampled permanent farm servants with the help of the simple univariate regression model in which each factor is used alone as the explanatory variable. This exercise has yielded many important insights about the role of different factors in influencing the wage rate of permanent farm servants. This procedure is quite useful as a preliminary exercise, but does not yield definitive results because the effect of other factors is not controlled or accounted far. The coefficients of a univariate regression model give us the gross impact of the explanatory variable on the dependent variable and in this gross impact the effect of many other factors is intermingled. To find out the net/pure impact of a factor on the dependent variable, the multiple regression analysis is the technique universally used. In the multivariate model the effect of other variables gets controlled and one gets the pure net affect of each factor in the form of its regression coefficient. To further analyse the role of different factors in the determination of wage rates of permanent farm servants, we have used the multiple regression model and the results of that exercise are presented and discussed in this section. In all we have estimated three different multivariate regression models: in the first all the relevant personal characteristics of permanent farm servants are structured together as the explanatory factors; in the second features of farmers (employers) and conditions of production are taken together as the determinants and the third is a mixed model in which selected personal characteristics and features of farmers (employers) and production conditions are used as the explanatory factors.

Role of Personal Characteristics of Permanent Farm Servants in Wage Rate Determination

The results of the multivariate analysis of the net role of personal characteristics of permanent farm servants in influencing their annual wage are presented in Table 3.7. It may be seen that the set of personal characteristics of permanent farm servants structured together as the explanatory variables explains two-third (66 per cent) of the variation in the wage rate of the sample permanent farm servants. Out of the bundle of personal characteristics of permanent farm servants the ones that are statistically significant and have the right expected signs are the two skills(tractor driving, supervision of casual labour), and marital status and caste. It may be seen that the coefficient skill of tractor driving has a positive sign and is significant at one per cent level; and so is the case of supervision of the casual labour dummy variable. Similarly, Binswanger[17] found the regular farm servants who performed skilled and multiple tasks on farms got more wages, e.g. a cowherd got less wages compared to ploughmen. So the indication given by preliminary univariate results about the positive impact of these two personal skills on the wage rate of permanent farm servants is confirmed by the multivariate results as well. Similarly, the results of the multivariate exercise presented in Table 3.7 confirm the univariate clues about the role of caste and marital status in wage rate determination. On the basis of these results, one can accept the hypothesis made about the role of these variables at the beginning of this study.

Table 3.7: (Model–I) Role of Personal Characteristics in Wage Rate Determination: Multivariate Analysis (N=240)

Explanatory Variables	*Dependent Variable (Y): Annual Wage Rate (Rs.)*	
	Equation – 1 (Dependent Variable in Natural Form)	*Equation – 2 (Dependent Variable in Log Form)*
Age	235.58	0.01
	(0.89)	(1.24)
Age^2	-3.53	-0.0002
	(0.99)	(1.45)
Do Tractor Driving on Farms (D_1): Yes=1, No=0	3524.74	0.14
	(3.31)***	(2.79)***
Knows All Electric Motor Operations (D_2): Yes=1, No=0	1220.12	0.05
	(0.77)	(0.74)
Supervises Casual Labour on Farms (D_3):Yes=1, No=0	7761.00	0.46
	(5.35)***	(6.85)***
Literacy Level (D_4): Literate=1, Illiterate=0	905.55	0.01
	(0.83)	(0.02)
Caste (D_5):Scheduled Caste=1, Others=0	2708.95	0.13
	(2.61)***	(2.40)**
Marital Status (D_6): Married=1; Unmarried=0	2997.36	0.17
	(2.66)***	(3.37)***
Indebted to Employers (D_7): Yes=1, No=0	–1681.28	–0.04
	(1.36)	(0.83)
Intercept	7276.60	9.11
R^2	0.58	0.66
$\bar{R}^2$	0.56	0.64
F_{values}	22.19***	39.89***

Note: (i) Figures in parentheses are t_{values}
(ii) F_{values} and t_{values} are significant at ***1% & **5%

In the case of formal literacy, the multivariate results confirm the earlier univariate conclusions that this factor does not play any significant role in wage rate determination. The positive impact of familiarity with the operation of power tubewells on the wage rate indicated by univariate results, however, is not confirmed by multiple regression results reported in Table 3.7.The possible reason for this is the high positive correlation between tractor driving and power tubewell operation skills.All permanent farm servants who drive tractors are also experts in operating power tubewells. The role of indebtedness in wage rate determination, however, is unclear because the multivariate coefficient of this variable in Table 3.7 is not significant even at 10 per cent level, although in the univariate model it had come out quite significant indicating that indebted permanent farm servants get higher wages than the debt free permanent farm servants. The most surprising result we get in this multivariate exercise is on the role of age in wage rate determination. In the non-linear univariate analysis, (Table 3.6), of the impact of age on the wage rate it was observed that age has a significant influence on the wage rate and the impact takes the form of an inverted U-shaped curve.

In fact, both the age variables in that exercise (Age and Age^2) turned out highly statistically significant and Age alone seemed to explain almost one-third of the variation in the wage rate of sample permanent farm servants. But in the multivariate context of Table 3.7 both Age and Age^2 variables have very low t_{values} and are not significant even at 10 per cent level; though they have the right signs. This result is quite puzzling and difficult to rationalize. May be the high correlation of Age with the experience-related variables, (tractor driving, power tubewell operation and supervision of casual labour) may be responsible for the odd results. Anyhow, we have to wait till the final (third) mixed model to say something more definitive on the role of age as a determinant of the wage rate of permanent farm servant in Punjab.

Role of Employer's Characteristics and Production Conditions in Wage Rate Determination

In addition to characteristics related to the person of the worker, the wage rate of a permanent farm servant is influenced by size and type of the farm on which he is employed and also by the production conditions on the employing farm. The role of the employer's characteristics and production conditions related factors in wage rate determination is analyzed in this section by structuring these factors in a multiple regression model. As many as nine variables are included in this model to capture the maximum number of employer and production conditions related factors. The results of this multivariate model are given in Table 3.8 and reveal that the set of nine employer and production conditions related variables explains only 38 per cent of the variation in wage rates of sample permanent farm servants; much less than was explained by the personal characteristics related factors in Table 3.7.

Out of the nine explanatory variables included in this model, five emerge as statistically significant. The significant positive influence of farm size on the annual wage received by workers is clearly confirmed even in the multivariate context, as has been suggested by the univariate results. The permanent farm servants working on the big farms get a significantly higher wage rate than their brethren working on the medium and small farms. The univariate result on the impact of the cropping pattern is again validated by multivariate results presented in Table 3.8; the permanent farm servants working on cotton growing farms receive significantly higher wages than those working on wheat, paddy and maize growing farms. These results on the positive impact of farm size and cotton-based cropping pattern on the wage rate of permanent farm servants support the hypothesis proposed earlier in the study on the role of these two factors. It is again revealed by multivariate results that permanent farm servants working on share contract basis earn a significantly bigger amount compared to those working on fixed cash wage contracts.

It is also revealed clearly by results given in Table 3.8 that permanent farm servants who continue working for the same farm year after year also earn a significantly higher wage rate compared to those who switch their employers every year. Similarly, permanent farm servants who have to perform night shift work in the Soni (Kharif) season get duly compensated in terms of significantly higher annual wage rates.

Out of the four variables that are found with low t_{values} and hence not significant even at 10 per cent, the three (employer owns motor operated tubewell, number of permanent farm servants working on the farm and number of male family

Table 3.8: (Model-II) Impact of Employer's Characteristics and Production Conditions on Wage Rate: Multivariate Analysis (N=240)

Explanatory Variables	*Dependent Variable (Y): Annual Wage Rate (Rs.)* Equation – 1 (Dependent Variable in Natural Form)	Equation – 2 (Dependent Variable in Log Form)
Farm Size (D_1): ≥10(Acres) =1; other=0	6446.69 (3.99)***	0.39 (4.58)***
Employer Owns Tractor (D_2): Yes=1, No=0	2702.19 (1.48)	0.17 (0.10)
Employer Owns Electric Motor (D_3): Yes=1, No=0	–279.46 (0.11)	–0.02 (0.97)
Cropping Pattern (D_4): Wheat – Cotton=1, Other=0	2511.54 (1.80)**	0.16 (2.55)**
Number of Permanent Farm Servants Working on the Farms	–311.99 (0.82)	-0.01 (0.92)
Number of Adult Male Members of Employer's Family Working on the Farms	496.75 (1.04)	0.03 (0.80)
Continuity of Employment with the Employer for the Last One Year (D_5): Yes=1, No=0	2317.84 (2.22)**	0.11 (2.11)**
Type of Contract (D_6): Cash Wage=1, Share Wage=0	-6200.66 (2.88)***	-0.21 (2.05)**
Work in Night Shifts during the Soni Season (D_7):Yes=1, No=0	6952.61 (2.77)***	0.38 (2.91)***
Intercept	10959.07	9.16
R^2	0.37	0.38
$\bar{R}^2$	0.33	0.34
F_{values}	8.87***	9.60***

Note: (i) Figures in parentheses are t_{values}.
(ii) F_{values} and t_{values} are significant at: ***1% and **5%.

members of employer's family working on the farm), remain consistent with their univariate performance. It may be recalled that even in the univariate regressions none of these three variables was found to be significant even at 10 per cent level. But the case of tractor owning farms is quite different, because the earlier presented univariate results have clearly revealed that permanent farm servants working on farms which own tractors earn significantly higher wages compared to those working on farms that use hired tractors. In the multivariate context of Table 3.8, the tractor ownership variable has very small t_{values} and hence not significant even at 10 per cent level. The main reason for this drastic change in the significance level of tractor ownership variable from the univariate to the multivariate context seems to be the high positive correlation between farm size variable and the tractor ownership variable, since almost all the big farms in our sample own tractors. The correlation between big farm size dummy variable and tractor ownership dummy variable was 0.24, which is fairly high considering 0, 1 nature of these two variables. So, in a way the positive significant impact of the farm size variable on the wage rate of permanent farm servants revealed by results given in Table 3.8 can be interpreted as the combined effect of all the factors (particularly ownership of modern machinery) that are strongly positively correlates with farm size.

Factors Determining the Wage Rate: The Mixed Model

After exploring the role of personal characteristics and employer-related characteristics separately, we structured all the factors in a multivariate model to search for the factors that play a significant role in the determination of the wage rate of permanent farm servants in Punjab. For this purpose many combinations of these factors were tried in order to arrive at a satisfactory explanation of variations in the wage rate observed among our sample permanent farm servants. Out of these many models that we estimated and tried the one that we found most satisfactory is presented in Table 3.9. The selection of this model, out of the many that we tried is based mainly on two criteria; the highest R^2 and the right signs and significance of the theoretically important explanatory factors. This model yielded the highest R^2 and the coefficients of the theoretically important factors have the right signs and are significant statistically at an acceptable level. It may be seen from Table 3.9 that the set of seven explanatory variables (Age and Age^2 being treated as a single factor) included in this model explain 70 per cent of the variation in the wage rate of sample permanent farm servants and that can be taken as a fairly high explanatory power by the usually accepted standards. Moreover, the inverted U-shaped impact of Age on the wage rate comes out quite clearly and significantly in this model.

Table 3.9: (Model-III) Factors Affecting Wage Rate: Multivariate Analysis (N=240)

Explanatory Variables	*Dependent Variable (Y): Annual Wage Rate (Rs.)*	
	Equation – 1 (Dependent Variable in Natural Form)	*Equation – 2 (Dependent Variable in Log Form)*
Age	298.63	0.02
	(1.18)	(1.97)*
Age^2	-4.08	-0.003
	(1.19)	(2.06)**
Marital Status: Married=1,	2641.53	0.15
Others=0	(2.43)**	(3.15) **
Drives Tractor on Farms:	3873.67	0.15
Yes=1, No=0	(3.90)***	(3.45)***
Operates Power-Driven	2339.48	0.12
Tubewell on Farm:Yes=1, No=0	(1.51)	(1.69)*
Supervises Casual Labour:	5941.76	0.36
Yes=1, No=0	(4.11)***	(5.60)***
Farm Size (Acres): Big Farm	4645.18	0.26
≥ 10=1, Others=0	(4.04)***	(4.99)***
Intercept	4380.49	8.93
R^2	0.61	0.72
$\bar{R}^2$	0.60	0.70
F_{values}	31.74***	47.36***

Note: (i) Figures in brackets are t_{values}
(ii) t & F_{values} are significant at: * 10%, **5% and ***1% level.

It may be recalled that in the purely personal characteristics model of Table 3.7, the impact of age has become somewhat unclear because of the low t_{values} of Age and Age^2 variables in that model. On the basis of results presented in Table 3.9 and of our earlier detailed unifactor analysis of the impact of age (Table 3.6) one can say with considerable confidence that the impact of age on earnings of permanent farm servants in Punjab takes a non-linear inverted U-shape whereby the wage rate increases with age upto the middle age level and then starts falling as the workers become older and older.

The significant positive impact of three professional skills (tractor driving, supervision of casual labour and operation of power tubewell) is also very clearly confirmed. It may be recalled that the coefficients of the first two or three variables have remained constantly significant with positive signs in the previous model (Table 3.7) in which these have been included. However, the coefficient of operation of power tubewell variable was not significant even at 10 per cent in Table 3.7.But in the mixed model of Table 3.7 it is significant at 5 per cent level in equation two and has a t_{value} greater than one even in equation one. So one can conclude the positive role of power tubewell operation skill is also confirmed. On the basis of these results, one may observe that in modern Punjab agriculture the training and skills of permanent farm servants in working as tractor drivers and in supervising casual labour on the farm get duly rewarded in the form of significantly higher annual wage rate. The significant positive impact of farm size (and of course its correlated factors not included here) is also clearly confirmed and one can conclude safely that in Punjab permanent farm servants working on big farms earn significantly more than those working on medium and small farms. The positive significant impact of marital status is also clearly confirmed by the results of Table 3.9. It may be recalled that the coefficient of this variable has been consistently positive and significant in all the models (univariate as well as multivariate) in which it was structured. So, one can say with confidence that in the Punjab rural side married permanent farm servants earn significantly more than the unmarried ones. This positive impact may be the mixed result of the positive correlation of age with the wage rate and the greater pressure of family consumption needs of married workers, compelling them to work harder and hence becoming more productive. Their higher productivity then gets translated into a higher wage rate. Before concluding, it may be pertinent to mention that in the final model that we selected and have presented (Table 3.9) we have not included the caste variable. The reasons for dropping the caste variable were partly theoretical and partly empirical. The caste variable turned out statistically significant (both in the univariate context as well as in the personal characteristics model), but with an unexpected positive sign that indicated a sort of reverse discrimination. The positive sign of the caste variable indicated that scheduled caste permanent farm servants earned significantly more than non-scheduled caste permanent farm servants. Although we tried to laid out an explanation for this but it did not seem very convincing. Moreover the inclusion of the caste variable resulted in making some of the theoretically important explanatory variables insignificant. On account of these two reasons, we ultimately decided to exclude the caste variable altogether. However, the unexpected positive sign of the caste variable and its positive significant influence on the wage rate of permanent farm servants calls for a more detailed separate exercise to fully uncover the role of caste in influencing wage rates of permanent farm servants in rural Punjab. However, that cannot be attempted here for obvious reasons.

NOTES

1. The studies conducted by Shalini Dhavle: "Hired Labour and Wage Rates for Farm Operations in Eleven Selected Rural Centres of Maharashtra". *Arthavijnana*, Vol. 6, No. 2, 1964, pp. 127-144, R.N. Soni: "The Recent Agricultural Revolution and the Agricultural Labour". *Indian Journal of Agricultural Economics*, Vol. 25, No. 3, 1970, pp. 23-28, Pranab Bardhan: "Variations in Agriculture Wages: A Note". *Economic and Political Weekly*, Vol. 8, No. 21, 1973, pp. 947-950 and Sheila Bhalla: "Real Wage Rates of Agricultural Labourers in Punjab – 1961-1977: A Preliminary Analysis". *Economic and Political Weekly*, Vol. 20, No. 26, 1979, pp. A57-A68 by using the secondary data of the Ministry of

Agriculture (Government of India) on agriculture wages or the data collected by state governments estimated periodic trends in real wage rates of the casual agricultural labourers in different states over the years. Some empirical studies like of David E. Sahn et al.: "The Effects of Human Capital on Wages, and the Determinants of Labour Supply in a Developing Country". *Journal of Development Economics,* Vol. 29, No. 2, 1988, pp. 157-83 and Daniel A. Sumner et al.: "Wage Rates in a Poor Rural Area with Emphasis on the Impact of Farm and Non-farm Experience". *Economic Development and Cultural Change,* Vol. 37, No. 4, 1989, pp. 709-718 applied the human capital model to analyse the wage differentials among farm and non-farm workers. At micro level for rural labour markets in India, the wage functions have been estimated by very few scholars like Kalpana Bardhan: "Factors Affecting Wage Rates for Agricultural Labour". *Economic and Political Weekly,* Vol. 8, No. 26, 1973, pp. A56-A64, Mark R. Rosenzweig: "Neoclassical Theory and the Optimizing Peasant: An Econometric Anlaysis of Market Family Labour Supply in a Developing Country". *Quarterly Journal of Economics,* Vol. 94, No. 1, 1980, pp. 31-55, James G. Ryan : *Wage Functions for Daily Labour Market Participants in Rural South India,* Mimeo,1980. and Indira Rajaraman: "Offered Wage and Recipient Attribute: Wage Functions for Rural Labour in India". *Journal of Development Economics,* Vol. 24, No. 1, 1986, pp. 179-195. No study in literature as such studied the wage functions of permanent farm servants separately.

2. The technical and managerial skills of the permanent farm servants enhanced their utility to the farmers compared to the casual labourers. The casual labourers cannot perform many of these functions satisfactorily. For details see, Shyamal Roy and Melvin, G. Blase: "Farm Tractorisation, Productivity and Labour Employment: A Case Study of Indian Punjab". *Journal of Development Studies,* Vol. 14, No. 2, 1978, pp. 193-209, Bina Aggarwal: "Agricultural Mechanization and Labour Use: A Disaggregated Approach". *International Labour Review,* Vol. 120, No. 1, 1981, pp. 115-127 and Mukesh Eswaran and Ashok Kotwal: "A Theory of Two-Tier Labour Markets in Agrarian Economies". *American Economic Review,* Vol. 75, No. 1, 1985, pp. 162-77.
3. Kalpana Bardhan: "Factors Affecting Wage Rates for Agricultural Labour". *Economic and Political Weekly,* Vol. 8, No. 26, 1973, pp. A 56-A64.
4. Pranab K. Bardhan: "Wages and Unemployment in a Poor

Agrarian Economy: A Theoretical and Empirical Analysis". *Journal of Political Economy*, Vol. 87, No. 3, 1979, pp. 479-500.

5. The most popular standard theories discuss the impact of wage rate on individuals productivity and nutritional status. The relationship was first described within an economic framework by H.A. Leibeinsten: *Economic Backwardness and Economic Growth*, 1957, in his explanation of the coexistence of surplus labour and downward wage rigidities in labour markets. The work of G.B. Rodgers: "Nutritionally Based Wage Determination in the Low Income Market". *Oxford Economic Papers*, Vol. 27, No. 1, 1975, pp. 61-81, J.A. Mirrlees: "A Pure Theory of Under Developed Economics" in Reynolds, Lloyd G. (ed.) *Agriculture in Development Theory*, 1975, J.E. Stiglitz: "The Efficiency Wage Hypothesis Surplus Labour and Distribution of Income in LDCs". *Oxford Economic Papers*, Vol. 28, No. 2, 1976, pp. 185-207 and C. Bliss and N. Stern: "Productivity, Wages and Nutrition: Part I & II: The Theory". *Journal of Development Economics*, Vol. 5, No. 4, 1978, pp. 331-362 and 363-398, revolves around the efficiency wage hypothesis which proposes an explanation for the coexistence of labour surpluses and downward wage rigidities for populations and adult calorie intakes. W. Arthur Lewis: "Economic Development with Unlimited Supplies of Labour". *The Manchester School of Economic and Social Studies*, Vol. 22, No. 2, 1954, pp. 139-191 propounded the theory of subsistence wage in the less developed economies, but Theoder W. Schultz: *Transforming Traditional Agriculture*, 1964, did not agree with his idea.
6. Karl Marx: *Critique of the Gotha Programme*, 1947, p.26.
7. For details see G.S. Becker: *Human Capital: A Theoretical and Empirical Analysis*, 1975 and C. Joll et al.: *Developments in Labour Market Analysis*, 1983.
8. C. Joll, et al., op.cit., p. 250.
9. L.W. Weiss: "Concentration and Labour Earnings". *American Economic Review*, Vol. 56, Nos.1&2, 1966, pp. 96-117.
10. H. Wachtel and C. Betsey: "Employment at Low Wages". *Review of Economics and Statistics*, Vol. 54, No. 2, 1972, pp. 121-129.
11. L. Smith and V. Briggs et al.: "Wage and Occupational Differences Between Black and White Men: Labour Market Discrimination in the Rural South". *Southern Economic Journal*, Vol. 45, No. 1, 1978, pp. 250-257.
12. G.J. Stigler: "Information in the Labour Market". *Journal of Political Economy*, Vol. 70, No. 5 (Part 2), 1962, pp. 94-105.

13. For details see Mark Blaug: "An Economic Analysis of Personal Earnings in Thailand". *Economic Development and Cultural Change,* Vol. 23, No. 1, 1974, pp. 1-31, N. Sören Blomquist: "Wage Rates and Personal Characteristics". *The Scandinavian Journal of Economics,* Vol. 81, No. 4, 1979, pp. 505-520, David E. Sahn et al.: "The Effects of Human Capital on Wages and the Determinants of Labour Supply in a Developing Country". *Journal of Development Economics,* Vol. 29, No. 2, 1988 pp. 157-83, Daniel, A. Sumner et al.: "Wage Rates in a Poor Rural Area with Emphasis on the Impact of Farm and Non-farm Experience". *Economic Development and Cultural Changes,* Vol. 37, No. 4, 1989, pp. 709-18 and Koshal Manjulik et al.: "Role of Education in Wage Determination in the Japanese Construction Sector". *The Indian Journal of Labour Economics,* Vol. 47, No. 4, 2004, pp. 833-841.
14. David E. Sahn et al., op.cit.
15. Gaurav Datt: *Wage and Employment Determination in Agricultural Labour Markets in India,* A Ph.D. Thesis, 1989, pp. 73-78.
16. Indira Rajaraman, op.cit.
17. Hans P. Binswanger: *Contractual Arrangements, Employment and Wages in Rural Labour Markets in Asia (ed.),* 1984, pp. 143-168.

4

Variations in the Wage Rate: Across Regions and Within Villages

In the previous Chapter 3 we analysed the variations in the wage rates of permanent farm servants in Punjab and the role of personal characteristics such as age, education, skill level, caste and of the attributes of their employers' households such as farm size and ownership of tractors, etc., in these variations. In the present chapter we shall explore the inter-regional and inter-village variations in the wage rates of permanent farm servants. Although a compact and small state, yet one finds considerable regional variations in Punjab in terms of agro-climatic conditions, agricultural productivity, cropping pattern, rainfall, urbanization, distribution of scheduled castes population, cultural milieu and tenurial history that may impact the wage rates of permanent farm servants. Similarly, wage rates of permanent farm servants are likely to be different across villages on account of the village-wise segmentation of the rural labour market. In most cases farmers of a village hire permanent farm servants residing in that very village; one rarely comes across a permanent farm servant of even a neighbouring village being employed by farmers of other villages. Moreover, villages in Punjab vary considerably in terms of population size, time of settlement, farm size, urban connectivity and proportion of landless and scheduled castes population.

The interaction of these factors with village-wise segmentation of the rural labour market is likely to produce considerable inter-village variations in the wage rates of permanent farm servants.

In the first part of this chapter regional variations in the wage rates of permanent farm servants are described and analysed; and in the second part a detailed analysis of inter-village variations in the wage rates of permanent farm servants is attempted.

Regional Variations in the Wage Rates of Permanent Farm Servants

In this section an attempt is made to provide a detailed and disaggregated picture of variations in wage rates of permanent farm servants across different regions of Punjab. In the literature one comes across many different schemes or methods for regionalization of a country or a state. In the specific context of Punjab the most often used scheme is to divide the state into a number of agro-climatic and geographical regions. Another approach has been to partition the state into distinct regions on the basis of the level of agricultural productivity, and we have, of course, the well known historical division of Punjab into Majha, Malwa and Doaba. The choice of a regionalization scheme depends on the objectives of the study, availability of data and the personal preferences of the researcher. For the sake of completeness and to provide the necessary background we first review briefly the regionalisation schemes used by some earlier researchers on Punjab agriculture. A frequently used method is to take each district as a separate regional entity and do district-wise analysis. Since districts are merely administrative units, so this method fails to capture the variations resulting from agro-climatic and other conditions. Its popularity is mainly because of easy availability of district-wise data. Another often used scheme is to divide the state into distinct agro-climatic and geographical regions. A well known attempt on these lines is by Gosal and Gopal Krishan[1] who divided Punjab into five agro-climatic and geographical regions on the basis of geographic, demographic and agro-climatic non-homogeneity. An important example of division of Punjab into agricultural productivity regions is by Grewal and Rangi.[2] They grouped the districts of Punjab into three broad agricultural productivity regions on the basis of high, medium and low productivity. In Punjab's traditional folklore, people have always divided the state into three cultural regions, namely Majha, Malwa and Doaba. In the present study we have employed all the above mentioned regional schemes, namely agro-climatic and geographic regions demarcated by Gosal and Gopal Krishan, agricultural productivity regions used by Grewal and Rangi and the traditional Majha, Malwa and Doaba regionalization on the basis of Punjab's tradition and folklore. These regionalization schemes are shown in Panels A, B and C of Map 2.

Variations Across Agro-Climatic and Geographical Regions

The division of Punjab into five agro-climatic and geographical regions is shown on Map 2 (Panel-A). These five regions are: (i) Shiwalik Foot Hills, (ii) Bist Doab, (iii) Upper Bari Doab, (iv) Northern Malwa, and (v) Southern Malwa. The relevant information on the wage rates of permanent farm servants in these five different regions of the state is presented in Table 4.1.

Table 4.1: Annual Mean Wage Rate of Permanent Farm Servants: Agro-Climate and Geographical Regions

Geographical Region	*Number of Sample Permanent Farm Servants*	*Mean Wage Rate (Rs.)*	*Standard Deviation (SD)*	*Coefficient of Variation (C.V.)*
Shiwalik Hills and Foot Hills	40 (16.67)	15,300	4,529.58	29.60
Bist Doab	32 (13.33)	17,369	7,757.30	44.66
Upper Bari Doab	32 (13.33)	17,362	6,123.21	35.27
Northern Malwa	32 (13.33)	23,627	5,017.78	21.24
Southern Malwa	104 (43.33)	26,874	6,620.55	24.64
All	240 (100)	22,153	7,977.30	36.01

Notes: (i) Source: Primary Survey (2007-08)
(ii) Figures in brackets are percentages

MAP 4.1

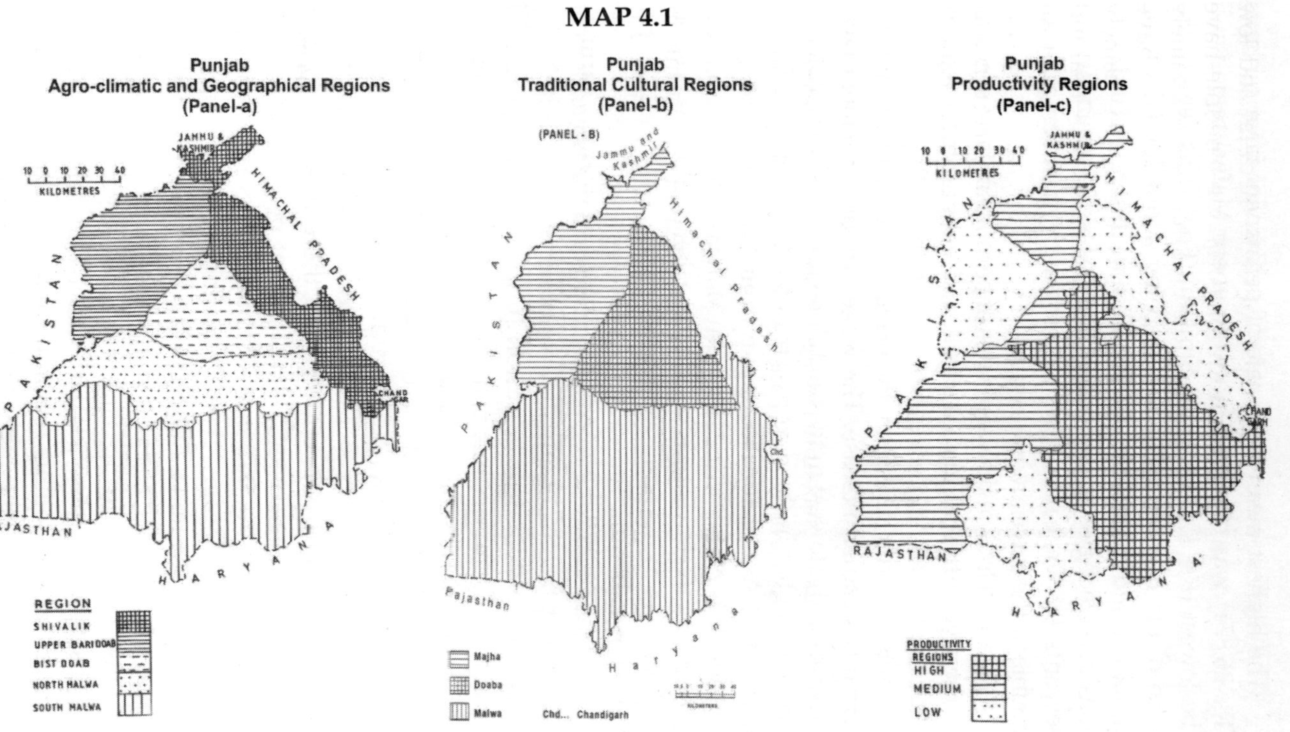
Punjab
Agro-climatic and Geographical Regions
(Panel-a)
JAMMU & KASHMIR
HIMACHAL PRADESH
PAKISTAN
RAJASTHAN
HARYANA
KILOMETRES
REGION
SHIVALIK
UPPER BARI DOAB
BIST DOAB
NORTH MALWA
SOUTH MALWA
Punjab
Traditional Cultural Regions
(Panel-b)
(PANEL - B)
Jammu and Kashmir
Himachal Pradesh
PAKISTAN
Rajasthan
Haryana
Majha
Doaba
Malwa
Chd... Chandigarh
Punjab
Productivity Regions
(Panel-c)
JAMMU & KASHMIR
HIMACHAL PRADESH
PAKISTAN
RAJASTHAN
HARYANA
KILOMETRES
PRODUCTIVITY REGIONS
HIGH
MEDIUM
LOW

The highest mean wage rate of permanent farm servants (Rs. 26,874) was observed in the Southern Malwa region and the lowest (Rs. 15,300) in the Shiwalik Foot Hills region; the ratio of the highest to the lowest being about 1.8. Given the small size and compactness of Punjab state this indeed indicates considerable regional variation in wage rates of permanent farm servants; the wage rate in the highest wage region being almost double of the lowest wage region.

A careful look at the wage rates of permanent farm servants in the five different agro-climatic and geographical regions indicates that as one moves from North to South, i.e. from the foothills towards Rajasthan, the wage rates of permanent farm servants steadily increase. The wage rate of permanent farm servants is the lowest in the foothill regions, it is marginally,14 per cent, higher in the next two regions (Bist Doab and Upper Bari Doab).As we further, move from North to South, it is considerably higher in the Northern Malwa regions (54 per cent higher than the lowest); as we move further South it rises to the highest level in the Southern Malwa region, where it is 76 per cent higher than the Shiwalik Foot Hills region.

Another feature of regional variations in the wage rates of permanent farm servants that we observe is that within the regions coefficient of variation (CV) of the wage rate of permanent farm servants is higher in three northern regions (Shiwalik foot hills, Bist Doab and Upper Bari Doab), compared to the two Southern regions (Northern Malwa and Southern Malwa). It means permanent farm servants in the two southern regions not only get higher wage rates than their counterparts in the three northern regions, but there is also a greater uniformity in their wage rates. It is not possible to do any statistical analysis of factors responsible for these inter-regional variations in the wage rates of permanent farm servants with just five observations. But one may venture a few tentative explanations on the basis of well-known features of these five regions. The level of agricultural productivity may be one possible factor, because it is well-known that farm productivity is lower in the foothills region compared to the two Malwa regions. Similarly, the cultivation of the high value cotton crop in the Southern Malwa region and the continuing prevalence of 'share-wage' contracts in that region may also be partly responsible for the higher wage rates of permanent farm servants in that region.

Variation Across Traditional-Cultural Regions

Next we compared the wage rates of permanent farm servants among the traditional cultural regions of Punjab. In the Punjab folklore and cultural traditions people have always viewed Punjab as consisting of three broad cultural regions: Doaba, Majha and Malwa (Panel-B in Map-2). The Doaba region consists of districts of Hoshiarpur, Jalandhar, Nawanshahr (Shaheed Bhagat Singh Nagar) and Kapurthala; the Majha region is made up of districts of Amritsar, Taran Taran and Gurdaspur, and the Malwa region consists of the entire area south of river Satluj upto the river Ghaggar. The origin of these regions, lies buried in Punjab's pre-history, but till recently the rural population of these three regions was not normally inter-marrying and to a large extent the tribes of agriculturists and landless who have settled in these regions are somewhat distinct. The agro-climatic conditions in these three regions also differ somewhat. The mean wage rates of permanent farm servants and other relevant information on these three regions is presented in Table 4.2 and reveals that the wage rates of permanent farm servants was the highest in the Malwa region (Rs. 25,316) compared to the Doaba and Majha regions.

The wage rates of permanent farm servants did not differ much between the Majha region (Rs. 17,362) and the Doaba region (Rs. 16,308). The wage rate of permanent farm servants in the Malwa region was almost 50 per cent higher compared to the other two regions. Furthermore, the variation in wage rates of permanent farm servants within each region was found to be lower in the Malwa region (Coefficient of variation= 27.35 per cent) compared to the Majha region (Coefficient of variation is 35.27 per cent) and the Doaba region (Coefficient of variation is 42.88 per cent). So the wage rate of permanent farm servants in the Malwa region was not only much higher compared to the other two regions, but was also more uniform within the region. On the whole the results of this comparison are in line with what is presented in the previous sub-section on wage rate variations across agro-climatic and geographical regions.

Table 4.2: Annual Mean Wage Rate of Permanent Farm Servants: Traditional Cultural Regions

Region	*Districts*	*Number of Sample Permanent Farm Servants*	*Mean Wage Rate (Rs.)*	*Standard Deviation (SD)*	*Coefficient of Variation (C.V.)*
Doaba	Hoshiarpur Jalandhar Nawanshahr Kapurthala	56 (23.33)	16,308	6,992.66	42.88
Majha	Amritsar Taran Taran Gurdaspur	32 (13.33)	17,362	6,123.21	35.27
Malwa	Bathinda Mansa Faridkot Moga Mukatsar Ferozepur Barnala Sangrur Ludhiana Ropar S.A.S. Nagar Patiala Fatehgarh Sahib	152 (63.33)	25,316	6,923.65	27.35
	All	240 (100)	22,153	7,977.30	36.01

Notes: (i) Source: Primary Survey (2007-2008)
(ii) Figures in brackets are percentages

Variations Across Productivity Regions

Finally, we compare the wage rates of permanent farm servants across the agricultural productivity regions of Punjab (Panel-C in Map 2). As mentioned earlier, we have employed agricultural productivity regions proposed by Grewal and Rangi for this purpose. The relevant information on agricultural productivity regions is provided in Table 4.3.

Table 4.3: Annual Mean Wage Rate of Permanent Farm Servants: Productivity Regions

Productivity Region	*Districts*	*Number of Sample Permanent Farm Servants*	*Mean Wage Rate (Rs.)*	*Standard Deviation (SD)*	*Coefficient of Variation (CV)*
High Productivity Region	Jalandhar Ludhiana Patiala Sangrur	88 (36.67)	23,455	7,279.99	31.04
Medium Productivity Region	Faridkot Ferozepur Gurdaspur Kapurthala	72 (30.00)	21,827	8,647.68	39.62
Low Productivity Region	Amritsar Bhatinda Ropar Hoshiarpur	80 (33.33)	20,976	8,089.26	38.56
All Regions	-	240 (100)	22,153	7,977.30	36.01

Notes: (i) Source: Primary Survey (2007-08)
(ii) Figures in brackets are percentages

It may be observed from this table that the productivity regions cut across and are spread over two or more than two agro-climatic and traditional cultural regions. A productivity region is also not always conterminous. For example, the low agricultural productivity region consists of the districts of Amritsar, Bhatinda, Ropar and Hoshiarpur, and the medium productivity region consists of districts of Faridkot, Ferozepur, Gurdaspur and Kapurthala. The high productivity region, of course, is conterminous and includes the districts of Jalandhar, Ludhiana, Patiala and Sangrur. As expected the wage rate of permanent farm servants was the highest in the high agricultural productivity region (Rs. 23,455) and the lowest in the low productivity region (Rs. 20,976), the medium productivity region falling in between. It may however be noted that the difference in the wage rates of permanent farm servants across the three productivity regions was not very pronounced; the highest productivity region wage rate being only about 11 per cent higher than the low productivity region wage rate. This is in sharp contrast to the wide difference in wage rates of permanent farm servants across agro-climatic geographical regions and the traditional cultural regions. It may be recalled from sub-section (1) that the difference between the highest and the lowest was about 76 per cent in the case of agro-climatic geographical regions, and about 50 per cent in the case of traditional-cultural regions. The above comparisons suggest that factors other than agricultural productivity may be playing a more important role in causing inter-regional variation in wage rates of permanent farm servants in Punjab. It is also noteworthy that the coefficient of variation (CV) of wage rates of permanent farm servants for the productivity regions are also quite close to each other, in contrast to the considerable difference in coefficient of variation (CV) noted in the case of the other two regionalization schemes used in the study.

To sum up the results of this section we may say that despite the small size and compact nature of Punjab, considerable inter-regional variations in wage rates of permanent farm servants are observed in the state. The most glaring difference in wage rates of permanent farm servants is observed between the south of Satluj located Malwa region and the north of Satluj located areas; in the Malwa region wage rate being almost 50 per cent higher than the other regions. The Malwa region is not only different from other regions in terms of agro-climatic conditions, but also to some extent in terms of traditions and culture. Moreover, out of the four districts with high agricultural productivity, three are located in the Malwa region. So, Malwa region is also characterized by higher agricultural productivity, compared to other regions of Punjab. The land holdings are also bigger, on the average, in the Malwa region compared to the other regions. Many factors seem to have combined to produce the situation of higher wage rates of permanent farm servants in the Malwa region compared to other regions of Punjab.

Inter-Village Variations in the Wage Rates of Permanent Farm Servants

The analysis presented in the previous section revealed considerable variations in the wage rates of permanent farm servants across the regions of Punjab. In this section variations in wage rates of permanent farm servants across villages are described and analysed. The rural population in India in general and in Punjab in particular is clustered village-wise. There are 12,278 inhabitated villages in Punjab as per census 2001 in Punjab. The population of a typical village is a mixture of a large number of land owning and cultivating households and a big group of scheduled castes whose main occupation is farm labour. Then there are smaller groups of a few families each engaged in artisan work and crafts and a few petty trader families. The majority of families belonging to a village have been living there for a long time and are intimately known to one another. Most of the permanent farm servants hired by farmers of a village belong to that very village, and one rarely encounters a permanent farm servant belonging to even a neighbouring village. So the market for permanent farm servants is essentially confined to the village population; with farmers of the village constituting the demand side and landless agricultural labour of the village making the supply side. This segmentation of farm labour market village-wise has been widely noted by scholars and is an accepted fact.[3] In view of the village-wise segmentation of the farm labour market it is very likely that there are considerable inter-village variations in the wage rates of permanent farm servants; because villages differ from one another considerably in terms of economic and demographic characteristics. We begin with a brief description of the economic and demographic profile of sample villages that will highlight the differences in the economic and demographic structure of sample villages. The extent of inter-village variations in the wage rates of permanent farm servants is described next and then the factors responsible for inter-village variations in the wage rates of permanent farm servants are analysed. At the end a brief analysis of intra-village variations in wage rates is also attempted.

Profile of Sample Villages

To capture the broad contours of profile and economic structure of sample villages, twelve characteristics on which data were available have been used. The summary data of the thirty sample villages on these twelve characteristics is presented in Table 4.4. The information from these twelve characteristics is summarized and analysed under five broad headings: (i) Village Size (ii) Caste and Occupational Structure (iii) Holding Size and Farm Type (iv) Cropping Pattern and Irrigation, (v) Land Productivity and (vi) Urban Connectivity and Literacy. The grouping of features is somewhat loose, but helps in considering the matter to promote the necessary background for analysis of inter-village variations in wage rates of permanent farm servants.

(i) Village Size: The size of the village can be proxied either by the size of population, or by the land area of the village. We preferred population size to indicate village size, because of the existence of the very large segment of landless population in each village, who constitute the supply side of the farm labour market in the village. It may be observed from Table 4.4 that villages in Punjab vary considerably in terms of size; in the sample the largest village (Fatta Maluka) with 5965 persons is nine times bigger in size than the smallest village (Ghoga) with only 600 persons in it. The considerable variations in village size is also indicated by the coefficient of variation (CV=56.82 per cent) given in the relevant column at the bottom of this table. So, in terms of size the village labour markets vary considerably across the state.

(ii) Caste and Occupational Structure: The caste structure is sought to be captured by a simple variable, namely the per cent of scheduled castes population in the village, and the occupational structure by three variables, namely per cent of male cultivators, per cent of male agricultural labourers and per cent of non-farm male labourers. Considerable variation in the per cent of scheduled caste population is clearly observable across the sample villages. The highest proportion of scheduled caste population (72.44 per cent of total population) is observed in village Hardo Sheikh and the lowest (0.80 per cent) in village Dalla Gauria. In about 50 per cent of sample villages the proportion of scheduled caste population is above the state average and in the remaining 50 per cent below the state average. The coefficient of variation (CV=38.44 per cent) given at the bottom of the column also indicates considerable inter-village variation in the scheduled caste population in the sample villages.

The occupational structure also differed markedly among the sample villages. The proportion of male cultivators varied from the high figure of 62.84 per cent in Kahan Singh Walla to the lowest figure of 13.18 per cent in village Dod; the ratio of highest to the lowest being almost five. Similarly, the proportion of male agricultural labourers varied from one extreme (43.14 per cent) in Barsat to the other extreme (1.07 per cent) in village Khiala Kalan. In the proportion of male non-farm labourers also considerable variation is noticeable among the sample village. One can safely say on the basis of information given in Table 4.4 that occupational structures varied considerably among the sample villages.

(iii) Holding Size and Farm Type: The size of holding also varied quite significantly among the sample villages. The ratio of the biggest holding size (21.67 acres) in village Pakhi Kalan to the smallest holding size (2.81 acres) in village Dader Sahib comes to more than seven. Similarly, considerable variation is observable in the degree of mechanization among the sample villages. In village Pakhi Kalan all the 100 per cent farmers had their own tractors, in sharp contrast to village Bijja where only 7 per cent of cultivating households owned tractors.

(iv) Cropping Pattern and Irrigation: The cropping pattern of a village depends on many factors out of which irrigation is probably the most important. Out of our sample of thirty villages, in six villages the entire cultivated area (100 per cent) was under irrigation, in 16 villages irrigated area was above 50 per cent but less than 100 per cent, and in the remaining villages

Table 4.4: Profile of Sample Villages

Name of Village	Total Population	Scheduled Caste Population (Percentage)	Percentage of Literate	Percentage of Male Cultivators	Percentage of Male Agriculture Labourers	Percentage of Male Non-Farm Workers	Size of Holding (Acres)	Percentage of Irrigated Area	Main Crops	Number of Tractors	Land Rent (Rs./ Acre)	Distance from Nearest Town (Kms)
Dehriwal	1628	13.51	57.37	40.44	24.89	34.67	3.48	37.38	W+P	60	8150	9
Dala Gauria	753	0.80	73.44	45.87	19.59	34.54	5.55	11.54	W+P	18	1000	10
Hardokhundpur	1472	32.13	66.24	18.49	37.90	43.61	7.90	91.54	W+P	16	7500	11
Padrana	2105	34.63	68.74	31.78	5.03	63.19	3.74	88.03	W+P	60	5000	04
Ghoga	600	38.50	68.83	29.42	22.99	47.59	4.58	50.00	W+P	15	12000	15
Das Grao	870	14.94	55.52	18.77	1.75	79.48	6.65	67.13	W+P	05	6450	08
Hardosheikh	1085	72.44	63.23	21.83	29.93	48.24	8.37	100	W+P	20	7500	06
Ugi	3576	47.54	56.96	23.29	26.34	50.37	8.10	82.90	W+P	75	10,000	13
Bagrian	1162	26.51	60.41	40.24	9.91	49.85	3.46	100	W+P	12	7000	03
Mutton	1177	24.47	61.11	35.02	22.22	42.76	8.64	33.26	W+P	16	8500	10
Mukandpur	3785	43.83	68.19	14.54	7.85	77.61	8.27	99.84	W+P	100	11000	08
Khiala Kalan	3428	33.40	48.16	43.01	1.07	55.92	4.37	100	W+P	100	10,000	10
Dader Sahib	2600	33.58	50.85	50.12	19.52	30.36	2.81	100	W+P	70	13500	20
Bijja	2667	42.26	64.64	29.16	12.52	57.87	3.70	100	W+P	20	13000	11
Heran	2746	43.41	64.13	27.92	28.38	43.70	6.65	93.71	W+P	75	11500	12
Dyalpura Bhaika	4554	38.10	46.07	48.47	24.67	26.86	8.11	86.98	W+C	100	11500	25
Malkana	4250	27.29	43.34	55.78	26.22	18.00	7.60	48.86	W+C	200	5500	16
Fatta Maluka	5965	31.20	38.80	57.94	26.93	15.13	5.11	55.94	W+C	300	10000	20
Makha Challan	1253	23.22	48.04	46.05	19.21	34.74	6.76	44.89	W+C	50	11500	22
Bhagu	3597	32.61	43.17	29.36	10.21	60.43	13.10	57.00	W+C	225	7500	16

Khai	4065	29.54	47.08	43.20	25.58	31.20	7.01	98.97	W+P	400	10,000	18
Dod	1235	39.68	49.15	13.13	8.10	78.72	7.17	78.89	W+P	25	10,000	5
Pakhi Kalan	3693	41.13	49.16	17.54	7.44	75.02	21.67	39.19	W+P	200	15,500	14
Midda	2781	30.78	51.52	55.98	27.23	16.79	7.67	94.43	W+C	250	7500	18
Kahan Singh Walla	862	17.87	57.66	62.84	22.12	15.04	3.27	100	W+P	75	12000	10
Barsat	1564	25.58	51.98	30.98	43.14	25.88	9.95	89.38	W+P	60	16250	13
Khanpur Gandian	1790	38.04	62.23	34.45	34.10	31.45	3.92	25.49	W+P	50	11000	07
Rurki	2015	40.99	54.99	27.58	28.19	44.23	9.31	69.12	W+P	85	16,000	12
Dhindsa	1604	35.10	42.52	55.62	41.67	2.71	4.11	75.66	W+P	70	11,000	14
Sehjra	3917	33.19	53.74	44.16	17.78	38.06	5.14	91.32	W+P	100	17500	16
CV	56.82	38.44	-	-	-	-	-	-	-	-	31.03	-

Source: Census of India (2001) and Primary Survey (2007-08). * W+P = Wheat and Paddy *W+ C = Wheat and Cotton

the irrigated area was less than 50 per cent. In our sample we have even a village with a very low (only 11.54 per cent) per cent of irrigated area. Contrary to the macro impression of irrigated area being 95 per cent in Punjab, we find considerable inter-village variation in intensity of irrigation among sample villages.

The sample villages also show considerable variation in the cropping pattern. In twenty-four villages out of thirty, wheat and paddy rotation was the dominant cropping pattern, in the remaining six villages cotton-wheat rotation cropping pattern prevailed. In some villages maize and sugarcane also claimed a significant share of the cropped area. On the whole, one can say that wheat-paddy rotation, and wheat-cotton rotations were the two main cropping patterns prevalent in the sample villages.

(v) Land Productivity: Land productivity plays an important role in determining the wage rate of agricultural labour. On account of many factors land productivity is likely to vary considerably across villages. The standard measure of land productivity used by agricultural economists is output per acre. But village-wise data on land productivity per acre were not available for our sample villages. On account of that we have used land rent per acre prevailing in the sample villages in the year of survey as a proxy for land productivity. Although many other factors also influence land rent per acre, yet land productivity per acre is its most important determinant and due to that it can be used as a rough measure of land productivity variations across the villages. The information given in Table 4.4 reveals considerable variation in land rent among the thirty sample villages. The highest land rent per acre (Rs. 17,500) was observed in village Sehjra and the lowest (Rs. 5,500) in village Malkana. The ratio of the highest to the lowest works out to more than three times and clearly indicate that land rent varied widely in the sample villages. This conclusion is also confirmed by the coefficient of variation (CV =31.03 per cent) given at the bottom of this table. On the basis of the above it may not be wrong to conclude that land productivity (or proxied by land rent) varied considerably among Punjab villages.

(vi) Urban Connectivity and Literacy: The proximity of a village to an urban centre provides opportunities to village landless for urban employment and hence likely to influence the village wage rate in the positive direction. The spread of literacy among the village population may also influence the wage rate of farm labour directly as well as through many indirect channels. The urban connectivity was measured by distance of the village from the nearest town. The data given in Table 4.4 reveal considerable differences among sample villages in urban connectivity. There were eleven villages that were situated at a distance of 15 kms or more from the nearest town; and there were seven villages that were situated at a distance of less than ten kilometres from the nearest town. The maximum distance of 25 kms is evident in the case of one village and the minimum of only 3 kms in the case of another. So in terms of urban connectivity also our sample villages differed among themselves considerably.

The literacy rate also varied considerably among the sample villages. It may be seen that in our sample the highest literacy rate (73.44 per cent) is observed in village Dalla Gauria, and the lowest (38.80 per cent) in village Fatta Maluka. The ratio of the highest to the lowest is almost twice and indicates considerable variation in the literacy rate among the sample villages. This variation in literacy rates is likely to influence the wage rates of permanent farm servants considerably across the villages.

Extent of Inter-Village and Intra-Village Variations in Wage Rates of Permanent Farm Servants

The extent of inter-village variations in some important features related to size and structure having been described in previous sub-sections, now we describe the extent of inter-village variations in wage rates of permanent farm servants. The summary information on mean wage rate, coefficient of variation (CV), maximum and minimum wage rate, etc. is presented in Table 4.5 for the thirty sample villages. It may be observed from this table that the highest mean wage rate (Rs. 31,985) in village Khanpur Gandian is almost four times the lowest mean wage rate (Rs. 8,961) in village Bagrian. This indicates very wide variation in wage rates of permanent farm servants across the sample villages. The coefficient of variation (CV) given at the bottom (29.14 per cent) also suggests that considerable inter-village variations in the wage rates of permanent farm servants. The mean wage rate for the sample villages taken together worked out to be Rs. 22,134 and in half the villages the mean wage rate was higher than this and in the other half lower than this.

Information on wage rate variation within each of the sample villages (intra-village variation) is also presented in Table 4.5 (last four columns). It may be observed that sample villages differed from one another considerably on this feature as well. The highest intra-village variation in the wage rate of permanent farm servants (CV=47.90 per cent) is observed in village Mukandpur, and the lowest (5.14 per cent) in village Khiala Kalan. The ratio of the maximum to minimum wage rate within a village given in the last column also differs widely across sample villages and indicates considerable intra-village variation in the wage rate of permanent farm servants. The ratio of maximum to minimum wage rate was the highest in village Dehriwal (3.64) and the lowest in village Khiala Kalan (1.13). In some villages the intra-village wage variation was greater than even the inter-village wage variation discussed in the preceding paragraph. We also tried to find out the relation between intra-village variation in the wage rate and the mean wage level prevailing in the village with the help of simple correlation analysis. The correlation between the village mean wage rate of permanent farm servants and coefficient of variation (CV) of wage rate within the village was found to be negative and significant [correlation = (-0.41) significant at 5 per cent level]. This suggests that intra-village variation in the wage rate of permanent farm servants was lower in villages that they have a higher mean wage rate and vice versa.[4]

Comparison of the Wage Rate of Permanent Farm Servants and Casual Labourers

In the course of our survey, we have also collected information on the wage rate of male casual labour[5] prevailing in the sample villages. A simple comparison of the wage rate of casual labour

Table 4.5: Inter-Intra Village Wise: Mean Wage Rate of Permanent Farm Servants (Rs.)

Name of Village	*Annual Mean Wage Rate (Rs.)*	*Maximum Wage Rate (Rs.) (i)*	*Minimum Wage Rate (Rs.) (ii)*	*Coefficient of Variation (CV)*	*Maximum to Minimum Wage Rate Ratio*
Dehriwal	13,533	21,982	6,033	46.19	3.64
Dala Gauria	14,606	21,633	8,097	32.81	2.67
Hardokhundpur	13,097	14,433	10,152	14.86	1.42
Padrana	14,529	26,433	8,673	35.43	3.05
Ghoga	18,000	22,344	8,673	34.60	2.58
Das Grao	15,892	19,809	11,553	22.16	1.71
Hardosheikh	26,799	29,697	23,073	10.76	1.29
Ugi	19,713	25,233	11,553	26.09	2.18
Bagrian	8,961	11,553	7,223	20.95	1.60
Mutton	16,843	30,273	11,841	45.02	2.56
Mukandpur	14,529	26,433	8,673	47.90	3.05
Khiala Kalan	22,838	24,472	21,705	5.14	1.13
Dader Sahib	18,470	26,664	11,553	37.44	2.31
Bijja	25,921	30,945	20,865	17.56	1.48
Heran	24,506	28,833	14,433	24.36	2.00
Dyalpura Bhaika	30,365	35,745	24,202	15.38	1.48
Malkana	31,380	45,892	12,967	42.81	3.54
Fatta Maluke	21,047	22,737	19,233	7.62	1.18
Makha Challan	24,451	29,793	20,433	16.47	1.46
Bhagu	31,681	35,793	26,304	14.89	1.36
Khai	25,395	32,630	20,784	17.34	1.57
Dod	25,426	30,801	21,633	13.06	1.42
Pakhi Kalan	31,319	40,353	25,425	19.00	1.59
Midda	25,474	28,353	23,904	8.30	1.19
Kahan Singh Walla	20,443	22,833	14,433	16.62	1.58
Barsat	20,653	26,637	11,433	29.26	2.33
Khanpur Gandian	31,985	39,633	25,329	21.37	1.56
Rurki	25,729	30,583	16,833	20.78	1.82
Dhindsa	21,407	24,472	15,633	15.85	1.57
Sehjra	30,046	35,313	20,588	18.87	1.72

All Villages

Mean (Rs.)	22,134
Maximum Mean Wage Rate (Rs.) [Village: Khanpur Gandian]	31,985
Minimum Mean Wage Rate (Rs.)[Village: Bagrian]	8,961
Coefficient of Variation (CV)	29.14
Maximum to Minimum Ratio	3.56

Source: Primary Survey (2007-08)

and that of permanent farm servants is presented in Table 4.6. Strictly speaking a comparison of the wage rate of casual labour and of permanent farm servants is valid neither theoretically, nor empirically. The nature of wage contract, working hours, working conditions and work responsibilities differ so greatly between casual labour and permanent farm servants that a comparison of their wage rates may not be valid. Moreover the availability and nature of data on the wage rates of these two categories also differ considerably making a comparison difficult. Still four considerations prompted us to attempt such a comparison. Firstly, in most cases these two types of agricultural labourers belong to the same caste and even the same families. Secondly, there may be many farm labourers who switch from casual labour to permanent farm servant work and vice versa over time as the rewards and availability and uncertainty of these two types of work change. Thirdly, even for a purely descriptive purpose such a comparison can throw some light on the question under investigation, namely inter-village variation in wage rates of permanent farm servants. Fourthly, some earlier researchers have also made such a comparison and arrived at certain generalizations. The relevant information on the wage rate of casual labour and permanent farm servants in the sample villages is presented in Table 4.6.

For purposes of comparison the annual wage rate of permanent farm servants was converted into per day basis, since the wage rate of casual labour is on a per day basis. It may be observed that in all the sample villages, except one, the wage rate of casual labour was higher than the per day earnings received by permanent farm servants. In 30 per cent of the villages the casual wage rate was 50 per cent or more higher than the daily earnings of permanent farm servants. On the whole, it may be concluded that the wage rate for casual work was on the average higher than the daily basis earnings of permanent farm servants.[6] This negative gap in the daily basis earnings of permanent farm servants may be partly due to certainty and continuity of employment (a premium for job security) and partly due to many lean periods in the year when there is very little farm work, but still permanent farm servants

Table 4.6: Wage Rate of Male Casual Agricultural Labourers and Daily Earnings of Permanent Farm Servants: A Village-Wise Comparison

Name of Village	*Average Daily Wage Rate of a Male Casual Agricultural Labourer (Rs.) (X)*	*Average Daily Earnings of a Permanent Farm Servant (Rs.) (Y)*	*Difference in (X) & (Y) (Rs.)*	*Percentage Difference in (X) & (Y)*
Dehriwal	80.00	35.00	45.00	56.25
Dala Gauria	90.00	40.00	50.00	55.56
Hardokhundpur	90.00	36.00	54.00	60.00
Padrana	85.00	39.00	46.00	54.12
Ghoga	120.00	49.00	71.00	59.17
Das Grao	90.00	44.00	46.00	51.11
Hardosheikh	50.00	73.00	(-)23.00	(-)46.00
Ugi	85.00	54.00	31.00	36.47
Bagrian	90.00	25.00	65.00	72.22
Mutton	90.00	46.00	44.00	48.49
Mukandpur	90.00	40.00	50.00	55.56
Khiala Kalan	75.00	63.00	12.00	16.00
Dader Sahib	80.00	51.00	29.00	36.25
Bijja	93.00	71.00	22.00	23.66
Heran	98.00	67.00	31.00	31.63
Dyalpura Bhaika	90.00	83.00	7.00	07.78
Malkana	100.00	86.00	14.00	14.00
Fatta Maluka	80.00	58.00	22.00	27.50
Makha Challan	70.00	67.00	03.00	04.29
Bhagu	95.00	87.00	08.00	8.42
Khai	100.00	70.00	30.00	30.00
Dud	103.00	70.00	33.00	32.04
Pakhi Kalan	90.00	86.00	04.00	04.44
Midda	83.00	70.00	13.00	15.66
Kahan Singh Walla	105.00	56.00	49.00	46.67
Barsat	85.00	57.00	28.00	32.94
Khanpur Gandian	90.00	87.00	03.00	03.33
Rurki	100.00	70.00	30.00	30.00
Dhindsa	90.00	59.00	31.00	34.44
Sehjra	120.00	82.00	38.00	31.67
Mean of All Villages	90.23	60.70		
r_{xy}	**0.12**			

Source: Primary Survey (2007-08)

keep receiving their remuneration.

We further explored the issue of correlation of daily remuneration of permanent farm servants and the casual wage rate across the villages. The correlation between daily remuneration of permanent farm servants and casual wage rate across the thirty villages was found to be small (0.12) and not significant statistically even at 10 per cent level, suggesting that factors determining inter-village variations in casual labour wage rates may be different from the factors that influence inter-village variations in the wage rates of permanent farm servants.[7]

Determinants of Inter-Village Variations in Wage Rates of Permanent Farm Servants

An attempt is made in this section to explain the factors responsible for the considerable inter-village variation in wage rates of permanent farm servants noted in the previous section. For this purpose the standard ordinary least square (OLS) regression analysis technique has been employed. Given the small number of observations in our sample of villages (N=30) only five or six explanatory variables could be legitimately included in the multiple regression model. This limited the number of factors whose influence could be analysed as a group in determining the inter-village variations in the wage rates of permanent farm servants. To overcome this limitation imposed by sample size, at least partly, we have used a pragmatic regression strategy. To begin with the effect of each explanatory variable on inter-village variations in wage rates of permanent farm servants was explored with the help of the univariate regression model. Next, the influence of each of the explanatory variables was assessed by controlling one by one some of the other important explanatory variables.

Finally two multivariate models were estimated to isolate the influence of important factors in determining the inter-village variations in the wage rates of permanent farm servants. On the basis of theory and clues from the existing literature eight variables were selected to explain the inter-village variations in the wage rates of permanent farm servants.

Description of Variables

The dependent and explanatory variables used in these regression exercises are briefly described here after:

I. Dependent Variable

Wage Rate of Permanent Farm Servants: It is the mean annual wage rate of permanent farm servants in a village. It includes the cash paid to the permanent farm servant as annual wage plus the monetary value of perks and perquisites received by him from the employer.

II. Explanatory Variables

(i) **Ratio of Agricultural Labourers to Cultivators:** Agriculture labourers and cultivators broadly represent the supply and demand side of farm labour in the village labour market. The ratio of male agriculture labourers to male cultivators in the village indicates the relative size of supply and demand sides of the village labour market.

(ii) **Proportion of Agricultural Labourers in Total Wage Labourers**: The landless of the village can either earn a living by working as farm labourers or/and by doing various types of non-farm labour work. The availability of non-farm employment is expected to influence the wage rate of permanent farm servants. This variable is defined as the proportion of male agricultural labourers in the village to all male labourers engaged in non-farm and farm labour work and indicates the relative availability of agricultural labour work to non-farm employment in the village.

(iii) **Extent of Migrant Labour:** The availability of migrant farm labourers in a village is expected to significantly influence the wage rate of permanent farm servants because it shifts the supply curve of permanent farm servants in the village rightwards and downwards. This variable is defined in terms of per cent of migrant permanent farm servants in total permanent farm servants in the village.

(iv) **Size of Holding**: Since most of the permanent farm servants are hired by bigger sized farms, so the relative number of bigger farms in a village is likely to influence the wage rates of permanent farm servants. This variable is defined as the mean size of holdings (in acres) in each village.

(v) **Tractor Ownership**: The use of tractors on a farm significantly influences the size and composition of labour used on the farms. Although almost all farms in Punjab use tractors, but all do not own one. This variable is defined as per cent of farms in the village owning tractors.

(vi) **Cropping Pattern**: The cropping pattern prevailing in a village is also likely to influence the wage rates of permanent farm servants (because different crops have different labour requirements). This variable is defined as a dummy taking value one if the cropping pattern in the village is dominated by wheat-cotton rotation and value zero in case of wheat-paddy cropping pattern.

(vii) **Land Productivity**: The value of output produced per acre is expected to significantly influence the wage rate of permanent farm servants. Owing to non-availability of village-wise data on per acre productivity, land rent per acre was used as a proxy for land productivity.

(viii) **Regional Influence Variable:** The analysis of regional variations in wage rates of permanent farm servants presented at the beginning of this chapter has revealed the important influence of regional factors on the wage rate. To capture this influence a regional dummy variable was devised. It takes value one for villages in the sub-mountainous foot hills region and value zero for villages in the other regions.

Regression Results: Univariate

To begin with the influence of each of the eight explanatory variables on the dependent variable was explored with the help of the simple univariate regression model. The results of this exercise are presented in Tables 4.7(A) and 4.7(B); the dependent variable in 4.7(A) is in natural form and in 4.7(B) in log form. The relative number of agricultural labourers to cultivators was found not to have any significant impact on the wage rates of permanent farm servants across the villages. Similarly, the relative number of agricultural labourers to all wage labourers in villages was also found not to have any significant influence on inter-village variations in wage rates of permanent farm servants.

Table 4.7(A): Factors Affecting Wage Rates of Permanent Farm Servants at Village Level [Univariate Analysis] (N=30)

Sr. No.	*Explanatory Variables*	*Dependent Variable (Y): Annual Mean Wage Rate of Permanent Farm Servants (Rs.)* Intercept (α)	Slope (β)	t_{values}	R^2
1.	Male Agriculture Labourers ÷ Male Cultivators	22319.77	–290.63	0.11	0.00
2.	Male Agriculture Labourers ÷ Male Agriculture Labourers + Male Non-Agriculture Workers	19753.77	7.65	1.63	0.09
3.	Percentage of Migrant Permanent Farm Servants	26625.35	-103.66	4.51***	0.42
4.	Size of Holding (Acres)	17164.91	723.00	2.40**	0.17
5.	Tractors (No.)	19433.38	28.45	2.47**	0.18
6.	Rent of Land (Rs./Acre)	14878.07	0.70	1.98*	0.12
7.	Cropping Pattern (Dummy): Wheat – Cotton=1 Wheat-Paddy = 0	20791.44	5752.30	2.20**	0.15
8.	Agro-Climatic Zone (Dummy): Sub-mountain = 1, Others = 0	23969.43	-9178.89	3.75***	0.33

Note: *, **, *** indicate significant at 10%, 5% and 1% levels for a two-tailed test.

As expected the greater presence of migrant permanent farm servants in a village lowered the wage rates of permanent farm servants; this variable has a significant (at 1 per cent level) coefficient with negative sign in the univariate regression results presented in Tables 4.7(A) and 4.7(B).

Table 4.7(B): Factors Affecting Wage Rates of Permanent Farm Servants at Village Level [Univariate Analysis] (N=30)

Sr. No.	Explanatory Variables	Dependent Variable (Y): Annual Mean Wage Rate of Permanent Farm Servants (Rs.)			
		Intercept (α)	Slope (β)	t_{values}	R^2
1.	Male Agriculture Labourers ÷ Male Cultivators	9.96	.0009	0.00	0.00
2.	Male Agriculture Labourers ÷ Male Agriculture Labourers + Male Non-Agriculture Workers	9.85	0.0003	1.50	0.07
3.	Percentage of Migrant Permanent Farm Servants	10.18	-0.005	4.48***	0.41
4.	Size of Holding (Acres)	9.73	0.03	2.20**	0.15
5.	Tractors (No.)	9.82	0.001	2.46**	0.18
6.	Rent of Land (Rs./Acre)	9.56	0.00003	2.22**	0.15
7.	Cropping Pattern (Dummy): Wheat-Cotton=1 Wheat-Paddy=0	9.89	0.28	2.14**	0.14
8.	Agro-Climatic Zone (Dummy): Sub-mountain = 1, Others = 0	10.05	-0.45	3.65***	0.32

Note:*, **, *** indicate significant at 10%, 5% and 1% levels for a two-tailed test.

It may be noted from Tables 4.7(A) and 4.7(B) that coefficient of size of holding variable is positive and significant (at 5 per cent level) and that the tractor ownership variable is positive and significant at 5 per cent level. The significant positive coefficient of land rent variable suggests a positive significant impact of land productivity on wage rates of permanent farm servants. The coefficient of the cropping pattern variable has a positive sign and is significant (at 5 per cent level) indicating that the wage rates of permanent farm servants were significantly higher in wheat-cotton cropping pattern villages compared to the wheat-paddy cropping pattern villages. The significant influence of regional factors on inter-village variation in the wage rate is also clearly revealed by these results. The coefficient of the sub-mountainous foothills dummy variable is negative and significant at 1 per cent level and suggests that on the average wage rates of permanent farm servants was lower in sub-mountainous region villages compared to the rest of Punjab villages. These results of univariate regression exercise provide many important clues regarding the influence of different factors on the inter-village variations in the wage rates of permanent farm servants. Though useful as a preliminary exercise, these results cannot be fully relied upon, because the influence of other factors is not controlled in a univariate regression model. In the next two sub-sections the influence of these factors is further explored by controlling the impact of other factors.

Multiple Regression Results-I

In the univariate results discussed in the preceding sub-section, six (out of eight) explanatory variables turned out significant (at different levels of confidence) and with the expected signs. To confirm these results the multiple regression analysis was employed. Since the number of observations in the inter-village sample is only thirty, so all the eight explanatory variables could not be tried simultaneously in the multiple regression model.

To overcome this limitation, we have used a two-stage multiple regression procedure. In the first step the impact of each of the eight explanatory variables on the dependent variable was assessed by controlling the influence of one of the other explanatory variables at a time. The results of this exercise are reported in Tables 4.8 to 4.15 and discussed in this sub-section. In the second step all the possible combinations of the eight explanatory variables were entered as regressors in sets of three or four and a number of alternative multiple regression models were estimated. Out of these many estimated multiple regression models we selected two on the basis of consistency of signs, statistical significance of explanatory variables and the size of R^2. These two regression models are reported in Tables 4.16 and 4.17 and discussed in the next sub-section.

In Tables 4.8(A) and 4.8(B) the influence of size of holding on inter-village variations in the wage rate of permanent farm servants is assessed by controlling (one by one) the influence of other seven explanatory variables. It may be seen that in all the seven equations, size of holding variable remains statistically

Table4.8(A): Factors Affecting Wage Rates of Permanent Farm Servants at Village Level: Variable Under Consideration is Size of Holding (Acres)

Explanatory Variables:	*Dependent Variable(Y):Annual Mean Wage Rate of Permanent Farm Servants (Rs.) Controlled Variables(One by One)*						
	Equation-1	*Equation-2*	*Equation-3*	*Equation-4*	*Equation-5*	*Equation-6*	*Equation-7*
Size of Holding (Acres) (Variable under Consideration)	544.99 (2.27)**	747.90 (2.41)**	615.50 (1.80)*	546.27 (1.79)*	665.42 (2.33)**	530.06 (2.02)*	625.94 (2.10)**
Percent of Migrant Permanent Farm Servants	-94.99 (4.37)***	-	-	-	-	-	-
Male Agriculture Labourers ÷ Male Cultivators	-	-1317.73 (0.50)	-	-	-	-	-
Male Agriculture Labourers ÷ Male Agriculture Labourers + Male Non-Agriculture Workers	-	-	3.55 (0.70)	-	-	-	-
Tractors (No.)	-	-	-	21.90 (2.14)**	-	-	-
Cropping Pattern (Dummy): Wheat- Cotton=1 Wheat-Paddy=0	-	-	-	-	5212.39 (2.14)**	-	-
Zone (Dummy): Sub-mountain=1;Others=0	-	-	-	-	-	-8148.12 (3.40)***	-
Rent of Land (Rs / Acre)	-	-	-	-	-	-	0.56 (1.63)
Intercept	22504.50	17837.67	16798.66	16301.27	16344.39	20120.51	12063.73
F_{values}	13.94***	2.93*	3.08*	4.90**	5.53***	9.89***	4.38**
R^2	0.51	0.18	0.19	0.27	0.54	0.42	0.25

Notes: (i) Figures in brackets are $_{tvalues}$ (ii) *, **, *** indicate significant at 10%, 5% and 1% levels for a two-tailed test.

Table 4.8(B): Factors Affecting Wage Rates of Permanent Farm Servants at Village Level: Variable Under Consideration is Size of Holding (Acres)

Explanatory Variables:	*Dependent Variable(Y): Log [Annual Mean Wage Rate of Permanent Farm Servants (Rs.)] Controlled Variables(One by One)*						
	Equation-1	*Equation-2*	*Equation-3*	*Equation-4*	*Equation-5*	*Equation-6*	*Equation-7*
Size of Holding (Acres) (Variable under Consideration)	0.02 (2.02)*	0.03 (2.20)**	0.02 (1.76)*	0.02 (1.79)*	0.03 (2.12)**	0.02 (1.80)*	0.03 (1.88)*
Percent of Migrant Permanent Farm Servants	-0.004 (4.30)***	-	-	-	-	-	-
Male Agriculture Labourers÷ Male Cultivators	-	-0.04 (0.35)	-	-	-	-	-
Male Agriculture Labourers÷ Male Agriculture Labourers + Male Non-Agriculture Workers	-	-	0.0001 (0.64)	-	-	-	-
Tractors(No.)	-	-	-	0.001 (1.91)*	-	-	-
Cropping Pattern (Dummy): Wheat-Cotton=1Wheat-Paddy=0	-	-	-	-	0.26 (2.06)*	-	-
Zone (Dummy):Sub-mountain=1 Others=0	-	-	-	-	-	-0.41 (3.37)***	-
Rent of Land (Rs/Acre)	-	-	-	-	-	-	0.00003 (1.62)
Intercept	9.99	9.75	9.71	9.68	9.69	9.88	9.43
F_{values}	12.73***	2.49	2.58*	4.45**	4.83**	9.01***	4.33**
R^2	0.49	0.15	0.16	0.25	0.26	0.40	0.25

Notes: (i) Figures in brackets are $_{tvalues}$ (ii) *, **, *** indicate significant at 10%, 5% and 1% levels for a two-tailed test.

significant and its sign (positive) remains consistent. On the basis of these results, one can infer that the positive influence of holding size variable on inter-village variations in the wage rates of permanent farm servants suggested by univariate results is further confirmed.

The results on tractor ownership variable reported in Tables 4.9(A) and 4.9(B) reveal that the significant positive impact of this variable holds in four equations in which the influence of size of holding, ratio of male agricultural labourers to male cultivators, per cent of male agricultural labour to all male wage labourers and rent of land respectively is controlled. In the other three regression equations the tractor ownership variable retains the positive sign but is not significant even at 10 per cent level of confidence. These mixed results do not warrant a firm conclusion on the positive impact of the tractor ownership variable on inter-village variations in the wage rates of permanent farm servants. However, one can say that the positive impact of the tractor ownership variable is indicated, but not fully confirmed.

The results on rent of land variable, which is used as a proxy for land productivity, are reported in Tables 4.10(A) and 4.10(B). Only in two equations, out of seven, the coefficient of this variable fails to show statistical significance even at 10 per cent level. These two equations are when the influence of zone and size of holding is controlled. In the remaining five regression equations it has a consistent positive sign and is significant at different levels of confidence. Even in the other two equations the sign of its coefficient remains consistently positive. On the basis of these results one may say that the positive impact of the land productivity variable on inter-village variations in wage rates of permanent farm servants is indicated, but not fully confirmed.

The influence of the cropping pattern on inter-village variations in the wage rates of permanent farm servants is explored in Tables 4.11(A) and 4.11(B). The cropping pattern variable has a positive sign in all the seven equations, and is also significant in four of these at different levels of confidence. So the positive impact of the cotton-wheat crop pattern on the wage rate is indicated, but not fully confirmed.

Table 4.9(A): Factors Affecting the Wage Rates of Permanent Farm Servants at Village Level: Variable Under Consideration is Tractor (No.)

Explanatory Variables:	*Dependent Variable(Y):Annual Mean Wage Rate of Permanent Farm Servants (Rs.) Controlled Variables(One by One)*						
	Equation-1	*Equation-2*	*Equation-3*	*Equation-4*	*Equation-5*	*Equation-6*	*Equation-7*
Tractors(No.)(Variable under Consideration)	21.90 (1.87)*	9.14 (0.81)	29.20 (2.44)**	25.60 (1.67)	21.12 (2.21)**	16.83 (1.56)	28.48 (2.62)**
Size of Holding (Acres)	546.27 (1.80)*	-	-	-	-	-	-
Percent of Migrant Permanent Farm Servants	-	-92.81 (3.43)***	-	-	-	-	-
Male Agriculture Labourers÷ Male Cultivators	-	-	897.07 (0.34)	-	-	-	-
Male Agriculture Labourers÷Male Agriculture Labourers + Male Non-Agriculture Workers	-	-	-	5.78 (1.29)	-	-	-
Cropping Pattern (Dummy): Wheat-Cotton=1 Wheat-Paddy=0	-	-	-	-	3663.78 (1.29)	-	-
Zone (Dummy): Sub-mountain=1; Others=0	-	-	-	-	-	-7792.31 (3.06)***	-
Rent of Land (Rs/Acre)	-	-	-	-	-	-	0.70 (2.17)**
Intercept	16301.27	25288.28	18788.10	17906.71	19274.47	22094.70	12167.50
F_{values}	4.90**	10.09***	2.99*	3.94**	3.94**	8.63***	5.79***
R^2	0.27	0.43	0.18	0.23	0.23	0.39	0.30

Notes: (i) Figures in brackets are $_{tvalues}$ (ii) *, **, *** indicate significant at 10%, 5% and 1% levels for a two-tailed test.

Table 4.9(B): Factors Affecting the Wage Rates of Permanent Farm Servants at Village Level: Variable Under Consideration is Tractor (No.)

Explanatory Variables:	*Dependent Variable(Y): Log [Annual Mean Wage Rate of Permanent Farm Servants (Rs.)] Controlled Variables(One by One)*						
	Equation-1	*Equation-2*	*Equation-3*	*Equation-4*	*Equation-5*	*Equation-6*	*Equation-7*
Tractors (No.) (Variable under Consideration)	0.001	0.0004	0.001	0.001	0.001	0.0008	0.001
	(1.90)*	(0.81)	(2.46)**	(2.21)**	(1.68)	(1.55)	(2.66)**
Size of Holding (Acres)	0.02	-	-	-	-	-	-
	(1.79)*						
Percent of Migrant Permanent Farm Servants	-	-0.004	-	-	-	-	-
		(3.47)***					
Male Agriculture Labourers÷ Male Cultivators	-	-	0.06	-	-	-	-
			(0.46)				
Male Agriculture Labourers÷Male Agriculture Labourers+Male Non-Agriculture Workers	-	-	-	0.0002	-	-	-
				(1.16)			
Cropping Pattern (Dummy): Wheat-Cotton=1 Wheat-Paddy=0	-	-	-	-	0.18	-	-
					(1.23)		
Zone (Dummy): Sub-mountain=1 Others=0	-	-	-	-	-	-0.39	-
						(3.01)***	
Rent of Land (Rs/Acre)	-	-	-	-	-	-	0.00003
							(2.44)**
Intercept	9.68	10.11	9.78	9.76	9.82	9.96	9.42
F_{values}	4.45**	9.84***	3.02*	3.71**	3.82**	8.40***	6.52***
R^2	0.25	0.42	0.18	0.22	0.22	0.38	0.33

Notes: (i) Figures in brackets are t_{values} (ii) *, **, *** indicate significant at 10%, 5% and 1% levels for a two-tailed test.

Table 4.10(A): Factors Affecting the Wage Rates of Permanent Farm Servants at Village Level: Variable Under Consideration is Rent of Land (Rs./Acre)

Explanatory Variables:	*Dependent Variable(Y):Annual Mean Wage Rate of Permanent Farm Servants (Rs.) Controlled Variables(One by One)*						
	Equation-1	*Equation-2*	*Equation-3*	*Equation-4*	*Equation-5*	*Equation-6*	*Equation-7*
Rent of Land (Rs./Acre) (Variable under Consideration)	0.56 (1.63)	0.60 (2.23)**	0.72 (1.98)*	0.63 (1.78)*	0.70 (2.18)**	0.89 (2.79)***	0.27 (0.80)
Size of Holding (Acres)	625.94 (2.10)**	-	-	-	-	-	-
Percentage of Migrant Permanent Farm Servants	-	-99.91 (4.56)***	-	-	-	-	-
Male Agriculture Labourers÷Male Cultivators	-	-	-995.09 (0.38)	-	-	-	-
Male Agriculture Labourers÷ Male Agriculture Labourers + Male Non-Agriculture Workers	-	-	-	6.45 (1.41)	-	-	-
Tractors(No.)	-	-	-	-	28.48 (2.62)**	-	-
Cropping Pattern (Dummy): Wheat-Cotton=1 Wheat-Paddy=0	-	-	-	-	-	7110.54 (2.97)***	-
Zone (Dummy): Sub-mountain=1 Others=0	-	-	-	-	-	-	-8307.08 (3.08)***
Intercept	12063.73	20201.20	15332.23	13632.84	12167.50	11213.92	21008.39
F_{values}	4.38**	13.72***	1.95	3.01*	3.34*	6.88***	7.28***
R^2	0.25	0.50	0.13	0.18	0.30	0.34	0.35

Notes: (i). Figures in brackets are t_{values} (ii) *, **, *** indicate significant at 10%, 5% and 1% levels for a two-tailed test.

Table 4.10(B): Factors Affecting the Wage Rates of Permanent Farm Servants at Village Level: Variable Under Consideration is Rent of Land (Rs./Acre)

Explanatory Variables:	*Dependent Variable(Y):Log [Annual Mean Wage Rate of Permanent Farm Servants (Rs.)] Controlled Variables(One by One)*						
	Equation-1	*Equation-2*	*Equation-3*	*Equation-4*	*Equation-5*	*Equation-6*	*Equation-7*
Rent of Land (Rs./Acre) (Variable under Consideration)	0.00003 (1.67)	0.00003 (2.54)**	0.00003 (2.20)**	0.00003 (2.03)*	0.00003 (2.44)**	0.00005 (3.08)***	0.00002 (1.07)
Size of Holding (Acres)	0.02 (1.88)**	-	-	-	-	-	-
Percentage of Migrant Permanent Farm Servants	-	-0.00004 (4.59)***	-	-	-	-	-
Male Agriculture Labourers÷Male Cultivators	-	-	-0.03 (0.29)	-	-	-	-
Male Agriculture Labourers÷Male Agriculture Labourers+Male Non-Agriculture Workers	-	-	-	0.0002 (1.27)	-	-	-
Tractors (No.)	-	-	-	-	0.001 (2.66)*	-	-
Cropping Pattern (Dummy): Wheat-Cotton=1 Wheat-Paddy=0	-	-	-	-	-	0.35 (3.02)***	-
Zone (Dummy): Sub-mountain=1; Others=0	-	-	-	-	-	-	-0.40 (2.95)***
Intercept	9.43	9.82	9.58	9.50	9.42	9.38	9.85
F_{values}	4.43**	14.72***	2.42	3.31**	6.52***	7.69***	7.46***
R^2	0.25	0.52	0.15	0.20	0.33	0.36	0.36

Notes: (i). Figures in brackets are t_{values} (ii) *, **, *** indicate significant at 10%, 5% and 1% levels for a two-tailed test.

Table 4.11(A): Factors Affecting the Wage Rates of Permanent Farm Servants at Village Level: Variable Under Consideration is Cropping Pattern

Explanatory Variables:	*Dependent Variable(Y):Annual Mean Wage Rate of Permanent Farm Servants (Rs.) Controlled Variables(One by One)*						
	Equation-1	*Equation-2*	*Equation-3*	*Equation-4*	*Equation-5*	*Equation-6*	*Equation-7*
Cropping Pattern (Dummy): Wheat-Cotton=1 Wheat-Paddy=0 (Variable under Consideration)	3663.77 (1.29)	922.72 (0.36)	5212.39 (2.14)**	5915.28 (2.18)**	6372.14 (2.56)**	3634.33 (1.55)	7110.54 (2.97)***
Tractors (No.)	21.12 (1.66)	-	-	-	-	-	-
Percentage of Migrant Permanent Farm Servants	-	-98.43 (3.59)**	-	-	-	-	-
Size of Holding (Acres)	-	-	665.42 (2.34)**	-	-	-	-
Male Agriculture Labourers÷ Male Cultivators	-	-	-	842.13 (0.31)	-	-	-
Male Agriculture Labourers÷Male Agriculture Labourers+Male Non-Agriculture Workers	-	-	-	-	8.97 (2.08)**	-	-
Zone (Dummy): Sub-mountain=1 Others=0	-	-	-	-	-	-8118.88 (3.27)***	-
Rent of Land (Rs/Acre)	-	-	-	-	-	-	0.89 (2.79)***
Intercept	19274.44	26183.46	16344.39	20214.12	17856.61	22909.41	11213.92
F_{Values}	3.94**	9.64***	5.53***	2.39	4.87**	8.62***	6.91***
R^2	0.23	0.42	0.29	0.15	0.27	0.39	0.34

Notes: (i) Figures in brackets are $_{tvalues}$ (ii) *, **, *** indicate significant at 10%, 5% and 1% levels for a two-tailed test.

Table 4.11(B): Factors Affecting the Wage Rates of Permanent Farm Servants at Village Level: Variable Under Consideration is Cropping Pattern

Explanatory Variables:	*Dependent Variable (Y): Log [Annual Mean Wage Rate of Permanent Farm Servants (Rs.)] Controlled Variables (One by One)*						
	Equation-1	*Equation-2*	*Equation-3*	*Equation-4*	*Equation-5*	*Equation-6*	*Equation-7*
Cropping Pattern (Dummy): Wheat-Cotton=1 Wheat-Paddy=0 (Variable under Consideration)	0.17 (1.23)	0.03 (0.28)	0.25 (2.06)**	0.29 (2.15)**	0.31 (2.45)**	0.18 (1.49)	0.35 (3.02)***
Tractors (No.)	0.001 (1.68)	-	-	-	-	-	-
Percentage of Migrant Permanent Farm Servants	-	-0.005 (3.60)***	-	-	-	-	-
Size of Holding (Acres)	-	-	0.03 (2.11)**	-	-	-	-
Male Agriculture Labourers÷Male Cultivators	-	-	-	0.05 (0.42)	-	-	-
Male Agriculture Labourers÷Male Agriculture Labourers+Male Non-Agriculture Workers	-	-	-	-	0.004 (1.91)*	-	-
Zone (Dummy): Sub-mountain=1 Others=0	-	-	-	-	-	-0.40 (3.17)**	-
Rent of Land (Rs/Acre)	-	-	-	-	-	-	0.00005 (3.08)***
Intercept	9.82	10.16	9.69	9.85	9.76	9.99	9.38
F_{Values}	3.85**	9.74***	4.81**	2.31	4.34**	8.25***	7.69***
R^2	0.22	0.42	0.26	0.15	0.24	0.37	0.36

Notes: (i) Figures in brackets are $_{tvalues}$ (ii) *, **, *** indicate significant at 10%, 5% and 1% levels for a two-tailed test.

Table 4.12 (A): Factors Affecting the Wage Rates of Permanent Farm Servants at Village Level:
Variable Under Consideration is Percentage of Migrant Permanent Farm Servants

Explanatory Variables:	*Dependent Variable(Y):Annual Mean Wage Rate of Permanent Farm Servants (Rs.) Controlled Variables(One by One)*						
	Equation-1	*Equation-2*	*Equation-3*	*Equation-4*	*Equation-5*	*Equation-6*	*Equation-7*
Percentage of Migrant Permanent Farm Servants (Variable under Consideration)	-94.99 (4.30)***	-108.56 (4.52)***	-98.43 (4.22)***	-92.81 (3.43)***	-98.43 (3.53)***	-83.32 (3.96)***	-99.91 (4.56)***
Size of Holding (Acres)	544.99 (2.27)**	-	-	-	-	-	-
Male Agriculture Labourers÷ Male Cultivators	-	1996.22 (0.90)	-	-	-	-	-
Male Agriculture Labourers÷Male Agriculture Labourers+ Male Non-Agriculture Workers	-	-	4.96 (1.32)	-	-	-	-
Tractors (No.)	-	-	-	9.14 (0.81)	-	-	-
Cropping Pattern (Dummy): Wheat-Cotton=1 Wheat-Paddy=0	-	-	-	-	922.72 (0.36)	-	-
Zone (Dummy): Sub-mountain=1 Others=0	-	-	-	-	-	-6748.68 (3.26)***	-
Rent of Land (Rs/Acre)	-	-	-	-	-	-	0.60 (2.22)**
Intercept	22504.50	25559.66	24854.90	25288.28	26183.46	27093.96	20201.20
F_{Values}	13.94***	10.22***	11.02***	10.09***	9.64***	18.58***	13.72***
R^2	0.51	0.43	0.45	0.43	0.42	0.58	0.50

Notes: (i) Figures in brackets are $_{tvalues}$ (ii) *, **, *** indicate significant at 10%, 5% and 1% levels for a two-tailed test.

Table 4.12(B): Factors Affecting the Wage Rates of Permanent Farm Servants at Village Level: Variable Under Consideration is Percentage of Migrant Permanent Farm Servants

Explanatory Variables:	*Dependent Variable(Y): Log [Annual Mean Wage Rate of Permanent Farm Servants (Rs.)] Controlled Variables(One by One)*						
	Equation-1	*Equation-2*	*Equation-3*	*Equation-4*	*Equation-5*	*Equation-6*	*Equation-7*
Percentage of Migrant Permanent Farm Servants (Variable under Consideration)	-0.004 (4.21)***	-0.005 (4.52)***	-0.003 (4.16)***	-0.0005 (3.38)***	-0.0005 (3.51)***	-0.004 (3.89)***	-0.0005 (4.59)***
Size of Holding (Acres)	0.02 (2.02)*	-	-	-	-	-	-
Male Agriculture Labourers÷ Male cultivators	-	0.12 (1.04)	-	-	-	-	-
Male Agriculture Labourers÷Male Agriculture Labourers+Male Non-Agriculture Workers	-	-	0.0002 (1.16)	-	-	-	-
Tractors(No.)	-	-	-	0.0005 (0.80)	-	-	-
Cropping Pattern (Dummy): Wheat-Cotton=1 Wheat-Paddy=0	-	-	-	-	0.04 (0.30)	-	-
Zone (Dummy): Sub-mountain=1 Others=0	-	-	-	-	-	-0.33 (3.18)***	-
Rent of Land (Rs/Acre)	-	-	-	-	-	-	0.00003 (2.54)**
Intercept	9.99	10.12	10.10	10.11	10.16	10.20	9.82
F_{Values}	12.73***	10.20***	10.43***	9.85***	9.37***	17.85***	14.72***
R^2	0.49	0.43	0.44	0.42	0.41	0.57	0.52

Notes: (i) Figures in brackets are $_{tvalues}$ (ii) *, **, *** indicate significant at 10%, 5% and 1% levels for a two-tailed test.

Table 4.13 (A): Factors Affecting the Wage Rates of Permanent Farm Servants at Village Level: Variable Under Consideration is Male Agriculture Labourers ÷ Male Cultivators

Explanatory Variables:	*Dependent Variable(Y):Annual Mean Wage Rate of Permanent Farm Servants (Rs.) Controlled Variables(One by One)*						
	Equation-1	*Equation-2*	*Equation-3*	*Equation-4*	*Equation-5*	*Equation-6*	*Equation-7*
Male Agriculture Labourers÷ Male Cultivators (Variable under Consideration)	-1317.73 (0.50)	1996.22 (0.90)	473.44 (0.17)	897.02 (0.34)	842.13 (0.31)	188.30 (0.08)	-995.09 (0.38)
Size of Holding (Acres)	747.90 (2.42)**	-	-	-	-	-	-
Percentage of Migrant Permanent Farm Servants	-	-108.56 (4.52)***	-	-	-	-	-
Male Agriculture Labourers÷Male Agriculture Labourers+Male Non-Agriculture Workers	-	-	7.79 (1.61)	-	-	-	-
Tractors (No.)	-	-	-	29.20 (2.44)**	-	-	-
Cropping Pattern (Dummy): Wheat-Cotton=1 Wheat-Paddy=0	-	-	-	-	5915.28 (2.18)**	-	-
Zone (Dummy): Sub-mountain=1 Others=0	-	-	-	-	-	-9189.98 (3.65)***	-
Rent of Land (Rs/Acre)	-	-	-	-	-	-	0.72 (1.98)*
Intercept	17837.67	25559.66	19406.85	18788.10	20214.12	23851.05	15332.23
F_{Values}	0.29	10.22***	1.30	2.99*	2.39	6.81***	1.95
R^2	0.18	0.43	0.09	0.18	0.15	0.34	0.13

Notes: (i) Figures in brackets are $_{tvalues}$ (ii) *, **, *** indicate significant at 10%, 5% and 1% levels for a two-tailed test.

Table 4.13 (B): Factors Affecting the Wage Rates of Permanent Farm Servants at Village Level: Variable Under Consideration is Male Agriculture Labourers ÷ Male Cultivators

Explanatory Variables:	*Dependent Variable(Y): Log[Annual Mean Wage Rate of Permanent Farm Servants (Rs.)] Controlled Variables(One by One)*						
	Equation-1	*Equation-2*	*Equation-3*	*Equation-4*	*Equation-5*	*Equation-6*	*Equation-7*
Male Agriculture Labourers÷Male Cultivators (Variable under Consideration)	-0.05 (0.35)	0.12 (1.04)	0.04 (0.26)	0.06 (0.46)	0.06 (0.42)	0.02 (0.21)	-0.04 (0.28)
Size of Holding (Acres)	0.03 (2.20)**	-	-	-	-	-	-
Percentage of Migrant Permanent Farm Servants	-	-0.005 (4.52)***	-	-	-	-	-
Male Agriculture Labourers÷Male Agriculture Labourers+Male Non-Agriculture Workers	-	-	0.0004 (1.50)	-	-	-	-
Tractors(No.)	-	-	-	0.001 (2.46)**	-	-	-
Cropping Pattern (Dummy): Wheat-Cotton=1 Wheat-Paddy=0	-	-	-	-	0.29 (2.15)**	-	-
Zone (Dummy): Sub-mountain=1 Others=0	-	-	-	-	-	-0.46 (3.64)***	-
Rent of Land (Rs/Acre)	-	-	-	-	-	-	0.00004 (2.19)**
Intercept	9.75	10.12	9.82	9.78	9.85	10.03	9.58
F_{Values}	2.41	10.20***	1.13	3.02*	2.31	6.64***	2.41
R^2	0.15	0.43	0.08	0.18	0.15	0.33	0.15

Notes: (i) Figures in brackets are $_{tvalues}$ (ii) *, **, *** indicate significant at 10%, 5% and 1% levels for a two-tailed test.

Table 4.14(A): Factors Affecting the Wage Rates of Permanent Farm Servants at Village Level: Variable Under Consideration is Male Agriculture Labourers ÷ Male Agriculture Labourers + Male Non-Agriculture Workers

Explanatory Variables:	*Dependent Variable(Y):Annual Mean Wage Rate of Permanent Farm Servants (Rs.) Controlled Variables(One by One)*						
	Equation-1	*Equation-2*	*Equation-3*	*Equation-4*	*Equation-5*	*Equation-6*	*Equation-7*
Male Agriculture Labourers÷ Male Agriculture Labourers+ Male Non-Agriculture Workers (Variable under Consideration)	7.79 (1.61)	3.55 (0.70)	4.96 (1.32)	5.78 (1.29)	8.97 (2.08)**	3.78 (0.91)	6.45 (1.41)
Male Agriculture Labourers÷ Male Cultivators	473.44 (0.17)	-	-	-	-	-	-
Size of Holding (Acres)	-	615.50 (1.81)*	-	-	-	-	-
Percentage of Migrant Permanent Farm Servants	-	-	-98.43 (4.28)***	-	-	-	-
Tractors (No.)	-	-	-	25.60 (2.20)**	-	-	-
Cropping Pattern (Dummy): Wheat-Cotton=1 Wheat-Paddy=0	-	-	-	-	6372.14 (2.56)**	-	-
Zone (Dummy): Sub-mountain=1 Others=0	-	-	-	-	-	-8539.40 (3.35)***	-
Rent of Land (Rs/Acre)	-	-	-	-	-	-	0.63 (1.78)*
Intercept	19406.85	16798.66	24854.90	17906.71	17856.61	22665.09	13632.84
F_{Values}	1.30	3.08*	11.02***	3.94**	4.87***	7.43***	3.01*
R^2	0.09	0.19	0.45	0.23	0.27	0.35	0.18

Notes: (i) Figures in brackets are $_{tvalues}$ (ii) *, **, *** indicate significant at 10%, 5% and 1% levels for a two-tailed test.

Table 4.14(B): Factors Affecting the Wage Rates of Permanent Farm Servants at Village Level: Variable Under Consideration is Male Agriculture Labourers ÷ Male Agriculture Labourers + Male Non-Agriculture Workers

Explanatory Variables:	*Dependent Variable(Y):Log [Annual Mean Wage Rate of Permanent Farm Servants (Rs.)] Controlled Variables(One by One)*						
	Equation-1	*Equation-2*	*Equation-3*	*Equation-4*	*Equation-5*	*Equation-6*	*Equation-7*
Male Agriculture Labourers÷ Male Agriculture Labourers+ Male Non-Agriculture Workers (Variable under Consideration)	0.0004 (1.50)	0.0002 (0.64)	0.0002 (1.16)	0.0003 (1.16)	0.0004 (1.92)*	0.0002 (0.77)	0.0003 (1.27)
Male Agriculture Labourers÷ Male Cultivators	0.03 (0.26)	-	-	-	-	-	-
Size of Holding (Acres)	-	0.03 (1.66)	-	-	-	-	-
Percentage of Migrant Permanent Farm Servants	-	-	-0.0005 (4.16)***	-	-	-	-
Tractors (No.)	-	-	-	0.0001 (2.20)**	-	-	-
Cropping Pattern (Dummy): Wheat-Cotton=1 Wheat-Paddy=0	-	-	-	-	0.31 (2.45)**	-	-
Zone (Dummy): Sub-mountain=1 Others=0	-	-	-	-	-	-0.43 (3.32)***	-
Rent of Land (Rs/Acre)	-	-	-	-	-	-	0.00004 (2.03)**
Intercept	9.82	9.71	10.10	9.76	9.76	9.99	9.51
F_{Values}	1.12	2.58*	10.43***	3.71**	0.44	7.05***	3.31*
R^2	0.08	0.16	0.44	0.22	0.24	0.34	0.20

Notes: (i) Figures in brackets are $_{tvalues}$ (ii) *, **, *** indicate significant at 10%, 5% and 1% levels for a two-tailed test.

Table4.15(A): Factors Affecting the Wage Rates of Permanent Farm Servants at Village Level: Variable Under Consideration is Zone (Dummy)

Explanatory Variables:	*Dependent Variable(Y):Annual Mean Wage Rate of Permanent Farm Servants (Rs.) Controlled Variables(One by One)*						
	Equation-1	*Equation-2*	*Equation-3*	*Equation-4*	*Equation-5*	*Equation-6*	*Equation-7*
Zone (Dummy): Sub-mountain=1 Others=0 (Variable under Consideration)	-8148.12 (3.43)***	-7792.31 (3.06)***	-8118.88 (3.27)***	-6748.68 (3.26)***	-9189.98 (3.69)***	-8539.40 (3.35)***	-8307.71 (3.08)***
Size of Holding (Acres)	530.06 (2.02)*	-	-	-	-	-	-
Tractors (No.)	-	16.83 (1.56)	-	-	-	-	-
Rent of Land (Rs/Acre)	-	-	0.23 (0.80)	-	-	-	-
Cropping Pattern (Dummy): Wheat-Cotton=1 Wheat-Paddy=0	-	-	-	3634.33 (1.55)	-	-	-
Percentage of Migrant Permanent Farm Servants	-	-	-	-	-83.32 (3.96)***	-	-
Male Agriculture Labourers÷ Male Cultivators	-	-	-	-	-	188.30 (0.08)	-
Male Agriculture Labourers÷ Male Agriculture Labourers+ Male Non-Agriculture Workers	-	-	-	-	-	-	3.71 (0.91)
Intercept	20120.51	22094.70	22909.41	27093.99	23851.05	22665.09	21008.39
F_{Values}	9.89***	8.63***	8.62***	18.58***	6.81***	7.43***	7.29***
R^2	0.42	0.39	0.35	0.39	0.58	0.36	0.35

Notes: (i) Figures in brackets are $_{tvalues}$ (ii) *, **, *** indicate significant at 10%, 5% and 1% levels for a two-tailed test.

Table 4.15(B): Factors Affecting the Wage Rates of Permanent Farm Servants at Village Level: Variable Under Consideration is Zone (Dummy)

Explanatory Variables:	*Dependent Variable(Y): Log [Annual Mean Wage Rate of Permanent Farm Servants (Rs.)] Controlled Variables(One by One)*						
	Equation-1	*Equation-2*	*Equation-3*	*Equation-4*	*Equation-5*	*Equation-6*	*Equation-7*
Zone (Dummy):Submountain=1 Others=0 (Variable under Consideration)	-0.41 (3.37)***	-0.39 (3.01)***	-0.40 (2.95)***	-0.40 (3.23)***	-0.33 (3.18)***	-0.46 (3.64)***	-0.43 (3.32)***
Size of Holding (Acres)	0.02 (1.80)*	-	-	-	-	-	-
Tractors (No.)	-	0.0008 (1.55)	-	-	-	-	-
Rent of Land (Rs/Acre)	-	-	0.00002 (1.07)	-	-	-	-
Cropping Pattern (Dummy): Wheat-Cotton=1 Wheat-Paddy=0	-	-	-	0.18 (1.49)	-	-	-
Percentage of Migrant Permanent Farm Servants	-	-	-	-	-0.004 (3.98)***	-	-
Male Agriculture Labourers÷ Male Cultivators	-	-	-	-	-	0.02 (0.21)	-
Male Agriculture Labourers÷ Male Agriculture Labourers+ Male Non-Agriculture Workers	-	-	-	-	-	-	0.0001 (0.45)
Intercept	9.88	9.96	9.85	9.99	10.20	10.03	9.99
F_{Values}	9.01***	8.40***	7.46***	8.25***	17.85***	6.64***	7.05***
R^2	0.40	0.38	0.36	0.38	0.57	0.33	0.34

Notes: (i) Figures in brackets are $_{tvalues}$ (ii) *, **, *** indicate significant at 10%, 5% and 1% levels for a two-tailed test.

The depressing effect of the greater proportion of migrant labourers in a village on the wage rates of permanent farm servants is further confirmed by these results [Tables 4.12(A) and 4.12(B)]. The coefficient of this variable has a consistent negative sign and is significant in all the seven equations.

The coefficient of the ratio of male agricultural labourers to cultivators variable remained non-significant in all the seven equations reported in Tables 4.13(A) and 4.13(B) which further confirmed the lack of influence of this factor revealed by univariate results reported earlier. The results reported in Tables 4.14(A) and 4.14(B) reveal a similar lack of significant influence of variable, "Proportion of agricultural labourers in total wage labourers" in the village on inter-village variation in wages of permanent farm servants. Even in the univariate regression results this variable failed to show statistical significance even at 10 per cent level. So, these two features of the village labour market do not seem to significantly influence inter-village variations in wage rates of permanent farm servants. The statistically significant influence of zone variable indicated earlier by univariate results was fully confirmed by this controlled variable exercise as well. It may be seen from Tables 4.15(A) and 4.15(B) that the coefficient of this variable remains negative and highly significant (at one per cent level) in all the seven equations. These results suggest that the lower wage rates of permanent farm servants in the foot hills zone was not due to factors such as size of holding, tractor ownership, land productivity or cropping pattern, etc. Because even when the influence of these variables was controlled (one by one) the zone dummy retained the negative sign and remained significant at one per cent level. It seems there are many other factors, apart from the above mentioned, that make wage rates of permanent farm servants lower in villages of foot-hills region.

To sum up the results of this sub-section we may conclude that the significant influence of three variables, namely (i) size of holding, (ii) proportion of migrant farm labourers, and (iii) the zone-dummy was fully confirmed. Similarly, the lack of influence of two variables, namely the ratio of male agricultural labourers to cultivators, and proportion of male agricultural labourers among all wage labourers in the village was also clearly confirmed. On the influence of tractor ownership, rent of land and cropping pattern the conclusion remains somewhat uncertain on account of the mixed results on these variables.

Multiple Regression Results-II

On the basis of clues suggested by the multiple regression analysis of the previous sub-section (in which influence of one variable at a time was controlled or held constant), we explored further by entering all the possible combinations, of three or four, of the eight explanatory variables as independent variables. Out of these many multiple regression models estimated, we chose two for final reporting and discussion on the basis of value of R^2 and consistency of signs and statistically significance of the explanatory variables in all three levels of regression analysis (i.e. univariate, multivariate-I and multivariate II). These models are reported in Tables 4.16 and 4.17. In the results presented in Table 4.16, three variables, namely size of holding, rent of land and per cent of migrant permanent farm servants in the village, are entered as explanatory variables. It may be seen that the sign of each of these variables is correct in the sense that it is in line with economic logic on the inter-village variations in the wage rates of permanent farm servants. Moreover the sign of each of these variables has remained consistent in all the models (univariate, multivariate - I and multivariate - II) in which these were used as explanatory variables. Each of these three variables is also statistically significant at varying levels of confidence.

In the results reported in Table 4.17, zone dummy is added to the three explanatory variables model of Table 4.16. It may be seen that as a result of the addition of zone dummy, rent of land variable lost its statistical significance, but retains the positive sign. However, the other two variables retain their significant status and right sign even in this model. It may be recalled that the zone dummy variable retained its negative sign and statistical significance in the earlier reported univariate and multivariate results. It seems part of the impact of the zone dummy on the wage rates of permanent farm servants is via rent of land or its principal the productivity of land.

Table 4.16: Impact of Supply and Demand Factors on the Wage Rates of Permanent Farm Servants at Village Level: Multiple Regression (Model-I) (N=30)

Dependent Variable: Annual Mean Wage Rate of Permanent Farm Servants (Rs.)		
Explanatory Variables:	*Annual Mean Wage Rate*	*Log(Annual Mean Wage Rate)*
Size of Land Holding (Acres)	460.24(1.98)*	0.02(1.79)*
Rent of Land (Rs./Acre)	0.50(1.92)*	0.03(2.25)**
Percentage of Migrant Permanent Farm Servants	-93.21(4.42)***	-0.004(4.41)***
Intercept	17774.75	9.72
F_{values}	11.44***	11.45***
R^2	0.58	0.58
$\overline{R}^{-2}$	0.53	0.53

Notes: (i) Figures in parentheses are t_{values}, (ii) *, **, *** indicate significant at 10%, 5% and 1% levels for a two-tailed test.

Table 4.17: Impact of Agro-Climatic Zone, Supply and Demand Factors on the Wage Rates of Permanent Farm Servants at Village Level: Multiple Regression (Model-II) (N=30)

Dependent Variable: Annual Mean Wage Rate of Permanent Farm Servants (Rs.)		
Explanatory Variables	*Annual Mean Wage Rate*	*Log(Annual Mean Wage Rate)*
Size of Land Holding (Acres)	404.39(1.88)*	0.02(1.57)
Rent of Land (Rs./Acre)	0.26(0.99)	0.00002(1.37)
Percentage of Migrant Permanent Farm Servants	-79.89(3.97)***	-0.004(3.94)***
Zone (Dummy): Sub-mountainous=1 Others = 0	-5220.18(2.42)**	-0.25(2.24)**
Intercept	21168.50	9.88
F_{values}	11.63***	11.16***
R^2	0.65	0.64
$\overline{R}^{-2}$	0.60	0.58
F_{values}	11.63***	11.16***

Note: (i) Figures in parentheses are t_{values}, (ii) *, **, *** indicate significant at 10%, 5% and 1% levels for a two-tailed test.

The R^2 value reported in Table 4.17 indicates that these four variables explain 65 per cent of the inter-village variation in the wage rates of permanent farm servants. Given the cross section nature of data used, R^2 equal to 0.65 can be taken as a fairly satisfactory fit of the model to the underlying data. However, the unexplained 35 per cent of the inter-village variation in the wage rates of permanent farm servants suggests that there are some other important determinants of inter-village variations in the wage rates of permanent farm servants that are not included in the models presented in Tables 4.16 and 4.17. That suggests a further probing of this issue is needed to get a fuller explanation of inter-village variations in the wage rates of permanent farm servants. But that cannot be attempted here for obvious reasons.

The results of this section may be summed up. It is clearly established that there are considerable inter-village variations in the wage rates of permanent farm servants in Punjab. Some of the factors responsible for this inter-village variation in the wage rates of permanent farm servants we have been able to isolate with the help of regression analysis. These are size of holding, productivity of land, proportion of migrant farm workers in the village and some zone-related factors proxied by the zone dummy. It was found that villages with bigger sized holdings also have a higher wage rate of permanent farm servants, on the average. Similarly, villages with higher land productivity were also found, on the average, to have a higher mean wage rate. The proportion of permanent migrant farm servants in the village was found to depress the wage rates of permanent farm servants, on the average. Finally, it was observed that villages falling in the sub-mountainous (foothills) zone had a lower mean wage rate of permanent farm servants, on the average, compared to villages located in the Punjab plains.

NOTES

1. The Foot Hills region which includes Shivalik hills and semi-hilly area are Ropar, Hoshiarpur and Gurdaspur districts especially tehsil Pathankot, is dissected by closely spaced seasonal streams that cause soil erosion and floods, suffers from water scarcity for irrigation purposes. The Upper Bari Doab

region consists of areas falling in Amritsar and Gurdaspur districts. The Bist-Doab region includes area which falls in districts—Kapurthala, Jalandhar and Nawanshahr. Northern Malwa consists of districts Moga, Ludhiana and tehsil of Zira in Ferozepur district. Southern Malwa comprises other districts. For details see, G.S. Gosal and Gopal Krishan: "Physical and Cultural Settings" in *Regional Disparities in Levels of Socio-Economic Development in Punjab*, 1984, pp. 11-29.

2. The study conducted by Grewal and Rangi pointed out that even in a small state like Punjab, there exists significant inter-district and inter-area differentials in value productivity in agriculture. Hence, the districts are divided into three productivity zones: high productivity, medium and low productivity zone. For details see S.S. Grewal and P.S. Rangi: "An Analytical Study of Growth of Punjab Agriculture", *Indian Journal of Agricultural Economics*, Vol. 38, No. 4, 1983, pp. 509-519.
3. The village-wise segmentation of the rural markets has been studied by Bardhan and Rudra in the villages of West Bengal. For details see Pranab Bardhan and Ashok Rudra: "Labour Mobility and the Boundaries of the Village Moral Economy", *Journal of Peasant Studies*, Vol. 13, No. 3, 1986, pp. 90-115.
4. Similarly, Rudra estimated the wide inter and intra-village-wise wage variations in the agriculture labour markets in West Bengal. For details see Ashok Rudra: *Extra Economic Constraints on Agricultural Labour: Results of an Intensive Survey in Some Villages Near Santiniketan, West Bengal*, 1982, pp. 38-79.
5. In this present study all the permanent farm servants are male so we took only the daily wage of male casual agricultural labourers to compare their daily earnings in surveyed villages with their male counterparts.
6. The findings of this study coincide with the findings of Basant and Pal. These scholars on the basis of Farm Management Studies Data and ICRISAT data found the daily wages of permanent farm servants lower than casual agricultural labourers. For details see Rakesh Basant: "Attached and Casual Labour Wage Rates". *Economic and Political Weekly*, Vol. 19, No. 9, 1984, pp. 390-396 and Sarmistha Pal: "Task Based Segmentation of Rural Labour Contracts: Theory and Evidence". *Bulletin of Economic Research*, Vol. 51, No. 1, 1999, pp. 67-94.
7. In literature it has accepted the market of casual agricultural labourers operates under the principle of supply and demand and it is entirely different from the market of permanent farm

servants. The difference in the mean wage rate of casual agricultural labourers and permanent farm servants has always been found statistically insignificant. For details see Ajit Kumar Ghose: "Wages and Employment in Indian Agriculture". *World Development*, Vol. 8, Nos. 5&6, 1980, pp. 413-428.

5

Working Conditions and Nature of Contract

The working conditions of permanent farm servants in post-green revolution Punjab are described and discussed in this chapter. The working conditions cover the whole spectrum of issues from the selection process to completion of the annual contract of a permanent farm servant that impact his person and earnings. The information on the working conditions of permanent farm servants is very scanty and scattered and no systematic picture is available. Therefore, the description in this chapter is based on the field survey of two hundred and forty permanent farm servants conducted in thirty villages of Punjab, itineraries, focus group discussions (FGDs), personal accounts of employers (farmers) and past studies relating to working conditions of permanent farm servants.

Mode of Selection of Permanent Farm Servants

In an almost perfectly competitive village labour market a permanent farm servant is selected by an employer for regular labour supply throughout the year. The selection process of permanent farm servants in the village labour market is quite complex and depends on a number of economic or non-economic factors. A farmer (employer) is always in search of a loyal, skilled, young and sturdy permanent farm servant, who may devote his maximum time and strength on the farm. Similarly, a permanent farm servant always wants of an employer who has a kind temperament, pays good wages and perks and renders timely social and financial help in an emergency.[1] In the survey of thirty villages the employers of surveyed permanent farm servants reported that nowadays it is a difficult task to get an efficient permanent farm servant. The prevailing wage rate and perks never satisfy them. Moreover, nowadays the young local labourers do not want to work on a long-term labour contract in agriculture. Their first preference is to work on the non-farm jobs (e.g. in the construction sector, industries and shops) in nearby towns. In the non-farm sector jobs the working hours are fixed and they get better wages compared to agriculture.[2] In the village labour market, the employers prefer to select those permanent farm servants who are skilled, punctual, ready to work at odd hours, do not hesitate to tumble and mire in dust or mud, well-mannered and having good habits and work diligently in all farm operations. A permanent farm servant, either migrant or local, who has such qualities is preferred.[3] Interestingly, a permanent farm servant (migrant or local) who can vouch for or affirm such qualities or reputation of a good worker in a village labour market is even enticed away by one employer from another.[4] On the other hand, the permanent farm servants said that they prefer to work on those farms where employers are not haughty and miserly, their young male family members behave well at farms and in homes, and the wages and perks are good and are paid in time. Further, the reputation of the head lady of an employer's household in giving sufficient and good quality food to permanent farm servants also matters in attracting permanent farm servants to a farmer. In the village labour market an employer or a permanent farm servant can easily get the required information about each other's reputation and personal qualities. The social interaction among permanent farm servants and farmers (employers) is intense in village labour markets. In a small community (village) everyone watches everyone, and a person's bad reputation tends to become known quickly in the whole village. In such a labour market both parties may be discouraged from opportunistic behaviour, given the high expected cost of losing one's reputation in the event of the probable discovery of dishonest behaviour.[5] In case of new migrant permanent farm servants it may be difficult for employers to get full information on their reputation and qualities at the time of selection. Similarly, the new migrants are also quite ignorant of the reputation of the farmer (employer) while entering into a contract. The mutual tying up of a permanent farm servant and farmer occurs through an informal process of interaction. The farmer sends feelers or direct offers to a number of permanent farm servants that pass his rating. Similarly each permanent farm servant also enquires directly or through someone else from a number of prospective employers and ultimately the tying up occurs and the wage rate and other conditions also settled.

Nature of Contract

The permanent farm servants after selection enter into a formal contract with their employers. Generally, the contract of a permanent farm servant is for one year and starts on May 1 and ends on April 30. The contract can be written or unwritten depending on the relationship and mutual trust of the hiring farmer household and the concerned permanent farm servant. In the surveyed villages, a majority of contracts between employing farmers and permanent farm servants were unwritten. The terms of contract are more stringent and very likely written in the case of those permanent farm servants who take some advance payment from their employers.[6] Some employers also mortgage some saleable asset of the permanent farm servants as surety for the advance amount; but this is not the popular practice. We have reproduced copies of some of the actual contracts in the appendices (Chapter 5) from the colonial period to the post-green revolution period in Punjab. From the reading of these contracts it seems that no major change has occurred in the terms of contract of permanent farm servants in Punjab except for the rise in wage rates. The advance payment of wages to permanent farm servants has remained a permanent feature of their terms of contract during the entire period. It is visible from the contract of 'siri' (share wage permanent farm servant) that he has a more binding agreement with his employer relatively to a cash wage permanent farm servant. At the time of contract negotiations, perquisites, wages in cash or kind are often based on local customs of the village. The terms of a contract like mode of wage payments, advance money taken, holidays and position of permanent farm servants in the labour hierarchy on the farm are pre-negotiated. If either side violates the terms of the contract, the village panchayat, is approached by either party for the enforcement of conditions of the contract. At the end of the year, unless a new contract has been agreed, both sides are automatically free to negotiate with any one else they like in the village.

Settlement of Wage Rates, Pattern of Wage Payments and Perks

In the labour market for permanent farm servants the wage rates are not collectively settled or contracted between permanent farm servants and farmers as groups. Rather each farmer (employer) and each permanent farm servant negotiates individually with the other party to settle the wage rate and perks to be paid to the permanent farm servant. That is why the wage rates of permanent farm servants vary considerably in a village, unlike the casual labour for which a single wage rate prevails for all. A few months before the date on which new contracts begin (May 1) each permanent farm servant starts getting feelers and offers from farmers (employers) depending on his reputation and rating in the village labour market. Similarly, farmers (employers) also start getting approached by permanent farm servants directly or by someone on their behalf for employment in the coming year, again depending on the reputation and rating of the farmers (employers) as good pay master. In the two-three months preceding the date on which new contracts start (May 1) the village labour market is buzzing with open and confidential negotiations between farmers and permanent farm servants for an advantageous contract for the next year. It is through this informal one to one negotiation that permanent farm servants are hired in the village labour market of Punjab. A few cases of break up of the contract even before joining the new job also occur in every village because of the permanent farm servant or the farmer finding a more attractive offer after the contract has been entered into with someone. Such cases of rescinding the contract earn a bad name for the permanent farm servant or the farmer who has gone back on his word. The share of a share wage permanent farm servant in total output and inputs varies from village to village and farm to farm and depends on customs of the village, size of the land holding of the farmer, and the ranking and rating of permanent farm servant as a worker and mutual bargaining between the farmer and permanent farm servants. The share wage contract was quite popular in the pre-green revolution period, but is gradually disappearing after the green revolution. In the paddy/ wheat belt the share wage contract has almost disappeared, but it is still lingering in the cotton belt. The reasons behind the disappearance of this type of contract have been discussed by Day[7] and Shergill.[8] These authors concluded that the mechanization of various farm operations reduced the demand of share wage permanent farm servants. The pattern of payment of wages to a permanent farm servant varies from village to village. In the surveyed villages the employers reported that a permanent farm servant always wants to get his entire wage in advance; and some of the local permanent farm servants do manage to get their whole wage in advance. But, not a single migrant permanent farm servant was paid even half of total wages in advance (Table 5.1).

Table 5.1: Pattern of Wage Payment of Permanent Farm Servants [N: Local = 134; Migrant = 106]

Advance/ Loan Status of Permanent Farm Servants	*Local Permanent Farm Servants*		*Migrant Permanent Farm Servants*		*All*	
	N	%	N	%	N	%
Some part of wages taken as advance	132	99	40	38	172	72
Some loan taken without interest	101	75	39	37	140	58
Some loan taken with interest	34	25	12	11	46	19

Source: Primary Survey (2007-2008)

In most cases the migrant permanent farm servants are paid wages on a monthly basis. The pattern of payment of wages to local permanent farm servants varies somewhat from village to village and in the different regions of Punjab. In the cotton belt and the Malwa zone the local permanent farm servants usually receive wages in two instalments; first instalment is paid in early May when the permanent farm servant joins the job with a new employer, and the second in the month of January around the *Lohri* festival. In other regions of the state one half of wages is paid at the time of joining the contract and the remaining part after the completion of the contract.

We have also tried to capture the types of perks which permanent farm servants get from their farmers (employers). In the colonial period, on the basis of official reports, we may say that permanent farm servants had special privileges and access to various perks like food, loans, clothes, turbans, blanket, shoes, fodder or a patch of land for growing fodder. Over the years and particularly after the green revolution, it seems the various perks have been curtailed and are dis-appearing. The information collected during the survey (Table 5.2) revealed that the most common perk the permanent farm servants get now is only food and tea during the day.

Table 5.2: Perks of Permanent Farm Servants in Punjab [N: Local = 134; Migrant = 106]

Perks Availability at Employer's Place	*Local Permanent Farm Servants*		*MigrantPermanent Farm Servants*		*All*	
	N	%	N	%	N	%
Food	127	95	104	98	231	96
Tea	127	95	101	90	201	96
Fodder/Bhusa	16	12	2	1.9	18	8
Cotton sticks/wood	16	12	2	1.9	18	8
Clothes	32	24	16	15	48	20
Shoes	32	24	16	15	48	20
Blankets/Turbans	-	-	-	-	-	-
Minor medical facilities	48	36	48	45	96	40
Medical facility at time of injury at farm	121	90	96	91	217	90

Source: Primary Survey (2007-2008)

A permanent farm servant who does not get food from the employer is usually given twenty kilograms of wheat, etc. per month in lieu of food. Some employers occasionally give them milk, butter, *lassi* (whey) and ghee also. On the big farms with many permanent farm servants, usually a special servant is hired to prepare food and tea for all the permanent farm servants working on it. The provision of food at worksite is not only a part of the village custom, but is profitable for the employer, as it results in saving time that will be lost if a permanent farm servant goes to his own home for tea and food. The permanent farm servants not only get plentiful food, but are also aware of its monetary value. Akerlof[9] rightly mentioned in this regard "A custom which gives utility to each party dies hard". Apart from food and tea, other perks like some green fodder, cotton-sticks/wood, vegetables and straw are occasionally given to the local permanent farm servants but are no longer a regular feature of contracts.

The permanent farm servants are not provided any medical facilities by the farmers (employers). In the case of minor ailments, like a cold or fever, they may be given some medicine by the farmer from his own stock to prevent their abstaining from work to go to a doctor. But in the case of more serious ailments the permanent farm servants spend from their own pockets. If a permanent farm servant faces any major accident on the farm at the time of spraying chemicals, repairing tubewells, driving agriculture machinery or snake bite, etc. then most farmers (employers) bear all the medical expenses, but some also try to evade these costs. In the event of death of a permanent farm servant in a farm accident or amputation, some compensation is paid to the permanent farm servant by the Punjab Agriculture Marketing Board (Punjab Mandi Board). But most farmers (employers) also make a lump sum payment to the accident victim worker.

Nature of Duties and Working Hours

It is implicit in the contract between a permanent farm servant and his employer that he is supposed to do all the farm operations at any time. The contract of the two parties is based more on personal relationship and understanding. The employer is understood to have assumed far-reaching obligations and a permanent farm servant having placed his whole energy and time at the disposal of his employer. The authority exercised by his employer over a permanent farm servant is regarded almost unlimited; the bindings of a permanent farm servant's obligations being undefined. A permanent farm servant performs multiple duties on the farm and he is expected to consider himself as an attached adopted member of the family who will take as much interest and pains in farm work as a family member does. He is assigned more responsible duties on the farm, at the time of sowing of crops, watering of plants, spraying chemicals, manuring the crops, arranging and supervising the casual labour, etc. He also takes care of all the milch animals on the farm. But he does not clean the cattle sheds and milk the milch animals. Moreover, on many farms he acts as a factotum. In the lean season sometimes he helps his employer in non-farm jobs also, e.g. he assists the masons if his employer builds a house. He repairs the animal stalls and sheds. He assists his employer in business if he runs a shop in the village.

To complete the farm operations in time he spends long hours, during the lean as well as peak season. In fact, the working hours of permanent farm servants wax and wane over the year. In our study, we came to know from the farmers and the retired permanent farm servants aged between 50 and 75 years that the numbers of working hours, after the mechanization of farming, have fallen in agriculture not only for farmers and their family members, but also for permanent farm servants. Earlier the employers and their permanent farm servants used to rise early in the morning before 5 am; and all the farm operations were done manually. Even female family members of farmers spent a number of hours providing food in fields to workers and doing other farm-related jobs. After the green revolution many farm operations have become mechanized and employers have become lethargic and wake up only after sunrise; the permanent farm servants also follow the lifestyle of their employers.

At present the number of working hours of a permanent farm servant depends on the following factors: type of crops, sources of irrigation, distance of the farm from the village and of different plots from each other, number of permanent farm servants working on the farm, number of family members of the employer's household working on the farm, level of mechanization of the farm and tenure of attachment of a permanent farm servant with one employer. During our field survey we came to know that in the wheat-paddy and wheat-cotton zone a permanent farm servant, during the lean period, reports for work between 6 am to 7 am at his employer's home. After taking the cattle out of the shed, he has breakfast and tea. After this the employer directs him to his daily routine. In the evening after dinner he goes back to his own home between 6 and 7 pm. So approximately it is an 11 to 12 hour working day.

The working hours of a permanent farm servant depend largely on the nature of crops grown on the farm. The wheat crop, from sowing to maturity, needs less care and accordingly the working hours of permanent farm servants are shorter during the wheat season. The sowing operation of this crop is completely mechanized and the need of irrigation is less in this crop. The harvesting and threshing of this crop is also mechanized. Similarly, in the case of cotton growing farms the working hours are not so long. At the time of cotton picking the working schedule of a permanent farm servant becomes hectic, but it is not as burdensome, as cotton picking is done by casual labour and a permanent farm servant only supervises and manages it. On the other hand, in paddy growing areas the working hours of a permanent farm servant during the paddy season are not only longer, but he also comes under stress due to the nature of this crop.[10] First, at the time of transplantation of paddy a permanent farm servant not only arranges casual labour but also works with them. Secondly, his working hours become more intense because this crop needs water at regular intervals for three months continuously. During the paddy season a permanent farm servant works almost day and night to manage water in the fields. He does not get any compensatory leave for night duty. During the paddy season a permanent farm servant rests only for a few hours during the day and has to do the night shift also quite frequently. The intensity of working hours also depends on the distance of the farm and its various plots from the employer's home. If the farm is far away from the village then he has to spend considerable time to commute to the fields to work there. The insufficient number of permanent farm servants and family members of the employer's family on a farm also increases the burden and working hours of a permanent farm servant. Moreover, the working hours of a permanent farm servant also depend on the length of his tenure on the farm. If he has been working on the same farm from year to year then he has to share more responsibilities and duties on the farm which results in his spending longer working hours.

Advances and Loans

As we have already discussed, permanent farm servants in Punjab take a part of their annual wage as advance at the time of joining the new farmer (employer). This practice is almost universal in the case of local permanent farm servants.[11] However, only a few migrant permanent farm servants are paid any part of their wage as an advance. Apart from this advance payment of a part of the annual wage, permanent farm servants, especially the local ones, usually, take a loan also from their employers, with or without interest (Table 5.1). Some scholars have called this loan-taking by permanent farm servants in Punjab as inter-linking of credit and labour markets.[12] Such loans are generally given on the basis of the relationship between the employer and the permanent farm servant. Moreover, an employer (farmer) also takes into consideration the credit reputation of the permanent farm servant's family in the village. These loans taken by permanent farm servants are mostly used by them to finance current consumption expenditure, to perform social ceremonies and to repay the loan due to the previous employer. The availability of a loan from an employer is one of the factors that induces a permanent farm servant to join a particular farmer (employer). The permanent farm servant is expected to clear his debt with the previous employer before leaving his employment and his new employer takes the responsibility of advancing him sufficient money to clear this debt.[13] In the surveyed villages we found that a majority of permanent farm servants had taken some loan from their employers with as well as without interest.

Holidays and Leave Enjoyed by Permanent Farm Servants

The facility of paid holidays and leave enjoyed by permanent farm servants varies from region to region and farmer to farmer (Table 5.3). In the surveyed villages of Majha and Doaba regions we found that paid leave and holidays enjoyed by permanent farm servants during the year are not fixed in the contract signed by permanent farm servants.

Table 5.3: Holidays/Leave Allowed to Permanent Farm Servants [N: Local = 134; Migrant = 106]

Zone	*Total Number of Permanent Farm Servants*		*Local Permanent Farm Servants Enjoying Holidays*		*Migrant Permanent Farm Servants Enjoying Holidays*		*All*	
	Local	*Migrant*	*N*	*%*	*N*	*%*	*N*	*%*
Majha	18 (13.43)	14 (13.21)	8	44	2	14	10	31
Malwa	108 (80.60)	44 (41.51)	71	66	7	16	78	51
Doaba	8 (5.97)	48 (45.28)	1	13	1	2	2	4
All	134 (100)	106 (100)	80	60	10	9	90	38

Notes: (i) Source: Primary Survey (2007-2008) (ii) Figures in parentheses are percentages

A permanent farm servant has to be always at the beck and call of his employer in Daniel's terminology.[14] In these two regions (Doaba and Majha) a permanent farm servant is allowed paid leave only when he is seriously ill, only for two or three days. Similarly, he is allowed to enjoy paid holidays for one or two days only in case of his attending social ceremonies. If a permanent farm servant is absent from duty for more than two or three days on account of illness or social ceremonies then he is required to provide a substitute, otherwise wages of the days he missed are deducted from his salary on a per day basis. In the Malwa zone, specially in southern Malwa, the general custom is to allow a permanent farm servant twelve paid holidays in a year on account of illness, domestic work and social ceremonies. Sometimes this is mentioned in the contract, but more often it is the informal understanding between employer and the permanent farm servant. An absence of permanent farm servants for a longer duration than twelve days results in deduction from his salary on a per day basis if he does not provide a substitute for those days.

In all the regions it is the standard practice that a permanent farm servant cannot absent himself without the prior permission of his employer, except in case of sudden illness. During the peak sowing and harvesting season no holiday is allowed to a permanent farm servant, he has to report for work even when mildly ill; only in case of serious illness he can abstain. Many farmers (employers) take a more lenient view of occasional absenteeism of permanent farm servants during the lean season, but some are very strict about this matter even in the lean season. The reputation of the permanent farm servant in taking too many and without permission holidays, and of the employer (farmer) in granting holidays also plays an important role in the availability of regular employment to permanent farm servants and the wage rate he gets, and also in the availability of the permanent farm servant for hiring by a farmer and the wage rate he has to pay.

Employer—Employee Relationship

The relationship of farmers (employers) and permanent farm servants (employees) vary from village to village and farm to farm. The relationship between permanent farm servants (employees) and farmers (employers) is usually more informal on the small and medium farms on account of more close interaction between the two. On a small farm or medium farm the employer and his other male family members work on the farm side by side with the permanent farm servant. Moreover, the standard of living and culture of the farmer is not markedly superior to permanent farm servants. As a result there is greater interaction and involvement of the two in personal and farm problems. On small and medium farms, permanent farm servants (employees) usually prepare tea on the farm during work time and they share tea and food sitting in close proximity of the employer and his male family members. The economic and cultural gap between the employer and the permanent farm servant is also relatively less on small and medium farms. A permanent farm servant freely goes to the inner quarters of the employer's house and even interacts with female members of the employer's family. In contrast to this, on big farms permanent farm servants have less interaction with their employers. The employer (farmer) almost never participates in manual work on the farm and performs only a supervisory role. The big farmer treats permanent farm servants as servants and maintains a distance from them. He only allocates work among them and keeps an eye over their functioning from a distance. He never mixes with his permanent farm servants, nor even takes tea or food in their company. His economic and cultural level is much higher than the permanent farm servants and permanent farm servant usually is tongue-tied in his presence and submissively takes orders. The female quarters of big farmers' households are forbidden territory for a permanent farm servant, who goes there only when specially called and is expected to keep his head down to avoid eye contact with female family members. Despite this economic and status gap between a big farmer (employer) and his permanent farm servants the mutual relationship is more often quite cordial and without any bitter feeling and resentment. The permanent farm servant being a local village man, mostly from the scheduled castes, understands and even appreciates this social gap between him and his employer and does not try to violate it. The big farmer (employer) is also often quite kind to his permanent farm servants and to keep his reputation in the village labour market treats them quite well. In a way a permanent farm servant feels more relaxed at a big farm than at a small or medium farm. The big farmer's (employer's) supervision is light and the permanent farm servant works virtually at his own will and pace along with other permanent farm servants and casual labour. So the pace and timing of work is more relaxed on a big farm than on a small or medium farm, where the employer (farmer) works along with the permanent farm servant on the farm, and consequently is more demanding in work output, and the permanent farm servant ends up spending longer hours and putting in more intensive labour effort.

The employer-employee relations between farmers (employers) and permanent farm servants (employees) are normal and cordial in most cases. But in every village there are a few farmers who are notorious for bad behaviour and even doing physical violence towards permanent farm servants. Similarly, there are a few permanent farm servants in every village who are known to be great work shirkers, prone to stealing from the farms and abstaining from work without permission. In such cases the employer-employee relations get strained and sometimes result in the dismissal of the permanent farm servant in the middle of the contract period or the permanent farm servant leaving his job in mid year. Such cases then go to the village panchayat for resolution and settlement.

The literature highlights the fact that agrarian unrest in post-green revolution Punjab has remained relatively low compared to other states.[15] In the pre-green revolution period there had been some conflicts between share wage permanent farm servants and their employers on the issue of their share in agriculture produce and perks.[16] No study has reported any major confrontation of permanent farm servants with their employers in post-green revolution Punjab.[17] The permanent farm servants did not participate even in the agitations launched by casual farm labourers from time to time.[18] The surveyed permanent farm servants reported that they never organized any agitation against their employers. Moreover, they never demanded collectively any increase in wage rates and perks at the village level. It means the relations between permanent farm servants and their employers are cordial and quite personal. Sometimes the friction between permanent farm servants and their employers stems from a fundamental conflict. The employer seeks to increase his control over permanent farm servants to get more work; the permanent farm servant seeks to limit his obligation and wants to preserve his independence.

Another major reason of conflict between a permanent farm servant and his employer is when a permanent farm servant shirks work on the farm and plods in various farm operations. That results in the employer scolding the permanent farm servant and sometimes using abusive language and even physical violence. Sometimes belligerent permanent farm servant takes revenge by breaking or concealing tools, clumsy execution of important tasks and maltreatment of milch animals on farms.

Participation of Permanent Farm Servants in Supervision of Casual Labour and Farm Decisions

The participation of permanent farm servants in supervision of casual labour and routine farm decisions depends on the size of the farm and training and temperament of the farmer. On the small and medium farms, the farmer (employer) directly works with his permanent farm servant and casual labourers and takes all the routine and bigger farm decisions himself. The permanent farm servant attached to such a farm does only manual work and has minimal participation in supervision of casual labour and routine farm decisions (Table 5.4).

Table 5.4: Number of Permanent Farm Servants Doing Supervision of Casual Labourers [N: Local = 134; Migrant = 106]

Zone	*Total Number of Permanent Farm Servants (N)*		*Local Permanent Farm Servants*		*Migrant Permanent Farm Servants*		*All*	
	Local	*Migrants*	*N*	*%*	*N*	*%*	*N*	*%*
Majha	18 (13.43)	14 (13.21)	13	72	11	79	24	75
Malwa	108 (80.60)	44 (41.51)	105	97	26	59	131	86
Doaba	8 (5.97)	48 (45.28)	8	100	13	27	21	38
All	134 (100)	106 (100)	126	94	50	47	176	73

Notes: (*i*) Source: Primary Survey (2007-2008)
(*ii*) Figures in parentheses are percentages

On the other hand, on big farms the involvement of the farmer (employer) in actual farm operations being minimal and remote, an experienced and loyal permanent farm servant assumes the role of a de facto, foreman. He not only supervises the casual labour, but also allocates work among other permanent farm servants, and even takes most of the routine on-the-spot farm decisions. His participation even in major farm decisions like cropping pattern, amount of fertilizers, weedicides etc. to be used is quite active and effective. Even the hiring of casual labourers is mostly left to one of the permanent farm servants who acts as a sort of foreman on the farm. This supervisory role of permanent farm servant assumes even greater importance in the case of share wage permanent farm servants because they are a sort of farmers' junior partners in the farm enterprise and they share expenditure on many inputs like fertilizers, weedicides and casual labour, etc.

Continuity of Employment

The wage contract between a permanent farm servant and his farmer (employer) is for one year from (May 1st to April 30th) of the following year; this is the universal custom in rural Punjab. As the previous year contract draws to a close, the contract between the two may or may not be renewed for the next year depending on their respective experience of mutual interaction in the previous year. In case both, permanent farm servant and the farmer (employer), are satisfied with each other's behaviour, working and earnings, then it is normally renewed for the next year with a revised wage rate; and sometimes even some of the other conditions are also revised.

In the surveyed villages we found 58 per cent of surveyed permanent farm servants were continuing with their farmers (employers) of the previous year (Table 5.5), and 42 per cent have shifted to new farmers (employers). The dominant pattern in Punjab, therefore, seems to be a permanent farm servant continuing for more than one year with the same farmer; but a sizeable proportion of permanent farm servants also shift to some other farmers next year. So the same pool of permanent farm servants of a village goes on rotating from farmer to farmer

Table 5.5: Continuity in Employment with One Employer of Permanent Farm Servants [N: Local = 134; Migrant = 106]

Zone	Number Total		Continuing with Same Employer from the Previous Year					
			Local Permanent Farm Servants		Migrant Permanent Farm Servants		All	
	Local	Migrants	N	%	N	%	N	%
Majha	18 (13.43)	14 (13.21)	8	44	5	36	13	41
Malwa	108 (80.60)	44 (41.51)	75	69	19	43	94	61
Doaba	8 (5.97)	48 (45.28)	5	63	28	58	33	59
All	134 (100)	106 (100)	88	66	52	49	140	58

Notes: (i) Source: Primary Survey (2007-2008)
(ii) Figures in parentheses are percentages

over the years; frequently a permanent farm servant returns to the same farmer again after a lapse of a few years.[19]

What explains this mobility of permanent farm servants from farm to farm? One reason can be the difficulty of renegotiating a higher wage rate with the earlier employer; it is embarrassing to ask for a higher wage from the existing employer, but easier to negotiate a higher wage with a new employer. The other reason can be the usual estrangement between permanent farm servant and farmer resulting from mutual interaction over the previous year; familiarity breeds contempt as they say. However, this shifting of permanent farm servants from one farm to another is often taken for granted as part of the institutional pattern prevailing in Punjab villages. The farmers feel that the permanent farm servant after becoming familiar with them over the year starts obeying less and working less hard. A new permanent farm servant works harder and is more obedient. The shifting of permanent farm servants from farm to farm every year has a sort of financial cost to the permanent farm servant because in our analysis of determination of the wage rate of the permanent farm servant it was found that those permanent farm servants that continue with the same employer year after year earn a significantly higher wage than others who move every year (See Tables 3.4A and 3.4B in Chapter 3). Given this negative wage premium on movement of permanent farm servants every year, the push factors that compel them to shift from one farmer to another must be quite weighty. The push factors include ill treatment by the employer, low quality of food supplied to permanent farm servants, long working hours, non- mechanization of hard operations like fodder cutting, non-availability of free days when needed, delay in payment of wages, inadequate provision for advance wages and loans.

The farm size wise continuity in employment of local permanent farm servants is maximum on farms of 2.5 to 15 acres of size (Table 5.6).

Table 5.6: Farm Size Wise Continuity in Employment of Permanent Farm Servants [N: Local = 134; Migrant = 106]

Farm Size (Acres)	*Number (Total)*		*Number Continuing with Same Employer from the Previous Year*					
			Local Permanent Farm Servants		*Migrant Permanent Farm Servants*		*All*	
	Local	*Migrants*	*N*	*%*	*N*	*%*	*N*	*%*
2.5-5.00	5 (4)	3 (3)	3	60	-	-	3	38
5.00-10.00	9 (7)	18 (17)	7	78	6	33	13	48
10.00-15.00	17 (13)	18 (17)	14	82	12	67	26	74
15.00-20.00	8 (6)	29 (27)	3	38	11	38	14	38
More than 20	95 (70)	38 (36)	60	63	23	61	83	62
All	134 (100)	106 (100)	87	65	52	49	139	58

Notes: (i) Source: Primary Survey (2007-2008) (ii) Figures in parentheses are percentages

On these farms 77 per cent of local permanent farm servants were continuously working with the same employers for more than one year. On the bigger farms the mobility of the permanent farm servants was higher and the continuity of employment lower. In migrant permanent farm servants continuity in employment on all farm size categories is low compared to locals, except in farm size category of 10 to 15 acres. The highest continuity of employment is observed on 10 to 15 acres farm size group where about 74 per cent of permanent farm servants had continued with the same employer from the previous year.

Mutual Relations Among Permanent Farm Servants Working on the Same Farm

On big farms a number of permanent farm servants work together. Sometimes the number of permanent farm servants on a big farm may be four or more than four. The maximum number of permanent farm servants working on a single farm in our sample was twelve; it was a big farm of 250 acres of operated area. On such farms the mutual relations among these permanent farm servants assume considerable importance not only for their own well-being, but also for productive efficiency of the farm. In most cases the relations among permanent farm servants working on the same farm are cordial because the employer (farmer) keeps this factor in mind while hiring and tries to hire only those who can work together amicably as a team. However, cases of verbal altercations or physical violence also occur among permanent farm servants working on the same farm. But such occurrences are quite rare; the normal state being cordial relations among permanent farm servants working on a farm. Even the relations between migrant permanent farm servants and local permanent farm servants working on the same farm are quite cordial and a migrant permanent farm servant is almost never despised or treated badly by local permanent farm servants working on the same farm. The mutual relations of the permanent farm servant are usually structured by a hierarchy and pecking order that gets established automatically when a number of persons are working together. On many big farms the employer (farmer) informally deputes one of the permanent farm servants as a leader or foreman and that helps in keeping discipline on the farm and in maintaining cordial relations among permanent farm servants on the farm. But sometimes the head permanent farm servant or the foreman finds it difficult to establish his authority over other permanent farm servants, who feel his equals and find it difficult to obey his orders. In such cases some sort of tension among the permanent farm servants working on a farm is always there, but is kept in control by the farmer (employer) in most cases. That is why in most cases big farmers prefer to hire permanent farm servants in consultation with their head permanent farm servant or foreman to create better mutual relations among permanent farm servants and improve the production efficiency of the farm.

NOTES

1. Otsuka Keijiro et al.: "Land and Labour Contracts in Agrarian Economies: Theories and Facts". *Journal of Economic Literature*, Vol. 30, No. 4, 1992, pp. 1965-2018.
2. Platteau discussed the relationship between the agricultural labourers and land owners from ancient times to till date with the model of 'aristocratic-patronage' in the Indian setting. The author found the lower castes who were previously dependent on land owners for their livelihood. With the new agricultural settings they are not only deviating from the 'patron-client' relations but also moving towards other occupations. Previously their relationships were cordial but now sometimes turn hostile too. For more details see Jean-Philippe Platteau: "An Indian Model of Aristocratic Patronage." *Oxford Economic Papers*, Vol. 47, No. 41, 1995, pp. 637-662.
3. The territorial domain of labour markets of permanent farm servants is generally the village. Almost all the local permanent farm servants are hired by farmers of a village who belong to that village. Within the village labour market, a farmer (employer) possesses almost complete information on the individual worker's characteristics. Similarly, a permanent farm servant is also equally well-informed about his employer's relevant characteristics. The transactions in such village labour markets have been studied by Pranab Bardhan and Ashok Rudra: "The Domain of Rural Labour Markets Results of a Survey in

West Bengal, 1981-82". *Economic and Political Weekly*, Vol. 20, Nos. 51&52, 1985, pp. A153-A154 & "Labour Mobility and the Boundaries of the Village Moral Economy". *Journal of Peasant Studies*, Vol. 13, No. 3, 1986, pp. 90-115 and see also J. Dreze, and A. Mukherjee: *Labour Contracts in Rural India: Theories and Evidence*, Discussion Paper No. 7, 1987, The Development Research Programme, LSE.

4. The farmers (employers) in a village are divided into factions and among them a lot of competition prevails to lure a permanent farm servant from one another. By enticing a permanent farm servant away from a rival employer, an employer feels proud and the latter employer feels a loss of prestige. This competition in the village labour market is quite universal and with this both the employer and employee get a bad reputation. The employers are more sufferers than employees. The employees even defame the employers in a group of villagers if farmers (employers) did not provide them proper perks and wages with these employers feel more humiliation and difficulty while hiring a permanent farm servant. For more details see Jan Breman: *Patronage and Exploitation: Changing Agrarian Relations in South Gujarat (India)*, 1974, pp. 35-92.
5. A permanent farm servant who has a good work history in the labour market, has no problem to get employment and credit. Moreover, he does not change his employer frequently. This situation may be discussed with George A. Akerlof: "The Market for 'Lemons': Quality Uncertainty and the Market Mechanism." *The Quarterly Journal of Economics*, Vol. 84, No. 3, 1970, pp. 488-500.
6. A state-wise comparison in the terms of contracts has been studied by Daniel. The author concluded that the terms of contract of permanent farm servants in Punjab are entirely different relatively to the rest of India. In Punjab the author found the permanent farm servants were not bound to employers due to debt as they were in Madhya Pradesh and some other states. For details see Daniel and Alice Thorner: *Land and Labour in India*, 1962, p. 24.
7. Richard H. Day: "The Economics of Technological Change and the Demise of the Share Cropper." *American Economic Review*, Vol. 57, No. 3, 1967, pp. 427-449.
8. H.S. Shergill: "Impact of New Technology on the Employment of Share-Wage Annual Servants on Punjab Farms". *Indian Journal of Labour Economics*, Vol. 29, No. 4, 1987, pp. 72-81.

9. George A. Akerlof: "A Theory of Social Custom of Which the Unemployment May Be One Consequence." *The Quarterly Journal of Economics*, Vol. 94, No. 4, 1980, pp. 749-775.
10. Our findings are near to the findings of Pal. She also estimated more use of permanent labour in paddy crop and of casual labour in cotton crop. For details see Sarmistha Pal: "Task-Based Segmentation of Rural Labour Contracts: Theory and Evidence." *Bulletin of Economic Research*, Vol. 51, No. 1, pp. 67-94.
11. On the contractual labour arrangements in the agrarian economy there are two views. First that a tied labour arrangements emerge in segmented labour markets due to involuntary unemployment in the lean season. For details see Arnab K. Basu: "Oligopsonistic Landlords, Segmented Labour Markets and the Persistence of Tied Labour Contracts." *American Journal of Agricultural Economics*, Vol. 84, No. 2, 2002, pp. 438-453. Second, view supports the long term labour arrangements are the outcomes of credit for details see Suman Sarkar: "India's Agricultural Development: An Alternative Path." *Economic and Political Weekly*, Vol. 21, No. 19, 1986, pp. 825-836.
12. The studies conclude that in the rural labour markets the relations are personalized and interlinked between labourers and landowners who are also the credit providers .For details see Gillian Hart: "Interlocking Transactions: Obstacles, Precursors or Instruments of Agrarian Capitalism." *Journal of Development Economics*, Vol. 23, No. 1, 1986, pp. 177-203 and Nadeem Naqvi and Frederick Wemhoner: "Power, Coercion and the Games Landlord Play". *Journal of Development Economics*, Vol. 47, No. 2, 1985, pp. 191-205. In case of Punjab in relations to other states interlinked transactions have been studied by Clive Bell and T.N. Srinivasan: "Inter-Linked Transactions in Rural Market: An Empirical Study of Andhra Pradesh, Bihar and Punjab". *Oxford Bulletin of Economics and Statistics*, Vol. 51, No. 1, 1989, pp. 73-83.
13. This practice is common all over rural India and well documented in literature. For example, see Kathleen Gough: *Rural Society in Southeast India*,1981, pp. 50-55
14. Daniel and Alice Thorner, op.cit.
15. For more details on agrarian conflict see T.K. Oomen: "Green Revolution and Agrarian Conflict" *Economic and Political Weekly*, Vol. 6, No. 26, 1971, pp. A99-A103.
16. Master Hari Singh: *Agricultural Workers' Struggle in Punjab*, 1980, p. 13.
17. For a permanent farm servant it is difficult to organize any protest

against his employer (farmer). A permanent farm servant has a close social relationship with his employer which serve the interests of both. For details see M. Achi Reddy: "Work and Leisure: Daily Working Hours of Agricultural Labourers: Nellore District (1860-1989)". *Indian Economic and Social History Review*, Vol. 28, No. 1, 1991, pp. 73-95. Secondly, it has been universally accepted that the agricultural workers' unions have been weakened due to their daily fight to survive which compelled them to compete with other workers for employment and accept any working conditions. The trade unions remained active only in tea transplantation in developed and less developed countries. For details we may see D.F Hodson:" Problems and Constraints of Agricultural Workers' Organizations within Differing Continents and Agricultures". *Journal of Agricultural Economics*, Vol. 24, No. 1, 1973, pp. 125-139, Martine Vanackere: "Conditions of Day Agricultural Labourers in Mexico". *International Labour Review*, Vol. 127, No. 1, 1988, pp. 91-110 and Varden Fuller and John W Mamer: "Constraints on California Farm Workers' Unionization". *Industrial Relations: A Journal of Economy and Society*, Vol. 17, No. 2, 1978, pp. 143-155. Further the mechanization and less labour intensive crops reduced the influence of labour unions in rural areas, for details see Joan P. Mencher: "Peasant and Agricultural Labourers: An Analytical Assessment of Issues Involved in Their Organizing." in T.N. Srinivasan and P.K. Bardhan (ed.): *Rural Poverty in South Asia*, 1988, pp. 526-546.

18. Sheila Bhalla: "New Relations of Production in Haryana." *Economic and Political Weekly*, Vol. 11, No. 13, 1976, pp. A23-A30.
19. In literature the spatial and temporal mobility of permanent farm servants is always considered obscure. For details on the mobility of farm servants see, A.S. Kussmaul: "The Ambiguous Mobility of Farm Servants". *The Economic History Review*, Vol. 34, No. 2 (New Series), 1981, pp. 222-235.

6

Migrant Permanent Farm Servants

In this chapter we compare the wage rates of local and migrant permanent farm servants. To begin with the available evidence on the estimated number and proportion of migrant agricultural labourers in Punjab is summarized. Next the profile of local and migrant permanent farm servants is described with the help of a number of salient features. Finally, the wage differentials between migrant and local permanent farm servants will be analysed with the help of dummy variable regression analysis.

Migrant Labour in Punjab Agriculture

In Punjab the big inflow of migrant agricultural labour has become a regular and permanent feature after the green revolution. The presence of migrant agricultural labour is very visible in the peak seasons, but many of them also work as permanent farm servants. On the magnitude of migrant agricultural labourers in Punjab no very authentic and universally accepted estimate is available. The different estimates available are briefly reviewed to arrive at a reasonable guess about the number and proportion of migrant agricultural labourers in the state.

According to the 1971 population census, in migration to rural areas of Punjab increased from 8 per cent in 1961 to 13 per cent in 1971. Out migration from rural areas of Punjab increased from 9 per cent in 1961 to 13 per cent in 1971.[1] The migration to rural areas of Punjab from other states was mainly due to the availability of job opportunities created by the green revolution, particularly at the peak harvesting and sowing seasons. Most of the migrants were initially seasonal workers, but many of them also started working as permanent farm servants and stayed continuously in the rural areas of Punjab. As mentioned by Johl,[2] Punjab agriculture absorbed much of migrant labour from eastern UP, Bihar, Haryana and Rajasthan. Some of the migrants worked on an annual basis at wage rates between Rs. 1,200 to Rs. 1,500 per year. A study conducted by Oberai and Singh[3] concluded that the inter-state migration tremendously increased in Punjab compared to inter-district migration within the state. The local rural labourers of Punjab started shifting to non-farm jobs and the migrants filled the gap and started working in agriculture.[4] Some scholars concluded that migrants come to Punjab to earn higher wages in the farming and non-farming sector.[5]

For the period of the 1990s we have three studies conducted by Gill, Khurana and Chopra. The study conducted by Gill[6] gives detailed information on wages and working conditions of migrant agricultural labourers in Punjab. The author found that the migrants come to Punjab during the peak seasons in agriculture. The migrants work on lower wages and they depress the wages of local agricultural labourers. The migrants have little interest in agricultural workers' unions. Khurana[7] gave a state-wise comparison of migrants in Punjab. He found 78 per cent of the migrants came from Bihar, 21 per cent belonged to Uttar Pradesh and 1 per cent were Bengalis. A majority of the migrants were in the age group of 15-40 years. The study conducted by Chopra[8] concluded that the migrants have been largely assimilated in Punjabi culture in the rural areas. A very recent study conducted by Sidhu et al.[9] found the large presence of migrant agricultural labourers in Punjab during the lean as well as peak seasons. Further, they found the migrants get lower wages compared to locals in farm operations.

From these studies it is clear that the flow of migrants from less developed eastern states continuously increased in the rural areas of Punjab after the 1970s. The migrants come into Punjab in search of higher wages and more employment. Some migrants came for short durations and some stayed continuously to work with farmers for a number of years. No study has reported any major conflict and confrontations between local and migrant agricultural labourers owing to economic or non-economic reasons.

Number of Migrant Agricultural Labourers in Punjab Agriculture: Various Estimates

There is no official estimate or information on the number of migrant agricultural labourers in Punjab. The census of India is the main source of data on migration characteristics of people in India, but that information is not very helpful because most of the migrant labourers in Punjab agriculture are seasonal workers and usually fail to get captured in the census figures. The NSSO (National Sample Survey Organization) conducted various surveys on migration in India during different years. But the methodology used did not remain uniform during different periods under these official surveys. Moreover, these sources do not provide us with information on the number of migrant agricultural labourers in rural areas. So one has to depend on surveys made by individual researchers to estimate the number of migrant agricultural labourers in Punjab. The estimates of migrant agricultural labourers made by different authors are summarized in Table 6.1. We have reported here estimates made by professional economists and also by journalists that have appeared in the form of monographs, newspaper articles and stories. The first study conducted by Johl[10] estimated the number of migrant agricultural labourers in Punjab at 1.35 lakh in 1974-75. This made the migrant agricultural labourers about 16.77 per cent of the total male agricultural labourers in Punjab in that year. For the year 1978-79, we have three studies on migrant agricultural labour. The first study was conducted by Rupal[11] and estimated the number of migrant agricultural labourers in Punjab at one lakh. On the basis of this estimate, migrant agricultural labourers constituted about 11.33 per cent of the total male agricultural labourers in the state. The second study was made by Muro[12] and estimated the number of migrant agricultural labourers in Punjab at 1.50 lakh; and their share in total male agricultural labourers at 16.99

per cent. The third study for the period 1978-79 was conducted by Grewal and Sidhu.[13] According to their estimate, in 1978-79, there were 2.19 lakh migrant agricultural labourers; which made 24.80 per cent of the total male agricultural labourers of the state.

For the decade of the 1980s we have three studies by Chum, Sidhu and Grewal, and Devinder Sharma. According to the Chum[14] study there were 4.50 lakh migrant agricultural labourers in Punjab in 1983-84. Out of the total male agricultural labourers in the state the share of migrants was 41.67 per cent. Sidhu and Grewal[15] estimated migrant agricultural labourers separately for the lean and peak periods. In the lean periods the authors estimated 2.86 lakh migrant labourers, which came to 26 per cent of the total male agricultural labourers in Punjab.

Table 6.1: Estimates of Migrant Agricultural Labourers in Punjab

S. No.	*Source*	*Year*	**Estimated Number of Migrant Agricultural Labourers in Punjab (Lakhs) (i)*	*** Total Male Agricultural Labourers in Punjab (Lakhs) (ii)*	*Percentage of Migrant Agricultural Labourers in Punjab [(i)÷(ii) x 100] (iii)*
1.	S. S.Johl (1975): *Gains of the Green Revolution: How They Have Been Shared in Punjab,* Department of Economics and Sociology, PAU, Ludhiana	1974-75	1.35	8.08	16.77
2.	Gurcharan Singh Rupal: Punjab: 'Canada for Bhaias', *The Punjabi Tribune,* April 23, 1979.	1978-79	1.00	8.83	11.33
3.	Ross Muro: 'The Problem of Success', *The Time,* May 28, 1979.	1978-79	1.50	8.83	16.99
4.	S.S. Grewal and M.S. Sidhu (1979): *A Study on Migrant Agricultural Labour in Punjab,* Department of Economics	1983-84	2.19	8.83	24.80

contd.

and Sociology, PAU, Ludhiana				
5. B.K. Chum: 'Violence Hits Farmers' Economy', *The Indian Express*, March 3,1984	1983-84	4.50	10.80	41.67
6. M.S. Sidhu and S.S. Grewal (1984): *A Study on Migrant Agricultural Labour in Punjab*, Department of Economics and Sociology, PAU, Ludhiana	1983-84	Lean Period: 2.86 Peak Period: 5.72	10.80	Lean Period : 26.48 Peak Period: 52.96
7. Devinder Sharma: 'Migrant Flow Unabated', *The Indian Express*, April 13, 1986	1985-86	6.00	11.00	54.55
8. M.S. Sidhu and P.S. Rangi et al. (1997): *A Study on Migrant Agricultural Labour in Punjab*, Department of Economics and Sociology, PAU, Ludhiana.	1995-96	Lean Period: 3.87 Peak Period: 7.74	12.63	Lean Period : 30.64 Peak Period: 61.28
9. M.S. Sidhu and A.S. Joshi et al. (2007): *A Study on Migrant Agricultural Labour in Punjab*, Department of Economics and Sociology, PAU, Ludhiana	2006-07	Lean Period: 4.21 Peak Period: 8.42	11.29	Lean Period : 37.29 Peak Period: 74.58

Notes: * Different studies have different estimates

** Census of India provides state-wise number of male agricultural labourers for various decades. With extrapolation and interpolation we estimated the number of male agricultural labourers for non-census years on the basis of census data.

For the peak periods they estimated 5.72 lakh migrant agricultural labourers; during the peak seasons the migrant farm labourers were more than fifty per cent of total farm labour in the state. For the 1985-86 year, Sharma[16] estimated 6 lakh migrant agricultural labourers in lean as well as in peak periods.

Two recent studies were conducted by Sidhu et al.[17] in 1995-

96 and in 2006-07. They estimated 3.87 lakh migrant agricultural labourers in the lean period and 7.74 lakh in peak periods during 1995-96. For 2006-07, they estimated 4.21 lakh migrants in the lean periods and 8.42 lakhs in the peak period. In 1995-96 the share of migrants in total male agricultural labourers of the state came to 30.64 per cent in the lean period and 61.28 per cent in the peak period. During this decade (1995-96 to 2006-07) the migrant agricultural labourers increased by almost 8 per cent in lean as well as in peak periods. Another recent study by Ghuman et al.[18] gives the estimate of migrant agricultural labourers in different cultural zones of the state, viz. Majha, Malwa and Doaba. This study found the maximum inflow of migrant casual and attached farm workers in the Malwa region and least in the Doaba region.

Regional Distribution of Migrant Agricultural Labourers

On the basis of estimates of migrant agricultural labourers in different districts of Punjab, Sidhu et al.[19] divided the districts into three categories as shown in Map 6.1. The first group comprises those districts where the concentration of migrant agricultural labourers was maximum. This group includes Jalandhar, Nawanshahr, Kapurthala, Ludhiana, Patiala and Fatehgarh Sahib districts. In these districts there were 2.45 lakh migrant agricultural labourers in 1995-96; and 2.73 lakh in 2006-07 (Table 6.2). In one decade (1995-96 to 2006-07), the number of migrant agricultural labourers increased by 11 per cent. The second group consists of Amritsar, Faridkot, Ferozepur, Moga, Sangrur and Mukatsar districts. This group represents a situation where the concentration of migrant agricultural labourers was moderate. In this group the number of migrant agricultural labourers was 0.50 lakhs in 1995-96; and increased to 0.64 lakhs in 2006-07. From 1995-96 to 2006-07, the number of migrants increased by 28 per cent in this group of districts.

MAP 6.1

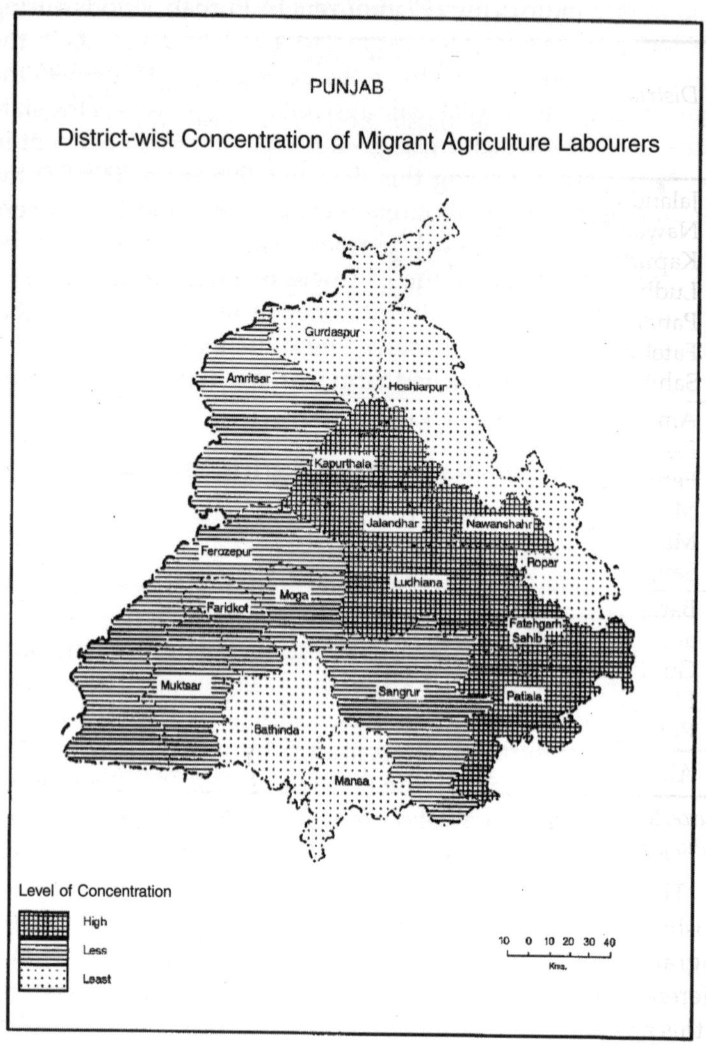

Source: M.S. Sidhu et al.: *A Study of Migrant Agricultural Labour in Punjab (1997, 2007)*, Punjab Agricultural University, Ludhiana.

Table 6.2: Districtwise Concentration of Migrant Agricultural Labourers in Punjab

S. No	District	*Level of Concentration in 1995-96*	*Level of Concentration in 2006-07*	*Year : 1995-96 Number (Lakhs)*	*Year : 1995-96 Proportion*	*Year : 2006-07 Number (Lakhs)*	*Year : 2006-07 Proportion*
1.	Jalandhar and Nawanshahr	High	High				
2.	Kapurthala	High	High				
3.	Ludhiana	High	High	2.45	74.92	2.73	72.61
4.	Patiala and Fatehgarh Sahib	High	High				
5.	Amritsar	Less	Less				
6.	Faridkot	Less	Less				
7.	Ferozepur, Moga and Muktsar	Less	Less	0.50	15.29	0.64	17.02
8.	Sangrur	Less	Less				
9.	Bathinda and Mansa	Least	Least				
10.	Gurdaspur	Least	Least	0.32	9.79	0.39	10.37
11.	Hoshiarpur	Least	Least				
12	Ropar	Least	Least				
	All	-	-	3.27	100	3.76	100

Source: M.S. Sidhu et al. (1997, 2007): *A Study on Migrant Agricultural Labour in Punjab*, Department of Economics & Sociology, PAU, Ludhiana.

The third group comprises Bathinda, Mansa, Gurdaspur, Hoshiarpur and Ropar districts. In this group the number of migrant agricultural labourers was the smallest. During the reference ten years, the number of migrant agricultural labourers in this group of districts increased from 0.32 lakhs to 0.39 lakhs. In this group, the proportion of migrants out of the total male agricultural labourers increased from 9.79 per cent to 10.37 percent; and their absolute number increased by 22 per cent.

Comparative Profile of Local and Migrant Permanent Farm Servants

The important features of the person and employment of migrant and local permanent farm servants are compared to reveal their comparative profile. This will not only provide the necessary background to the subsequent analysis of their respective wage determination, but also show how these two types of permanent farm servants differ from each other. For this purpose features like age, caste, marital status, wage rate, nature of wage contract, literacy level, technical/ managerial skills, profile of employers, credit dependency on employer and tenure of employment are compared. The summary information on these features for the two types of permanent farm servants is given in Table 7.3, and the statistical significance of the difference in the features of the two types is tested with the help of the dummy variable regression model given below and the results are reported in Table 6.4.[20]

$$Y = a_0 + (a_1 - a_0) D$$

Where Y is the relevant feature of the profile of permanent farm servants, and D is a dummy variable taking value '1' for migrants and '0' for local permanent farm servants.

In migration literature it is universally accepted that young people have a higher propensity to out migrate. This is shown by comparison of the age of migrants and local workers of our sample. The migrant permanent farm servants are younger compared to local permanent farm servants. The mean age of local permanent farm servants is 34 years and of the migrant permanent farm servants is only 25 years (Table 6.3). This difference of nine years in the mean ages of the two is highly significant at 1 per cent level (Table 6.4).

This is further confirmed by the comparison of the maximum age of the two types. The maximum age (65 years) of local permanent farm servants is twenty years higher than the maximum age of migrant permanent farm servants, though their minimum age is almost the same. So we can confidently say that the migrant permanent farm servants working on Punjab farms are much younger compared to the local permanent farm servants.

Table 6.3: Sample Permanent Farm Servants: Migrant and Local (Summary Statistics)

S.No. Characteristics	*Local Permanent Farm Servants (i)*	*Migrant Permanent Farm Servants (ii)*	*Difference (ii)-(i)*
I. Age Profile			
1. Mean Age	34.00	25.00	(-)9
2. Maximum Age	65.00	45.00	(-)20
3. Minimum Age	15.00	14.00	(-)01
II Mean Wage Rate (Rs)	25270	18188	(-)7082
III Caste Status			
1. Scheduled Castes	93%	32%	(-)61%
IV Marital Status			
1. Married	69%	49%	(-)20%
V Nature of Wage Contract			
1. Fixed Cash Wage Contract	89%	100%	(+)11%
VI Literacy Level			
1 Literate	17%	27%	(+)10%
VII Technical Managerial Skills			
1. Drives tractor on farms	44%	18%	(-)26%
2. Can handle the electric motor operated tubewells	94%	76%	(-)18%
3. Supervises casual labour on the farms	91%	53%	(-)38%
VIII Employer's Profile			
1. Employers having tractors	92%	83%	(-)9%
2. Employers having electric operated tube wells	93%	97%	(+)4%
IX Operated Area with Employers (Acres)			
1. More than or equal to ten acres	85%	76%	(-) 9%
X Credit Dependence on Employers			
1. Total advance taken (Mean)	11512	3523	(-) 7989
2. Advance taken free of interest (Mean)	8488	2417	(-) 6071
3. Advance taken on interest (Mean)	3024	1106	(-) 1918
XI Worked for the Same Employer Previous Year Also	66%	49%	(-) 17%
Number	134	106	

Source: Primary Survey (2007-08)

The difference in the annual mean wage rate of local and migrant permanent farm servants is of Rs.7082; which is highly significant at 1 per cent level (Table 6.4). It supports our hypothesis that a migrant permanent farm servant gets lower wages than a local permanent farm servant. A local permanent farm servant on the average earns 39 per cent more than a migrant permanent farm servant working on Punjab farms. So, the significantly lower wage rate received by migrant permanent farm servants compared to local permanent farm servants is clearly established by our sample data.

The caste complexion of these two groups of permanent farm servants is also different. Almost all the local permanent farm servants (93 per cent) belong to the scheduled castes. A majority of the migrant permanent farm servants (68 per cent), however, belong to the non-scheduled castes. This difference in their caste complexion is also significant at 1 per cent level (Table 6.4). Even if we discount for the misreporting of caste status by some migrant permanent farm servants, the difference in the proportion of scheduled castes in the two groups is so large that one can still draw the conclusion that almost all the local permanent farm servants are scheduled castes, but among the migrant permanent farm servants, non-scheduled castes are equally represented, if not predominating.

The marital status of the two types of permanent farm servants is also different from each other and the difference is significant at 5 per cent level (Table 6.4). A majority of local permanent farm servants (69 per cent) are married men, whereas only 49 per cent of migrant permanent farm servants reported being married. The difference of 20 per cent in the proportion of married is also significant at 5 per cent level (Table 6.4).

In a way even the married migrant permanent farm servants were in a state of forced de facto unmarried state as they were not accompanied by their spouses in most cases. So the migrant permanent farm servant being de facto single lived at employer's farm or barn and was virtually twenty-four hour servants. The local married permanent farm servants join their families in the evening and work only in the day time, except in emergency night duties for irrigation, etc.

Table 6.4: Differences in Mean Characteristics of Local and Migrant Permanent Farm Servants [Regression Analysis] (N=240)

S. No.	*Characteristics (Y)*	*Intercept (a)*	*Differential intercept coefficient(b)*	t_{values}	R^2
1.	Age (Years)	34	-9.00	5.60***	0.18
2.	Annual mean wage Rate (Rs)	25270	-7082	5.99***	0.20
3.	Caste (Dummy): Scheduled Caste=1	0.93	-0.61	10.12***	0.41
4.	Marital status (Dummy): Married = 1	0.69	-0.20	2.59**	0.04
5.	Literacy level (Dummy): Literate= 1	0.17	0.10	1.58	0.02
6.	Nature of wage contract (Dummy): Cash wage=1	0.89	0.11	2.80***	0.05
7.	Drives tractor on farms (Dummy): Yes=1	0.44	-0.26	3.46***	0.08
8.	Knows all electric motor operated tubewell (Dummy): Yes=1	0.94	-0.18	3.30***	0.07
9.	Supervises casual labour on farms (Dummy): Yes=1	0.91	-0.38	5.69***	0.18
10.	Farm Size (Dummy): ≥10 (Acres) =1	0.85	-0.09	1.35	0.02
11.	Employer's own tractors (Dummy):Yes=1	0.92	-0.09	1.56	0.02
12.	Employer's own electric motors (Dummy): Yes=1	0.93	0.04	1.16	0.01
13.	Total advance taken from employer (Rs.)	11512	-7989	5.39***	0.19
14.	Advance taken from employer free of interest (Rs.)	8488	-6071	5.88***	0.19
15.	Advance taken from employer with interest (Rs.)	3024	-1918	1.89*	0.02
16.	Continuity in employment with one employer (Dummy): Yes=1	0.66	-0.17	2.11**	0.03

Notes: (*i*) Form of estimated equation: $Y = a_0 + (a_1 - a_0) D$, where D=1 for migrants and 0 for local permanent farm servants.
(*ii*) *, **, ***, indicate respectively significant at 10%, 5% and 1% level for a two-tailed test.

There are two types of labour contract on which a permanent farm servant is hired in Punjab: the share wage contract and the cash wage contract. The share wage contract was very popular in the pre-independence period, but has gradually gone out of favour, particularly after the green revolution. In recent years the cash wage contract has emerged as the dominant type of contract for hiring permanent farm servants. However, share-wage contract is still continuing in the cotton-wheat belt of Punjab. All the migrant permanent farm servants in our sample were working on the cash wage contract. Among the local permanent farm servants, 89 per cent were working on the cash wage contract and 11 per cent on share-wage contract. The difference of 11 per cent in the proportion working on cash wage contract was found to be statistically significant at 1 per cent level (Table 6.4).

The overall literacy rate does not seem to be significantly different in local and migrant permanent farm servants. In our sample only 17 per cent local and 27 per cent migrant permanent farm servants reported being literate. The difference in proportion of literate between the two groups was not significant even at 10 per cent level. So we may conclude that in literacy two types of permanent farm servants were almost similar.

The technical and managerial skill differences in local and migrant permanent farm servants were captured by focusing on three characteristics, viz. tractor driving skill, knowledge of electric motor operations and supervision of casual labour and other farm operations. All these three characteristics bring out the difference in the technical/ managerial skills between the local and migrant permanent farm servants. The information given in Table 6.3 makes it clear that the local permanent farm servants have more expertise in tractor driving compared to migrant permanent farm servants. In our sample 44 per cent of local permanent farm servants reported driving tractors on the farms; whereas only 18 per cent of the migrant permanent farm servants were performing this job. The difference in these proportions was found significant at 1 per cent level (Table 6.4). The difference in the knowledge of the electric motor operated tubewell between the two groups, however, is less pronounced. Whereas 94 per cent of local permanent farm servants could operate electric motor operated tubewell independently, only 76 per cent migrant permanent farm servants reported having that expertise. This difference of 18 per cent was found to be significant at 1 per cent level (Table 6.4). The capacity to supervise casual labourers working on the farm, in the absence of the employer, was much higher among the local permanent farm servants, than migrant permanent farm servants. In the absence of the employer a local permanent farm servant not only takes care of casual labourers, but also supervises other farm operations. In peak seasons he arranges casual labour and directs them in fields. As many as 91 per cent of local permanent farm servants reported doing this supervisory work on the farms, compared to only 53 per cent of migrant permanent farm servants doing the same. The difference between these two proportions was found to be statistically significant at one per cent level (Table 6.4). So, we can conclude that almost all the local permanent farm servants not only do manual work on the farms, but also supervise casual labour; but only about half of the migrant permanent farm servants were doing so.

The profile of the employers (who have hired permanent farm servants) is only slightly different for the two groups. It may be seen (Table 6.3) that 92 per cent of the employers of local permanent farm servants have tractors and 93 per cent electric motor operated tubewells on their farms. On the other hand, about 83 per cent of employers of migrant permanent farm servants have tractors and 97 per cent have electric motor operated tubewells on their farm. The difference in the proportion of employers of these two types of permanent farm servants owning tractors and electric motor operated tubewells, however, was not significant even at 10 per cent level. So far as the degree of mechanization of the employing farm is concerned no significant difference is found between local and migrant permanent farm servants.

The difference in the size of the employer's farm was also found not to be significant even at 10 per cent level (Table 6.4). About 85 per cent of farms employing local permanent farm servants were operating ten acres or more land, compared to 76 per cent of farms employing migrant permanent farm servants, and the difference in these two proportions was not significant even at 10 per cent level.

It is well known that the permanent farm servants take some amount of advance from their employers at the time of joining the job. The two types of permanent farm servants were also compared on this feature of their wage contract. The mean amount of advance taken by local permanent farm servants was Rs. 11,512 and by migrant permanent farm servants Rs. 3,523. The difference in the mean amounts (Rs. 7,989) of the two groups is significant at 1 per cent level (Table 6.4). These two groups also differ significantly even in the mean advance taken on interest and free of interest. It may be observed from Table 6.4 that the mean difference in both these components of advance is significant; at 1 per cent level in the case of free of interest advance, and at 10 per cent level in the case of advance taken on interest payment basis. These two types of permanent farm servants also differ significantly in continuity of employment with the same employer. As many as 66 per cent of local permanent farm servants were working with the same farmer with whom they were attached the previous year; compared to that only 49 per cent of migrant permanent farm servants reported such a continuity of employment. The difference between these two proportions (17 per cent) was found to be statistically significantly at 5 per cent level (Table 6.4).

From this detailed comparison of characteristics of local and migrant permanent farm servants their respective profiles can be described approximately. The migrant permanent farm servants are on the average a younger lot working on a lower annual wage and always on a cash wage contract. The skill level of migrant permanent farm servants is generally lower compared to the local permanent farm servants, although the type of farmers (employers) and size and type of farm on which they work does not differ significantly from the local permanent farm servants. The migrant permanent farm servants more often belong to some non-scheduled caste social groups and are frequently bachelors compared to local permanent farm servants. The migrant permanent farm servants also change their employers from year to year more often and take a smaller advance at the time of joining the job compared to local permanent farm servants.

Comparison of Wage Structure of Local and Migrant Permanent Farm Servants

The migrant permanent farm servants get a much lower mean wage rate than local permanent farm servants emerged clearly in the last section. In this section we compare the entire wage structure of these two types of permanent farm servants. The relevant information is summarized in Table 6.5 and shows that whereas 7.54 per cent of migrant permanent farm servants are in the lowest wage range of Rs. 5,000-10,000; only 2.98 per cent of local permanent farm servants are in the same position.

Table 6.5: Structure of Sample Local and Migrant Permanent Farm Servants by Wage Rate (Rs.)

Wage Rate (Rs./ Annum)	*Local Permanent Farm Servants*			*Migrant Permanent Farm Servants*		
	Proportion	*N*	*Mean Wage (Rs.)*	*Proportion*	*N*	*Mean Wage (Rs.)*
5,000-10,000	2.98	4	7354	7.54	8	7982
10,000-15,000	7.46	10	12605	42.45	45	12844
15,000-20,000	4.48	6	18038	7.55	8	18264
20,000-25,000	39.55	53	22767	24.53	26	22591
25,000-30,000	22.39	30	27130	13.21	14	27578
30,000-35,000	14.18	19	31546	2.83	3	32285
35,000-40,000	5.97	8	37073	1.89	2	35314
40,000-45,000	2.24	3	41794	-	-	-
45,000-50,000	0.75	1	45893	-	-	-
All	100	134	25270	100	106	18188

Source: Primary Survey (2007-2008)

In the next higher wage range of Rs.10,000-15,000, there are 42.45 per cent migrant permanent farm servants, but only 7.46 per cent local permanent farm servants. Almost fifty per cent of the migrant permanent farm servants are in these two lower wage categories. Conversely more than eighty per cent of the local permanent farm servants are in the high wage range of Rs. 15,000-35,000. About 3 per cent of local permanent farm servants were getting the highest wage between Rs. 40,000 to Rs. 50,000, but not even a single migrant permanent farm servant falls in the highest wage category of Rs. 40,000-50,000. From the information presented in Table 6.5 it is clear that most of the migrant permanent farm servants are concentrated on the lower rungs of wage distribution, and most of the local permanent farm servants in the higher range of wage distribution. This finding is interesting and important in view of the fact that the size and type of farms on which the two types of permanent farm servants work do not differ significantly.

The difference in the wage structure of these two types of permanent farm servants is highlighted further by the information given in Table 6.6. The median wage rate of local permanent farm servants is about 58 per cent higher than the migrant permanent farm servants. The minimum wage rate of these two types differs less (only by 17 per cent), but the maximum wage differs much more. The maximum wage of local permanent farm servant was 30 per cent higher than that of the migrant permanent farm servant. Furthermore, there is smaller internal variation in the wage rate of local permanent farm servants (CV = 28.79 per cent) compared to migrant permanent farm servants (CV = 38.81 per cent).

Table 6.6: Summary Statistics of Wage Rate of Local and Migrant Permanent Farm Servants

Statistics	*Local Permanent Farm Servants (i)*	*Migrant Permanent Farm Servants (ii)*	*Ratios (i) ÷ (ii)*
Mean Wage (Rs)	25,270	18,188	1.39
Median Wage (Rs)	24,648	15,634	1.58
Minimum Wage Rate (Rs.)	6,034	7,234	0.83
Maximum Wage Rate (Rs.)	45,893	35,314	1.29
Ratio of Maximum to Minimum Wage Rate (Rs.)	7.61	4.89	-
Coefficient of Variation (CV)	28.79	38.81	-
Number	134	106	-

Source: Primary Survey (2007-2008)

Zone-wise Comparison of Wage Rate of Permanent Farm Servants: Local and Migrant

The zone-wise differentials in the wage rates of local and migrant permanent farm servants are presented in Table 6.7. The descriptive statistics indicate wide variations in wage rates of local and migrant permanent farm servants within and among the zones. In the sub-mountainous zone the migrant permanent farm servants get more than the local permanent farm servants, on the average, though the minimum and maximum wage of the two is quite similar. However there is greater internal variation (CV=41.03 per cent) in the wage rate of local permanent farm servants, compared to the migrant permanent farm servants (CV=28.17 per cent).

The situation is just the reverse in the central plains zone where migrant permanent farm servants get, on the average, much less than local permanent farm servants. The minimum wage of the two types differs widely, though the maximum wage of the two is quite similar. The internal variation in the wage rate of local permanent farm servants is much smaller (CV=16.67 per cent) in this zone, compared to migrant permanent farm servants (CV=40.21 per cent).

The comparative position of wage rate of the two groups in the Malwa zone is almost similar to the central plains zone. The local permanent farm servants get higher mean wage and have lesser internal variation in the wage distribution. However, the gap in the wage rate of local permanent farm servants and migrant permanent farm servants in the Malwa zone is less pronounced than in the central plains zone.

The above comparison of the various aspects of wage distribution of local and migrant permanent farm servants has revealed that the lower wage rate of migrant permanent farm servants is not a universal phenomena prevailing in all parts of the state. In the sub-mountainous zone the migrant permanent farm servants get more than local permanent farm servants, on the average; in the Malwa zone the migrant permanent farm servants get less than local permanent farm servants; but the gap is not very wide; however in the central plains zone the

Table 6.7: Zone-wise Wage Rates of Local and Migrant Permanent Farm Servants in Punjab

Zone	*Local Permanent Farm Servants*					*Migrant Permanent Farm Servants*				
	N	*Minimum Wage Rate (Rs)*	*Maximum Wage Rate (Rs)*	*Mean (Rs)*	*Coefficient of Variation*	*N*	*Minimum Wage Rate (Rs)*	*Maximum Wage Rate (Rs)*	*Mean (Rs)*	*Coefficient of Variation*
Sub-Mountainous	14 (10.45)	6,034	22,210	13,507	41.03%	34 (32.08)	8,098	22,786	15,484	28.17%
Central Plain	26 (19.40)	18,514	30,946	24,423	16.67%	55 (51.89)	7,234	29,698	17,776	40.21%
Malwa	94 (70.15)	12,967	45,893	27,294	23.57%	17 (16.04)	11,434	35,314	24,623	30.33%
Total	134 (100)					106 (100)				

Notes:
(i) Source: Primary Survey (2007-2008)
(ii) Figures in brackets are percentages

migrant permanent farm servant gets a glaringly low wage compared to the local permanent farm servants.

Analysis of Wage Differentials Between Migrant and Local Permanent Farm Servants

In this section, we not only estimate the average amount of difference in the wage rates of migrant and local permanent farm servants, but also analyse the sources of that wage differentials, i.e. analyse the reasons for migrant permanent farm servants getting a lower wage, on the average, than the local permanent farm servants. In the literature wage differentials in Indian agriculture labour markets have been mainly noticed with respect to sex or caste,[21] but very few scholars have paid attention to wage differences between migrant and local farm workers.[22] We did not find any study relating to permanent farm servants which studied the wage differentials between migrant and locals owing to economic and non-economic factors. According to some scholars the wage differentials between local and migrant farm workers arise mainly due to their personal traits. For example, Schultz opined, *"Most migratory farm workers earn very little indeed by comparison with other workers. Many of them have virtually no schooling, are in poor health, are unskilled and have little ability to do useful work"*[23]. Similarly, contradictory views prevail in Punjab on the productivity and efficiency of migrant permanent farm servants compared to local permanent farm servants. Many farmers think migrant workers are more hard working, efficient and reliable. But many others have a less favourable view of them and consider them inferior to local permanent farm servants in efficiency and skills essentials for farm operations. These two opposing views about the efficiency and usefulness of migrant permanent farm servants, notwithstanding, it is a universally accepted fact that migrant permanent farm servants, on the average, are paid a lower annual wage compared to local permanent farm servants in rural Punjab. Our sample data also show clearly that migrant permanent farm servants, on the average, get a lower annual wage than local permanent farm servants. We have tried to quantify this gap in wages of migrant and local permanent farm servants. For this purpose the mean wage rates of migrant and local permanent farm servants are compared with the help of the dummy variable regression model and the results are reported in Table 6.8. Out of the coefficients reported in this table, the intercept term (α_0) gives the annual mean wage rate of the local permanent farm servants and the differential intercept (α_1-α_0) coefficient gives the difference in the mean wage rate of migrant and local permanent farm servants. It may be seen that this difference in the wage rate of migrant permanent farm servants and local permanent farm servants comes to Rs. 7,082; compared to the annual mean wage rate of Rs. 25,270 of local permanent farm servants, the annual mean wage rate of migrant permanent farm servants was only Rs. 18,188 (Equation-1, Table 6.8).

Table 6.8: Comparison of Mean Wage Rates of Local and Migrant Permanent Farm Servants [Dummy Variable Regression Results] (N = 240)

Definition of Estimated Coefficients	*Dependent Variable (Y): Annual Wage Rate (Rs.)*	
	Equation-1 (Dependent Variable in Simple Form)	*Equation-2 (Dependent Variable in Log Form)*
($\alpha_1 - \alpha_0$) Differential intercept coefficient [Difference in wage rate of migrant permanent farm servants from local permanent farm servants]	-7082 (5.99)***	-0.36 (5.92)***
Intercept (α_0) [Mean Wage Rate of Local Permanent Farm Servants]	25270	10.09
R^2	0.20	0.19

Notes: (i) Form of model estimated: $Y = \alpha_0 + (\alpha_1 - \alpha_0) D$, D takes value '1' for migrant permanent farm servants and value '0' for local permanent farm servants.

(ii) Figures in parentheses are t_{values}.

(iii) *** indicates significant at 1% level for a two-tailed test.

It may also be noted that this gap or difference between the mean wage rate of migrant and local permanent farm servants is significant at 1 per cent level for a two-tailed test. The results reported in Table 6.8 leave little doubt about migrant permanent farm servants getting, on the average, a much lower annual wage compared to local permanent farm servants. The annual mean wage of migrant permanent farm servants (Rs. 18,188) was about 28 per cent lower than that of local permanent farm servants (Rs. 25,270). The results also clearly show that this difference in the mean wage of migrant and local permanent farm servants is significant at 1 per cent level.

The difference in the mean wage of migrant and local permanent farm servants revealed by results reported in Table 6.8 is in line with our own observations in the field survey and the general impression in Punjab rural areas, that migrant workers usually get lower wages than the local permanent farm servants. The difference in the mean wage rate of migrant and local permanent farm servants may be mainly due to two sets of factors. The migrant permanent farm servants may have lower average productivity than the local permanent farm servants because of their inferior farm level skills and due to their employment on farms with lower productivity levels. The other reason for the lower mean wage of migrant permanent farm servants may be that despite their almost similar skill level they are paid less simply because of being migrants.

By using the simple econometric procedure known as analysis of covariance,[24] we have tried to find out whether or not and to what extent the wage differential between migrant and local permanent farm servants is due to the differences in their personal characteristics and features of the farms employing them. This is done by inserting a number of variables representing personal attributes of permanent farm servants and their employing farms as the control variables in the model reported in Table 6.9. The results of this exercise are reported in Table 6.9.

The control variables entered are age, marital status, tractor driving skill, electric tubewell operation skill, and casual labour supervision skills, farm size, and zone dummies. The results reported in Table 6.9, suggest clearly that most of the difference between the annual mean wage rate of migrant and local permanent farm servants is accounted for by their personal characters and features of their employing farms. It may be seen from Table 6.9 that once the impact of age, marital status, tractor driving, electric motor operated tubewells and casual labour supervision skills and location (zone-wise) and size of the employing farms is controlled, the coefficient of the migrant

Table 6.9: Factors Affecting Wage Rates of Local and Migrant Permanent Farm Servants [Dependent Variable = Annual Mean Wage Rate (Rs.)] (N = 240)

Explanatory Variables	*Coefficients*
Migrant (Dummy)	-1451.92
Migrant =1, Local = 0	(1.41)
Controlled Variables	
Age (Years)	-7.02
	(0.16)
Marital Status (Dummy):	2667.19
Married=1, Unmarried = 0	(2.79)***
Drives Tractor on Farms (Dummy):	3377.76
Yes=1, No=0	(3.58)***
Familiar with Electric Motor Operations (Dummy):	1569.61
Yes=1, No=0	(1.06)
Supervises Casual Labour (Dummy):	5167.52
Yes=1, No=0	(3.79)***
Farm Size (Dummy): (Acres)	3739.38
≥10 = 1, other =0	(3.34)***
Zone-1 (Dummy):	-4705.17
Sub-mountain = 1, Other=0	(3.53)***
Zone=2 (Dummy)	-2252.95
Central Plain = 1, Other = 0	(2.13)**
Intercept	13800.25
R^2	0.66
$\bar{R}^2$	0.64
F_{values}	30.33***

Notes:

(i) Form of equation estimated: $Y = \alpha_0 + (\alpha_1 - \alpha_0) D + \beta_1 x1 + \beta_2 x_2 .....+ u_i$

(ii) Figures in parentheses are t_{values}.

(iii) t & F_{values} are significant at *10%, **5% & ***1%.

dummy is not only reduced to almost one-fourth in size (compared to its value in Table 6.8), but also is not significant even at 10 per cent level. The results reported in Table 6.9 were corroborated even when we entered the dependent variable (wage rate) in log form. The log form results are reported in Table 6.10, and are fully in line with results given in Table 6.9. These results clearly suggest that the difference in the mean wage rate of migrant and local permanent farm servants in

Table 6.10: Factors Affecting Wage Rates of Local and Migrant Permanent Farm Servants [Dependent Variable =Log (Annual Mean Wage Rate) (Rs.)] (N = 240)

Explanatory Variables	*Coefficients*
Migrant (Dummy)	-0.006
Migrant =1, Local = 0	(1.34)
Controlled Variables	
Age (Years)	-0.001
	(0.60)
Marital Status (Dummy):	0.16
Married=1, Unmarried = 0	(3.72)***
Drives Tractor on Farms (Dummy):	0.14
Yes=1, No=0	(3.15)***
Familiar with Electric Motor Operations (Dummy):	0.08
Yes=1, No=0	(1.24)
Supervises Casual Labour (Dummy):	0.34
Yes=1, No=0	(5.35)***
Farm Size (Dummy): (Acres)	0.22
≥10 = 1, Other =0	(3.73)***
Zone-1 (Dummy):	-0.20
Sub-mountain = 1, Other=0	(3.24)***
Zone=2 (Dummy):	-0.008
Central Plain = 1, Other = 0	(1.79)*
Intercept	9.41
R^2	0.72
$\bar{R}^2$	0.71
F_{values}	40.68***

Notes:

(i) Form of equation estimated: $Y = \alpha_0 + (\alpha_1 - \alpha_0) D + \beta_1 x1 + \beta_2 x_2 \ldots.. + u_i$

(ii) Figures in parentheses are t_{values}.

(iii) t & F_{values} are significant at *10%, **5% & ***1%.

Punjab (observed in Table 6.8), does not seem to be due to their migrant status per se, but due to their different personal attributes and features of their employing farms. This result is in line with findings of Bardhan and Rudra.[25] They also found no significant difference in the wage rates of agricultural labourers in West Bengal due to their migrant status. The migrants were even paid higher wages relatively to locals owing to their special skills in ploughing or transplantation of paddy, etc. On the basis of results presented in Table 6.9, we can say that out of the total difference (Rs. 7,082) in the mean wage of migrant and local permanent farm servants, Rs. 5,630 is due to difference in their personal characteristics, features of employing farms and zonal location, and only Rs. 1,452 due to other unexplained factors. But even this unexplained difference of Rs. 1,452 is not statistically significant even at 10 per cent level and may be entirely due to random factors.

The main conclusions of this chapter are now summarized. A sizeable proportion of permanent farm servants in Punjab agriculture are migrants from UP, Bihar etc. and these migrant permanent farm servants are found in all regions of Punjab. The comparison of wage rates of migrant permanent farm servants and local permanent farm servants clearly revealed that the migrant permanent farm servants, on the average, got a lower annual wage than the local permanent farm servants. The annual mean wage of migrant permanent farm servants (Rs. 18,188) was about 28 per cent lower than the annual mean wage of local permanent farm servants (Rs. 25,270). The analysis of the difference in the mean wage of migrant permanent farm servants and local permanent farm servants revealed that most of it (79.50 per cent) was due to differences in their productivity-related factor endowments such as age, skill in tractor driving, tubewell operation and casual labour supervision, etc., and characteristics related to employing farms and regional location. Only a small part (20.50 per cent) was due to other unexplained factors that may also include the sheer discrimination on account of migrant status. However, this remaining 20.50 per cent difference in the mean wage rate of migrant permanent farm servants and local permanent farm servants was not statistically significant even at 10 per cent level, and therefore may be due to random factors. On the whole, therefore one can say that migrant permanent farm servants do not suffer any marked wage discrimination in the Punjab farm labour market on account of their migrant status.

NOTES

1. The inflow of migrant agricultural labourers continuously increased in rural Punjab from 1961 to 1971. This interstate flow of migrants has been explained in the *Special Monograph on Birth Place Migration in India,* Census of India, 1971.
2. S.S. Johl: "Gains of the Green Revolution: How They Have Been Shared in Punjab". *Journal of Development Studies,* Vol. 11, No. 3, 1975, pp. 178-189.
3. A.S. Oberai and H.K. Manmohan Singh: "Migration Flows in Punjab's Green Revolution Belt": *Economic and Political Weekly,* Vol. 15, No. 13, 1980, pp. A2-A12.
4. H., Laxminarayan: "The Impact of Agricultural Development on Employment: A Case Study of Punjab." *The Developing Economies,* Vol. 20, No. 1, 1982, pp. 40-51.
5. Indermit Gill: "Migrant Labour: A Mirror Survey of Jullunder and East Champaran." *Economic and Political Weekly,* Vol. 19, Nos. 24 & 25, 1984, pp. 961-964.
6. S.S. Gill: *Migrant Labour in Rural Punjab,* 1990.
7. M.R. Khurana: "Employment/Earning Pattern of the Migrant Labour in Rural Punjab" in *Agricultural Development & Employment Patterns in India: A Comparative Analysis of Punjab & Bihar,* 1992, pp. 190-211.
8. Radhika Chopra: "Maps of Experience: Narratives of Migration in an Indian Village." *Economic and Political Weekly,* Vol. 30, No. 49, 1995, pp. 3156-3162.
9. M.S. Sidhu et al.: *A Study on Migrant Agricultural Labour in Punjab,* 2007.
10. S.S. Johl: *Gains of the Green Revolution: How They Have Been Shared in Punjab,* 1975.
11. Gurcharan Singh Rupal: "Punjab: Canada for Bhaias", *The Punjabi Tribune,* April 23, 1979.
12. Ross Muro: "The Problem of Success", *The Time,* May 28, 1979.
13. S.S. Grewal and M.S. Sidhu: *A Study on Migrant Agricultural Labour in Punjab,* 1979.
14. B.K. Chum: "Violence Hits Farmers Economy", *The Indian*

Express, March 3, 1984.

15. M.S. Sidhu and S.S. Grewal: *A Study on Migrant Agricultural Labour in Punjab*, 1984.
16. Devinder Sharma: "Migrant Flow Unabated", *The Indian Express*, April 13, 1986.
17. M.S. Sidhu and P.S. Rangi et al.: *A Study on Migrant Agricultural Labour in Punjab*, 1997.
18. Ranjit Singh Ghuman et al.: *Status of Local Agricultural Labour in Punjab*, 2007.
19. M.S. Sidhu et al., op .cit.
20. Damodar N. Gujarati: "Regression on Dummy Variables" in *Basic Econometrics*, 1995, pp. 499-502.
21. Foster and Rosenzweig concluded that in Indian rural labour markets of casual agricultural labourers, discrimination prevails while providing wages between male, female, upper caste and lower caste casual agricultural labourers. For more details, see Andrew D. Foster and Mark R. Rosenzweig: "Information Flows and Discrimination in Labour Markets in Rural Areas in Developing Countries." *Proceedings of the World Bank Annual Conference on Development Economics*, 1992, pp. 173-203.
22. Sidhu et al. calculated difference of 2 per cent in the annual wage rate of a migrant and local permanent farm servant. For details see Sidhu et al., op. cit., 2007, pp. 40-50.
23. Theodore W Schultz: "Investment in Human Capital." *American Economic Review*, Vol. 51, No. 1, 1961, p. 2.
24. Damodar N. Gujarati, op.cit., pp. 502-505.
25. Pranab Kumar Bardhan and Ashok Rudra: "Labour Employment and Wages in Agriculture: Results of a Survey in West Bengal, 1979". *Economic and Political Weekly*, Vol. 15, Nos. 45 & 46, 1980, pp. 1943-1949.

7

Conclusions and Policy Implications

This present book is focused on the permanent farm servants in Punjab. The institution of permanent farm servants emerged in Punjab, along with casual agricultural labourers, in the last decades of the 19th century. Although about one-fourth of the hired labour used in Punjab agriculture is of permanent farm servants, but almost no information is available on their wage rates and working conditions.

Findings of Past Studies

To carry out the study we first of all reviewed the relevant literature on permanent farm servants (Chapter 1). In fact there are very few studies directly on permanent farm servants, especially relating to Punjab. So we had to search for studies in which some relevant information on permanent farm servants is given as a by product of the main theme; that is usually the wage rate, etc. of casual agricultural labourers. The main conclusions from this review of literature are:

1. A majority of the studies discussed the permanent farm servants only marginally along with their main focus on casual agricultural labourers.
2. Most of the studies suggest that the daily earnings of permanent farm servants are less than male casual agricultural labourers.
3. Some studies discussed the impact of new technology, especially of tractors, power-operated tube wells and HYV seeds on the employment of casual agricultural

labourers and permanent farm servants. The employment of casual agricultural labourers increased relatively more than that of permanent farm servants. Tractorization had a favourable impact on the employment of permanent farm servants relatively to casual labour.
4. A few scholars discussed the terms of contract, pattern of employment and changes in pattern of wage payments of permanent farm servants. No study reported that permanent farm servants were under any bondage to their employers due to heavy debt.
5. Finally, some studies reported that permanent farm servants are mainly hired on the big farms in Punjab and other states.

Emergence and Growth of Permanent Farm Servants

After reviewing the relevant literature, we made an attempt to find out (Chapter 2), how the institution of permanent farm servants emerged in Punjab and how its role has changed overtime. The commercialization of Punjab agriculture after the annexation of Punjab by the British in 1849, and the changes in the tenure system and the conversion of land revenue from kind to cash basis resulted in the disintegration of the traditional *jajmani* or *sepi* system under which the village landless has been associated with farmers for work on the farms. This created the ground for the emergence of the new type of agricultural labourers by the closing years of the 19th century. Even in the closing years of the 19th century the permanent farm servants were found in some districts, but not in all the districts of Punjab. The salient features of the system of employment of permanent farm servants in the early years of the 20th century were:

1. From the beginning of the 20th century not only the number of permanent farm servants grew, but this type of agricultural labourer made its appearance in all the districts of Punjab, along with the casual agricultural labourers.
2. In the early years of the 20th century, the use of permanent farm servants was prevalent more in the

Doaba region of Punjab.

3. The permanent farm servants were hired both on fixed annual cash wage as well as on a share of the crops basis. The cash wage contract was more popular in the Doaba region and the share wage contract in Malwa region.
4. A great majority of the permanent farm servants (almost three-fourth) were from the scheduled castes. Almost all the permanent farm servants worked in the village of their residence; very few got employment even in the adjoining villages.
5. The pattern of wages, perks and employment of permanent farm servants differed from village to village and from farm to farm within a village. A considerable inter-personal difference in wage of permanent farm servants was also an established pattern.
6. Compared to other states/regions of India, the institution of hired agricultural labourers was less developed in Punjab. The proportion of agricultural labourers in total agricultural population in Punjab was 14.5 per cent, while in Bombay it was 57 per cent, and in Madras it was just 54 per cent, during the 1920s.
7. From the early years of the 20th century to the middle of the 1970s, the share of permanent farm servants in total hired labourers used on Punjab farms did not change much; it hovered around thirty per cent. However, during the green revolution period, it declined to about 25 per cent by 2005-2006.
8. The caste composition of permanent farm servants, however, has not changed significantly over the last one century. The great majority (about 70 per cent) of permanent farm servants in Punjab belong to scheduled castes and particularly to Chamar, Chura and Mazhbi castes of scheduled castes.
9. There is no consensus among scholars about the long-term survival of the institution of permanent farm servants, and also on its desirability in agriculture vis-à-vis daily wage casual labourers.

The Wage Rate of Permanent Farm Servants: Structure and Determinants

The pattern and determinants of the annual wage rate of permanent farm servants in Punjab are discussed in Chapter 3, on the basis of primary data on 240 randomly selected permanent farm servants from thirty villages of Punjab. The annual wage rate of permanent farm servants in Punjab in 2007-08 (the year of primary survey) varied from Rs. 6,033 (minimum) to Rs. 45,892 (maximum); the mean wage rate being Rs. 22,153 and the median wage rate being Rs. 22,793. More than half the permanent farm servants (56.30 per cent to be exact), were getting an annual wage rate between Rs. 12,000 to Rs. 26,000. The considerable variation in the annual wage rate of permanent farm servants (maximum/minimum ratio = 7.61) is explained by many factors like age, technical and managerial skills, marital status, size and mechanization of employing farm. Both univariate and multiple regression analysis were used to isolate the main determinants of the wage rate of permanent farm servants. It was found that the age of a permanent farm servant had a major significant influence on his annual wage; the age-wage relationship being non-linear inverted U-shaped. The annual wage of permanent farm servants increases with age up to the middle age level, and then declines as the age of a permanent farm servant advances further. The technical and managerial skills of permanent farm servants (e.g. tractor driving, power tube well operation, and supervision of casual labour) were found to have a positive significant impact on the annual wage of the permanent farm servants. The mean annual wage (Rs. 27,896) of skilled (tractor drivers) permanent farm servants was about 44 per cent higher than that of the non-skilled (Rs. 19,368) permanent farm servants. The mean annual wage of a married (Rs. 25,505) permanent farm servant was also significantly higher than that of unmarried (Rs. 17,126) permanent farm servant. The big size of the farm also made a significant impact on the annual wage of permanent farm servants. The permanent farm servants employed on big and usually tractor owning farms were getting a significantly higher annual wage than those working on medium and small farms.

These six factors (age, marital status, tractor driving, power tube well operation, casual labour supervision and size of the employing farm) explained about 70 per cent of the total variation in the annual wage of permanent farm servants.

Variations in the Wage Rate: Across Regions and Within Villages

The inter-regional and inter-village variations in the annual wage of permanent farm servants are discussed in Chapter 4. In Punjab the labour market for permanent farm servants is segmented village-wise; one rarely finds a local permanent farm servant working in a village to which he does not belong. However, the migrant permanent farm servants often shift to other villages after working for a few years in a particular village. So in a way the migrant permanent farm servants provide some inter-linkage among village agricultural labour markets that are otherwise segmented. Further, there is considerable regional variation in agro-climatic and socio-economic conditions in Punjab despite its small size. For analysing regional variations in the annual wage of permanent farm servants we used three regional schemes: (1) Cultural regions (Malwa, Doaba, and Majha); (2) Agro-climatic regions (Foothills, Bist Doab, Upper Bari Doab, northern Malwa and southern Malwa); (3) Agricultural productivity regions (high, medium and low productivity zones). Considerable variation in the annual wage of permanent farm servants was found among the cultural regions; the highest mean wage in Malwa (Rs. 25,316) was 55 per cent higher than the lowest mean wage in the Doaba region (Rs. 16,308). Similarly, the highest mean wage in the southern Malwa agro-climatic zone (Rs. 26,874) was 75.65 per cent higher than the lowest mean wage in the Foothills zone (Rs. 15,300). The mean wage in the high agricultural productivity zone (Rs. 23,455) was 11.82 per cent higher than the mean wage in the lowest agricultural productivity zone (Rs. 20,976). So the annual wage of permanent farm servants varied considerably among the cultural, agro-climatic and agricultural productivity regions.

Considerable inter-village as well as intra-village variations in the annual wage of permanent farm servants was revealed by our sample data. In the sample of thirty villages the highest mean wage of permanent farm servants was found in village Khanpur Gandian (Rs. 31,985) in district Patiala and the lowest mean wage in village Bagrian (Rs. 8,960) in district Kapurthala; the ratio of the highest to the lowest being 3.98. Although the annual wage of permanent farm servants varied within the village in all the sample villages, but the degree of intra-village variation in the annual wage of permanent farm servants differed from village to village. The lowest coefficient of variation, (a measure of intra-village variation in wage of permanent farm servants), was found in village Khiala Kalan (5.14 per cent) in district Amritsar and the highest CV was observed in village Dheriwal (46.19 per cent) in district Gurdaspur. We also compared the wage rate of casual labourers and permanent farm servants in the cross section of thirty villages. On daily wage basis the wage rate of casual labourers was higher than that of permanent farm servants. The inter-village variations in the annual wage of permanent farm servants were analysed to find out the factors responsible for these variations. Both univariate and multiple regression were used for this purpose. The main factors responsible for inter-village variations in the annual wage of permanent farm servants were: mean size of holding in the village, land productivity, and proportion of migrant permanent farm servants in the village. It was found that villages with bigger mean holding size also have higher mean annual wage of permanent farm servants. Similarly, villages with higher land productivity were also found to have higher mean annual wage of permanent farm servants. The higher proportion of migrant permanent farm servants in a village lowered the annual mean wage of permanent farm servants in the village. Finally, it was found that villages located in the foothills zone had a lower mean wage of permanent farm servants compared to villages located in the Punjab plains.

Working Conditions and Nature of Contract

The nature of labour contract and working conditions of

permanent farm servants working on Punjab farms are described in Chapter 5 on the basis of information collected through the primary survey and focus group discussions in the surveyed villages. Most of the permanent farm servants in Punjab are now hired on an annual cash wage contract, though the share wage contract is still lingering in a few cases in the Malwa belt of the state. The contract is usually unwritten, but the written form is also used by some of the farmers (employers), especially by those who give advance wages to permanent farm servants. Most of the farmers (employers) allow a few days of paid leave to their permanent farm servants on account of illness and social ceremonies. The duration of the annual contract of permanent farm servants runs from the first day of May to the last day of April. In the few cases of breach of contract (in between the year), the dispute is settled by the village panchayat. The mode of selection of permanent farm servants is informal of one to one negotiation between the farmers and permanent farm servants. In many cases a permanent farm servant continues in the employment of the same farmer for a number of years. The payment of the annual wage is normally in two instalments; one half at the time of joining the farm on May 1st, and the other half after the harvesting of the Kharif crop. However, the migrant permanent farm servants are usually paid on a monthly basis. The local permanent farm servants also borrow some money from the farmers (employers) free of interest as well as on interest payment basis. Most of the permanent farm servants are also provided two meals and tea twice a day by the farmers (employers). The working hours of permanent farm servants run from early morning till late evening; and he has to also do a night shift when necessary for watering the crops. The pace of work, however, is slow and relaxed except during the peak operations. However, a permanent farm servant is required to be present on the farm even when there is no specific task to be performed. Some of the permanent farm servants also participate in the hiring and supervision of casual labour on the farm and also in day-to-day decisions on the routine farm operations. The relations of a permanent farm servant with his farmer (employer) are usually cordial due to both belonging to the same village and knowing each other quite well. On big farms, where three/ four or even more permanent farm servants are working together, one of them acts as a sort of informal leader or foreman to coordinate the work to be done by the team of permanent farm servants and the casual labour.

Migrant Permanent Farm Servants and Their Wage Rate

The wages of migrant permanent farm servants and local permanent farm servants are compared and analysed in Chapter 5. There has been a great influx of migrant labourers in rural Punjab over the green revolution period: the latest estimate for 2006-07 (M.S. Sidhu et al., 2007) puts the number of migrant agricultural labourers at 4.21 lakh in the lean period and 8.42 lakh in the peak season. Most of the migrant agricultural labourers work as casual workers, but some of them also stay on almost permanently and get employed as permanent farm servants. In our sample of 240 permanent farm servants about 44 per cent (number 106) were migrants. The comparison of mean wage of migrant permanent farm servant (Rs. 18,188) and local permanent farm servant (Rs. 25,270) revealed that migrant permanent farm servants get, on the overage, about 28 per cent less than the local permanent farm servants. The regression analysis of difference in the mean wage of migrant permanent farm servants and local permanent farm servants revealed that the lower wage earned by migrant permanent farm servants compared to local permanent farm servants was largely due to the difference in their personal characteristics such as age, marital status, technical and managerial skills (tractor driving, power tube well operations, supervision of casual labour), size of the employing farm and region of location. Once the influence of these factors is controlled, by inserting these factors as control variables in the regression model, the difference in the annual wage of the migrant permanent farm servants and local permanent farm servants becomes small and statistically not significant even at 10 per cent level. The analysis of the difference in the mean wage rate of migrant permanent farm servants and local permanent farm servants revealed that most of (79.50 per cent) the total wage differential between migrant permanent farm servants and local permanent farm servants is accounted for by the difference in personal endowments such as age, marital status, tractor driving skill, power tube well operation skill, casual labour supervision skill, size of the employing farm and region of location. The remaining 20.50 per cent of wage differential is attributable to other unexplained factors that may also include the sheer discrimination on account of migrant status. However, this remaining 20.50 per cent difference in the mean wage rate of local and migrant permanent farm servants was not statistically significant even at 10 per cent level.

The overall conclusion that emerged from this dummy variable regression analysis was that migrant permanent farm servants do not seem to suffer and face any serious wage discrimination in the market for permanent farm servants in Punjab agriculture. They earn lower wages mainly on account of their relatively poor endowments and skills compared to local permanent farm servants.

Policy Implications

The detailed investigation of the wage structure and working conditions of permanent farm servants presented in this study led to some policy implications that are outlined below:

1. The existence and importance of permanent farm servants in Punjab agriculture has been ignored by researchers and policy makers. This study shows that they constitute about one-fourth of the hired labour and perform the more skilled functions on the farm. So, government should officially recognize the existence of this important type of hired agricultural labour and government statistical agencies should regularly collect and publish data on the wage rate and working conditions of permanent farm servants in Punjab. At the time of census and other rural surveys separate data should be collected and published on permanent farm servants and daily wage labourers.
2. At present the labour contract of permanent farm servants is mostly unwritten. The government should

make a written contract between permanent farm servants and employing farm mandatory, with all the conditions explicitly stated. This contract should be enforceable through court of law in case of a dispute between a permanent farm servant and his employer.

3. The accident insurance of permanent farm servants should be made mandatory on the employer; the cost of insurance being shared equally (one-third each) by permanent farm servants, employing farmers and the Punjab Mandi Board. The Punjab Mandi Board should implement this accident insurance scheme.
4. The social welfare department of the government should formulate a special contributory pension scheme for permanent farm servants: the contribution being shared equally (one-third each) by permanent farm servants, employing farmer and the government. The pension should start on a permanent farm servant reaching the age of 50 years or after a permanent farm servant having completed 30 years service, whichever is earlier.
5. The skilled permanent farm servants earn a significantly higher wage than the unskilled ones. At present there is no formal systematic system of imparting skills to permanent farm servants. Some of them manage to acquire these skills through trial and error and at the sweet will of the employer, but a large number remain unskilled. The government should open training programmes in every tehsil to impart the necessary skills to permanent farm servants not only free of cost, but also paying them a minimum wage during the training period to compensate for the lost earnings. This will not only enable permanent farm servants to earn higher wages, but will also help in raising labour productivity in agriculture.

Appendices

CHAPTER 1

1.1 Methodology Used in the Study

In the literature on rural labour markets in developing countries five broad schools of thought can be discerned, viz. neoclassical, new institutionalist, Marxist political economy, formalized political economy and feminist. There are many studies that also followed a mixture of the various methodological standpoints. In the present study we have not followed any of these specific methodological approaches, but have used a straightforward descriptive and analytical approach. This is in our view the best approach given the complexity of rural labour markets. The rural labour markets are fairly complex because these are segmented as well as inter-linked at one and the same time. Moreover, the markets for the two types of agricultural labour, casual and permanent farm servants interact in very complex ways. So in the present study we have preferred to analyse the factual position of the market for permanent farm servants in Punjab and refrained from using and testing any ideologically guided hypotheses and formulations. Therefore, the methodology which we have used in this study is largely empirical rather than theoretical. This is in line with the latest methodological trends in research on labour economics. For carrying out the empirical analysis, we have used simple statistical techniques such as simple tabular forms, univariate and multivariate regression analysis.

To examine the impact of various factors such as age, skill

level, etc., on the wage rate of permanent farm servants we have used multiple regression analysis. The difference in the wage rate of migrant permanent farm servants and local permanent farm servants was examined with the help of dummy variables.

1.2 Data Sources and Sample Design

For carrying out the objectives of this study the secondary data as well as primary data have been used. The secondary sources of data are mainly the Settlement Reports and District Gazetteers. These Settlement Reports and the District Gazetteers contain useful descriptive information on permanent farm servants and daily farm labour used in Punjab agriculture in the late 19th century and early 20th century. Other secondary sources of information are the census for various years starting with 1901, village studies conducted by the Punjab Board of Economic Enquiry during colonial period, and studies in the Economics of Farm Management in Punjab for the mid-1960s.

For analysing the level and determinants of wages and for the present working conditions of permanent farm servants we mainly relied on our own primary survey conducted in May/ June 2008. The primary data were collected from a random sample of 240 permanent farm servants located in thirty villages of Punjab. For selecting the villages, Punjab was divided into five almost homogeneous agro-climatic zones, and from each zone the number of villages selected was approximately in proportion to the number of male agricultural labourers in the zone as per Census of 2001. However, to make the sample truly representative to the number of villages selected was slightly greater (than the exact proportion of male agricultural labourers) from zones that have greater internal variation in agro-climatic conditions like the foothills zone. The names and location of selected villages is given in Map 1 (Appendix 1.4). From each village eight permanent farm servants were selected randomly by arranging the holdings in the villages in descending order of area operated. From these 240 randomly selected permanent farm servants information was collected on all the relevant aspects of their person (such as age and education, etc.) and on the nature of employment contracts, wage rates, working conditions, nature of work done, and duties performed on the farms, share of output received (in case of share wage permanent farm servants), share of inputs paid to the employers, names of input shared and other relevant aspects on a carefully designed and pre-tested questionnaire. The collected information pertains to the agricultural year 2007-08 and was collected in May/June, 2008 after the harvesting of wheat was over.

1.3. Sample Design

Zone	*Districts in the Zone*	*Proportion of Male Agricultural Labourers*	*Number of Villages Selected*	*Sample to be Taken from Each Village*
Zone-I (Shiwalik Foot Hills Zone)	Gurdaspur Hoshiarpur Ropar SAS Nagar (Mohali)	15.7%	6	6x8=48
Zone-II (Central Plain Zone)	Amritsar Tarn Taran Kapurthala Jalandhar Nawanshahr Ludhiana	28.20%	9	9x8=72
Zone-III (Southern Plain Zone)	Bathinda Mansa	10.7%	4	4x8=32
Zone-IV (Eastern Plain Zone)	Sangrur Barnala Patlala Fatehgarh Sahib	19.10%	5	5x8=40
Zone-V (Western Plain Zone)	Ferozepur Faridkot Mukatsar Moga	26.30%	6	6x8=48
Total	20	100	30	30x8=240

Source: Census (2001)

1.4 Location of Sample Villages

Map 1.1

CHAPTER 3

3.1 Estimated Wage Rate of Permanent Farm Servants

$Y = -7995.17 + 1776.67\ Age - 22.51\ Age^2$

Age (Years)	*Y [Estimated Wage Rate (Rs.)]*
10	7,520.23
11	8,824.49
12	10,083.43
13	11,297.35
14	12,466.25
15	13,590.13
16	14,668.99
17	15,702.83
18	16,691.65
19	17,635.45
20	18,534.23
21	19,387.99
22	20,196.73
23	20,960.45
24	21,679.15
25	22,352.83
26	22,981.49
27	23,565.13
28	24,103.75
29	24,597.35
30	25,045.93
31	25,449.49
32	25,808.03
33	26,121.55
34	26,390.05
35	26,613.53
36	26,791.99
37	26,925.43
38	27,013.85
39	**27,057.25**
40	27,055.63
41	27,008.99
42	26,917.33
43	26,780.65
44	26,598.95
45	26,372.23

Contd...

46	26,100.49
47	25,783.73
48	25,421.95
49	25,015.15
50	24,565.33
51	24,066.49
52	23,524.63
53	22,937.75
54	22,305.85
55	21,628.93
56	20,906.94
57	20,140.03
58	19,328.05
59	18,471.05
60	17,569.03
61	16,621.99
62	15,629.93
63	14,592.85
64	13,510.75
65	12,383.63
66	11,211.49
67	9,994.33
68	8,732.15
69	7,424.95
70	6,072.73

CHAPTER 5

5.1 Working Conditions of Permanent Farm Servants in Surveyed Villages (A Profile)

Zone	*Name of Village*	*Dominant Form of Contract: Written=Yes Oral=No*	*Employer Provides Food and Tea*	*Get Vegetables From Farm*	*Get Fodder. & Bhusa/ Wood*	*Get Some Paid Holidays*	*Number of Holidays Fixed in Contract*	*Permanent Farm Servants Has to Use His Own Utensils*	*Working hours* Lean Period (Hrs.)	Peak Period (Hrs.)	*Female Family Members and Children Provide Free Labour on Farms*	*Any Union of Permanent Farm Servants in the Village*	*Any Protest in Village to Raise Share/ Wage of Permanent Farm Servants in Last 5 Years*
Majha	Khiala Kalan	Yes	Yes	Yes	Yes	Yes	Nil	No	9-10	>12	No	No	No
	Dader Sahib	Yes	Yes	Yes	No	Yes	Nil	No	9-10	>12	No	No	No
	Dala Gauria	No	Yes	No	No	Yes	Nil	Yes	9-10	>12	No	No	No
	Dehriwal	No	Yes	Yes	Yes	Yes	Nil	Yes	9-10	>12	No	No	No
Malwa	Das Graon	No	Yes	No	No	Yes	Nil	Yes	9-10	>12	No	No	No
	Goga	No	Yes	No	No	Yes	Nil	Yes	9-10	>12	No	No	No
	Barsat	Yes	Yes	Yes	Not sure	Yes	Nil	Yes	9-10	>12	No	No	No
	Khanpur Gandian	Yes	Yes	Yes	Yes	Yes	Nil	Yes	9-10	>12	No	No	No
	Rurki	No	Yes	No	No	Yes	Nil	Yes	9-10	>12	No	No	No
	Sehjra	Yes	Yes	Yes	No	Yes	10	Yes	9-10	>12	No	No	No
	Dhindsa	Yes	Yes	Yes	Yes	Yes	12	Yes	9-10	>12	No	No	No

Contd...

	Fata Maluka	Yes	Yes	Yes	Yes	Yes	12	Yes	9-10	>12	No	No	No
	Makha Challan	Yes	Yes	Yes	Not sure	Yes	12	Yes	9-10	>12	No	No	No
	Malkana	Yes	Yes	Yes	Not sure	Yes	10	Yes	9-10	>12	No	No	No
	Dyalpur Bhaika	Yes	Yes	Yes	Not sure	Yes	12	Yes	9-10	>12	No	No	No
	Khai	Yes	Yes	Yes	Yes	Yes	12	Yes	9-10	>12	No	No	No
	Bhagu	Yes	Yes	Yes	Yes	Yes	12	Yes	9-10	>12	No	No	No
	Dod	Yes	Yes	Yes	Not sure	Yes	Nil	Yes	9-10	>12	No	No	No
	Pakhi Kalan	Yes	Yes	Yes	Not sure	Yes	Nil	Yes	9-10	>12	No	No	No
	Mida	Yes	Yes	Yes	Yes	Yes	Nil	Yes	9-10	>12	No	No	No
	Heran	No	Yes	No	No	Yes	Nil	Yes	9-10	>12	No	No	No
	Bija	No	Yes	No	No	Yes	Nil	No	9-10	>12	No	No	No
	Kahan singh wala	No	Yes	Yes	No	Yes	10	Yes	9-10	>12	No	No	No
Doaba	Hardo-khundpur	No	Yes	No	No	Yes	Nil	Yes	9-10	>12	No	No	No
	Padrana	No	Yes	No	No	Yes	Nil	Yes	9-10	>12	No	No	No
	Mutton	No	Yes	No	No	Yes	Nil	Yes	9-10	>12	No	No	No
	Mukandpur	No	Yes	No	No	Yes	Nil	Yes	9-10	>12	No	No	No
	Hardoshek	No	Yes	No	No	Yes	Nil	Yes	9-10	>12	No	No	No
	Ugi	No	Yes	No	No	Yes	Nil	Yes	9-10	>12	No	No	No
	Bagrian	No	Yes	No	No	Yes	Nil	Yes	9-10	>12	No	No	No

Source: Primary Survey (2007-2008)

5.2 Terms of Contract Between Farmer (Employer) and Employee (Siri) Share Wage Permanent Farm Servant During Colonial Period in Punjab

I, Chaugutta, son of Karmun – by caste weaver – am a resident of village Suner, Tehsil Zira. I have today taken a cash sum of Rs. 60, the half of which is 30, as debt from Tehl Singh, son of Hazara Singh, of Suner, Tehsil Zira, to meet my household expenses. I promise that I will repay the above – mentioned sum, on which no interest will be charged, before Nimani (1st of Har), 1990 (Bikrami). The interest charge has been excused for the reason that I will be working as a siri with Tehl Singh. I further promise that I will continue with Tehl Singh up to Nimani, 1990 and will look after his cattle and serve him generally as I am ordered. My share of the produce will be one fifth of the total grain produced from one hal; in fodder I will have no share. I will take my food at the house of Tehl Singh and will not absent myself from work without his permission. In case I do I shall be responsible for any wages Tehl Singh may pay during the days of my absence. If it is found necessary, I shall sleep at night beside the cattle. Sick leave of only 3 days during the whole year will be allowed to me. In days of absence over and above this period, the wages of any labour that may be employed will have to be paid by me. In case I leave off work and go away before the aforesaid Nimani, the condition that no interest is chargeable from me, will not stand, and I shall be liable to 50 per cent interest which along with the principal I will pay whenever the same is demanded. This document is written to serve as an evidence of the contract.

Dated: 29th June, 1932. (Thumb Impression of Chaugutta)
Witness: Atma Ram, Age: 25 years.
Son of Harbans Das,
Resident of Suner.

Source: *A Village Study of Suner (District Ferozepur)*, The Board of Economic Inquiry, 1936, p. 24.

5.3 Terms of Contract, Between Farmer (Employer) and Employee (Cash Wage Permanent Farm Servant) During Pre–Green Revolution Period in Punjab

Agreement

It is hereby agreed that I ……., son of ……, caste….., a resident of …….. will serve for a period of one year. With …… of ….. from 1-4-1951 to 31-3-1952.

Conditions are detailed as follows:

1. Pay will be Rs. 25 a month
2. I shall be allowed an advance of Rs. 100
3. In case I leave my service, I shall repay an advance taken by me.
4. I shall take one short and one chaddar [coverlet] every six months.

I have given this in writing as my agreement so that it can be made use if need arise.

Signed Today, Dated: 1-4-1951

Witness Thumb impression Witness

Source: Daniel and Alice Thorner: *Land and Labour in India,* 1962, p. 24, Asia Publishing House, Bombay.

APPENDIX 5.4

APPENDIX 5.4
(Translated)

Terms of Contract Between Farmer (Employer) and Employee (Siri) Share Wage Permanent Farm Servant During the Post–Green Revolution Period in Punjab

Village* ———— Tehsil———— District————

It is hereby agreed that I Bachan son of Bishan will work as a siri (Share Wage Permanent Farm Servant) from June 5, 1973 to June 15, 1974. I took an advance of Rs. 1000/- from my employer and have to return this amount up to June 15, 1974. If I don't return the advance then my house will be forfeited.

I fully accept the term and condition of a contract.

Evidence – 1
Evidence – 2

Siri
(Bachan)
Thumb information
Date:
Contract written by:
Sukhwant Singh Dhaliwal
(Sarpanch), Dated: August 31, 73

Advance money (Rs. 1000/-) returned on June 9, 1974 to employer [Written by: Sukhwant Singh Dhaliwal]

Source: Accounts of a Farm.
*Keeping in mind the ethics of research, we have not mentioned the name of a village and district in appendices 5.4 to 5.5

APPENDIX 5.5

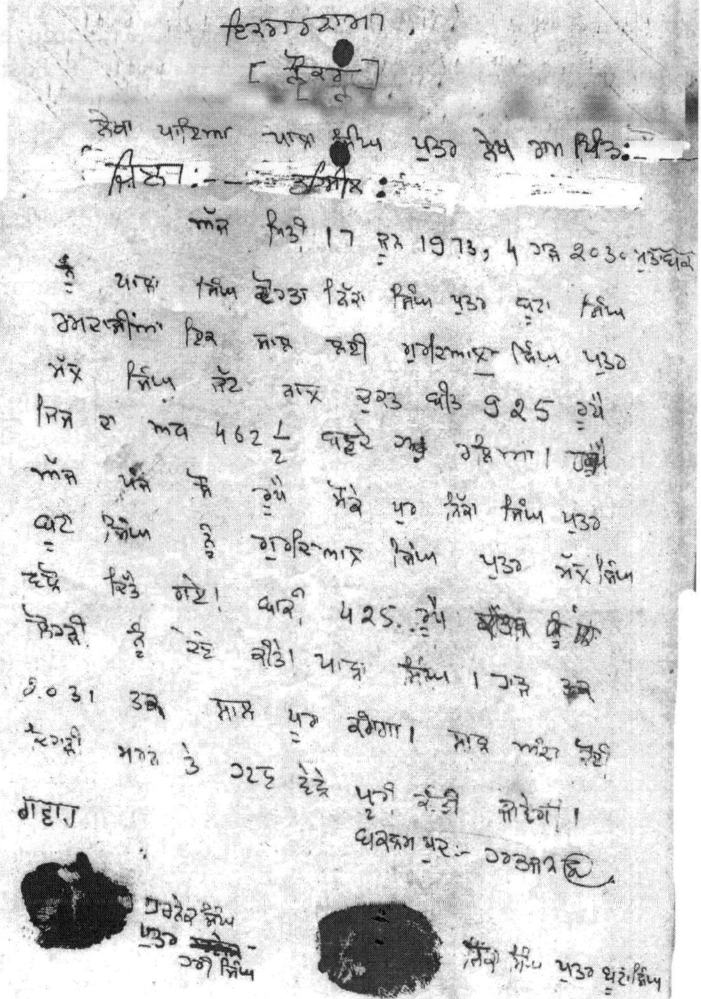

APPENDIX 5.5
(Translated)

Terms of Contract Between Farmer (Employer) and Employee (Cash Wage Permanent Farm Servant) During thePost Green Revolution Period in Punjab

Village————Tehsil————District—————

On June 17,1973 [Har 4, 2030], I Pala Singh grandson of S. Nika Singh s\o S. Buta Singh Ramdasia by caste will work as a cash wage permanent farm servant with S. Gurdial s\o Mal Singh Jat Sikh by caste. Pala Singh will get annual wages of Rs. 925. Today Nika Singh on behalf of Pala Singh received Rs. 500/- as advance. Remaining Rs. 425 will be given on Lohiri. Pala Singh will come into contract from Har 1, 2031 or June 1, 1973. The absents during a year will be compensated in form of work at the end of a year

Contract written by:
(Harbajhan Singh)

Evidence:

(Thumb impression)
Harnek Singh S/o Hari Singh

On Behalf of Cash
wage permanent Farm servant
Contract Signed by:

Thumb impression
(Nikka Singh S/o Buta Singh)

Source: Accounts of a Farm.

Bibliography

Acharya, S.S. (1973): "Green Revolution and Farm Employment", *Indian Journal of Agricultural Economics*, Vol. 28, No. 3, pp. 30-45.

Aggarwal, Bina (1981): "Agricultural Mechanization and Labour Use: A Disaggregated Approach". *International Labour Review*, Vol. 120, No. 1, pp. 115-127.

Aggarwal, Pratap C. (1971): "Impact of Green Revolution on Landless Labour: A Note". *Economic and Political Weekly*, Vol. 6, No. 47, pp. 2363-2365.

Akerlof, George A. (1970): "The Market for 'Lemons': Quality Uncertainty and the Market Mechanism." *The Quarterly Journal of Economics*, Vol. 84, No. 3, pp. 488-500.

Akerlof, George A. (1980): "A Theory of Social Custom, of Which the Unemployment May Be One Consequence." *The Quarterly Journal of Economics*, Vol. 94, No. 4, pp. 749-775.

Alagh, Y.K., Bhalla, G.S. and Bhaduri, Amit (1978): "Agricultural Growth and Manpower Absorption in India". in *Labour Absorption in Indian Agriculture: Some Exploratory Investigations (ed)*, ILO-ARTEP, ILO, Bangkok, pp. 119-164.

Alexander, K.C. (1973): "Emerging Farmer-Labour Relations in Kuttanad". *Economic and Political Weekly*, Vol. 8, No. 34, pp. 1551-1560.

Bagchi, Amiya Kumar (1976): "De-industrialization in India in the Nineteenth Century: Some Theoretical Implications". *Journal of Development Studies*, Vol. 12, No. 2, pp. 135-164.

Banerjee, Biswajit and Knight, J.B. (1985): "Caste Discrimination in the Indian Urban Market." *Journal of Development Economics*, Vol. 17, No. 3, pp. 277-307.

Banerjee, Himadri (1977): "Agricultural Labourers of the Punjab During the Second Half of the Nineteenth Century." *The Panjab Past and Present*, Part-I (Serial No. 21), pp. 96-116.

Banga, Indu (1978): *The Agrarian System of the Sikhs (Late 18th and Early 19th Century)*, Manohar Publications, Delhi.

Bardhan, Kalpana (1973): "Factors Affecting Wage Rates for Agricultural Labour". *Economic and Political Weekly*, Vol. 8, No. 26, pp. A56-A64.

Bardhan, Pranab (1973): "Variations in Agriculture Wages: A Note". *Economic and Political Weekly*, Vol. 8, No. 21, pp. 947-950.

Bardhan, Pranab (2003): *Poverty, Agrarian Structure and Political Economy in India*, Oxford University Press, New Delhi.

Bardhan, Pranab and Rudra, Ashok (1981): "Terms and Conditions of Labour Contracts in Indian Agriculture: Results of a Survey in West Bengal, 1979". *Oxford Bulletin of Economics and Statistics*, Vol. 43, No. 1, pp. 89-111.

Bardhan, Pranab and Rudra, Ashok (1985): "The Domain of Rural Labour Markets: Results of a Survey in West-Bengal, 1981-82". *Economic and Political Weekly*, Vol. 20, Nos.51& 52, pp. A153-A154.

Bardhan, Pranab K. (1979): "Labour Supply Functions in Poor Agrarian Economy". *American Economic Review*, Vol. 69, No. 1, pp. 73-83.

Bardhan, Pranab K. (1979): "Wages and Unemployment in a Poor Agrarian Economy: A Theoretical and Empirical Analysis." *Journal of Political Economy*, Vol. 87, No. 3, pp. 479-500.

Bardhan, Pranab K. (1980): "Interlocking Factor Markets and Agrarian Development: A Review of Issues". *Oxford Economic Papers*, Vol. 32, No. 1, pp. 82-98.

Bardhan, Pranab K. (1984): *Land, Labour and Rural Poverty*, Oxford University Press, Delhi.

Bardhan, Pranab Kumar and Rudra, Ashok (1980): "Labour Employment and Wages in Agriculture: Results of a Survey in West Bengal, 1979". *Economic and Political Weekly*, Vol. 15, Nos. 45 & 46, pp. 1943-1949.

Bardhan, Pranab, and Rudra, Ashok (1986). "Labour Mobility and the Boundaries of the Village Moral Economy". *Journal of Peasant Studies*, Vol. 13, No. 3, pp. 90-115.

Basant, Rakesh (1983): "Attached Labour and the Classification of Agricultural Labour: Some Issues" *Indian Journal of Labour Economics*, Vol. 26, Nos. 1&2, pp. 129-145.

Basant, Rakesh (1984): "Attached and Casual Labour Wage Rates". *Economic and Political Weekly*, Vol. 19, No. 9, pp. 390-396.

Basu, Arnab K. (2002): "Oligopsonistic Landlords, Segmented Labour Markets and the Persistence of Tied Labour Contracts." *American Journal of Agricultural Economics*, Vol. 84, No. 2, pp. 438-453.

Basu, Kaushik (1983): "The Emergence of Isolation and Interlinkage in Rural Markets". *Oxford Economic Papers*, Vol. 35, No. 2, pp. 262-280.

Basu, Kaushik (1994): *Agrarian Questions (ed.)*, Oxford University Press, New Delhi.

Becker, G.S. (1975): *Human Capital: A Theoretical and Empirical Analysis*, National Bureau of Economic Research, New York.

Bell, Clive and Srinivasan, T.N. (1985): *The Demand for Attached Farm Servants in Andhra Pradesh, Bihar and Punjab*, World Bank, Working Paper No. 11, Washington (D.C.).

Bell, Clive and Srinivasan, T.N. (1989): "Interlinked Transactions in Rural Markets: An Empirical Study of Andhra Pradesh, Bihar and Punjab". *Oxford Bulletin of Economics and Statistics*, Vol. 51, No. 1, pp. 73-83.

Bhalla, Sheila (1976): "New Relations of Production in Haryana". *Economic and Political Weekly*, Vol. 11, No. 13, pp. A23-A30.

Bhalla, Sheila (1979): "Real Wage Rates of Agricultural Labourers in Punjab: 1961-1977: A Preliminary Analysis". *Economic and Political Weekly*, Vol. 14, No. 26, pp. A57-A68.

Bharadwaj, Krishna (1991): *Production Conditions in Indian Agriculture: A Study Based on Farm Management Surveys*, K.P. Bagchi & Company, Calcutta.

Binswanger, Hans P. and Rosenzweig, Mark R. (1984): *Contractual Arrangements, Employment and Wages in Rural Labour Markets in Asia (ed.)*, Yale University Press, New Haven.

Blaug, Mark (1974): "An Economic Analysis of Personal Earnings in Thailand". *Economic Development and Cultural Change*, Vol. 23, No. 1, pp. 1-31.

Blinder, Alan S. (1973): "Wage Discrimination: Reduced Form and Structural Estimates". *Journal of Human Resources*, Vol. 8, No. 4, pp. 436-555.

Bliss, C. and Stern, N. (1978): "Productivity, Wages and Nutrition: The Theory, Part I & Part II". *Journal of Development Economics*, Vol. 5, No. 4, pp. 331-362 & 363-398.

Blomquist, N. Sorën (1979): "Wage Rates and Personal Characteristics". *The Scandinavian Journal of Economics*, Vol. 81, No. 4, pp. 505-520.

Booth, Anne and Sundrum, R.M. (1985): *Labour Absorption in Agriculture: Theoretical Analysis and Empirical Investigations*, Oxford University Press, Delhi.

Breen, Richard (1983): "Farm Servanthood in Ireland: 1900-40." *The Economic History Review*, Vol. 36, No. 1, pp. 87-102.

Breman, Jan (1974): *Patronage and Exploitation: Changing Agrarian Relations in South Gujarat (India)*, University of California Press, London.

Calvert, H. (1922): *The Wealth and Welfare of the Punjab,* Civil and Military Gazetteer Press, Lahore.

Campbell, George (1853): *Modern India (2nd Edition),* W. Clowes & Sons, London

Carter, Marina (1995): *Servants, Sirdars and Settlers: Indians in Mauritius, 1834-1874,* Oxford University Press, Delhi.

Caunce, Stephen(1997): "Farm Servants and the Development of Capitalism in English Agriculture." *Agriculture History Review,* Vol. 45, No. 1, pp. 49-60.

Chadha, G.K. (1979): *Production Gains of New Agricultural Technology: A Farm Sizewise Analysis of Punjab Experience,* Publication Bureau, Panjab University, Chandigarh.

Chadha, G.K. (1986): *The Ṣtate and Rural Economic Transformation: The Case of Punjab, 1950-85,* Sage Publications, New Delhi.

Chatterjee, Biswajit and Kundu, Amit (2001): "Changing Agrarian Structure and the Choice Between Local Labourer and Migrant Labourer". *Indian Journal of Labour Economics,* Vol. 44, No. 4, pp. 873-880.

Chattopadhyay, Manabendu (1977)): "Wage Rates of Two Groups of Agricultural Labourers". *Economic and Political Weekly,* Vol. 12, No. 13, pp. A20-A22.

Chattopadhyay, Manabendu (1984): "Transformations of Labour Use in Indian Agriculture". *Cambridge Journal of Economics,* Vol. 8, No. 3, pp. 289-296.

Chopra, Kusum (1974): "Tractorization and Changes in Factor Inputs: A Case Study of Punjab". *Economic and Political Weekly,* Vol. 9, No. 52, pp. A119-A127.

Chopra, Radhika (1995): "Maps of Experience: Narratives of Migration in an Indian Village." *Economic and Political* Weekly, Vol. 30, No. 49, pp. 3156-3162.

Chum, B.K. (1984): "Violence Hits Farmers Economy", *The Indian Express,* March 3.

Collins, Jane L., and Krippner, Greta R. (1999): "Permanent Labour Contracts in Agriculture: Flexibility and Subordination in a New Export Crop." *Comparative Studies in Society and History,* Vol. 41, No. 3, pp. 510-534.

Daniel and Thorner, Alice (1962): *Land and Labour in India,* Asia Publishing House, Bombay.

Darling, Malcolm (1925): *The Punjab Peasant in Prosperity and Debt,* South Asia Book, Columbia.

Darling, Malcolm (1934): *Wisdom and Waste in the Punjab Village,* Oxford University Press, London.

Dasgupta, Biplab (1984): "Agricultural Labour Under Colonial, Semi-Capitalist and Capitalist Conditions: A Case Study of West Bengal". *Economic and Political Weekly*, Vol. 19, No. 39, pp. A129-A148.

Datt, Gaurav (1989): *Wage and Employment Determination in Agricultural Labour Markets in India*, A Ph.D. Thesis, Australian National University (ANU), Canberra (Australia).

Day, Richard, H. (1967): "The Economics of Technological Change and the Demise of the Share Cropper." *American Economic Review*, Vol. 57, No. 3, pp. 427-449.

Dhavle, Shalini (1964): "Hired Labour and Wage Rates for Farm Operations in Eleven Selected Rural Centres of Maharashtra". *Arthavijnana*, Vol. 6, No. 2, pp. 127-144.

Dreze, J. and Mukherjee, A. (1987): *Labour Contracts in Rural India: Theories and Evidence*, Discussion Paper No. 7, The Development Research Programme, LSE.

Dreze, Jean and Lanjouw, Peter (1992): "Economic Mobility and Agricultural Labour in Rural India: A Case Study," *Indian Economic Review*, Vol. 27, Special Number, pp. 25-54.

Dribe, Martin and Lundh, Christer (2005): "People on the Move: Determinants of Servant Migration in Nineteenth-century Sweden". *Continuity and Change*, Vol. 20, No. 1, pp. 53–91.

Dutt, R. Palme (1947): *India Today*, People's Publishing House, Bombay.

Eswaran, Mukesh and Kotwal, Ashok (1985): "A Theory of Contractual Structure in Agriculture". *American Economic Review*, Vol. 75, No. 3, pp. 352-367.

Eswaran, Mukesh and Kotwal, Ashok (1985): "A Theory of Two Tier Labour Markets in Agrarian Economies". *American Economic Review*, Vol. 75, No. 1, pp. 162-77.

Foster, Andrew, D. and Rosenzweigh, Mark, R. (1992): "Information Flows and Discrimination in Labour Markets in Rural Areas in Developing Countries." *Proceedings of the World Bank Annual Conference on Development Economics*, pp. 173-203.

Frankel, Francine (1971): *India's Green Revolution: Economic Gains and Political Costs*, Princeton University Press, New Jersey.

Fuller, Varden and Mamer, John, W. (1978): "Constraints on California Farm Workers Unionization". *Industrial Relations: A Journal of Economy and Society*, Vol. 17, No. 2, pp. 143-155.

Gabbard, Susan, M. and Perloff, Jeffrey, M. (1997): "The Effects of Pay and Work Conditions on Farmworker Retention". *Industrial Relations: A Journal of Economy and Society*, Vol. 36, No. 4, pp. 474-488.

Ghose, Ajit Kumar (1980): "Wages and Employment in Indian Agriculture". *World Development*, Vol. 8, Nos. 5&6, pp. 413-428.

Ghuman, Ranjit Singh, Singh, Inderjeet and Singh, Lakhwinder (2007): *Status of Local Agricultural Labour in Punjab*, Department of Economics, Punjabi University, Patiala.

Gill, Indermit (1984): "Migrant Labour: A Mirror Survey of Jullunder and East Champaran." *Economic and Political Weekly*, Vol. 19, Nos. 24 & 25, pp. 961-964.

Gill, S.S. (1960): "Unemployment and Underemployment of Permanent Farm Workers" *Arthavijnana*, Vol. 2, No. 4, pp. 249-261.

Gill, S.S. (1990): *Migrant Labour in Rural Punjab*, Deptt. of Economics, Punjabi University, Patiala.

Gosal, G.S. and Krishan, Gopal (1984): *Regional Disparities in Levels of Socio-Economic Development in Punjab*, Vishal Publications, Kurukshetra.

Gough, Kathleen. (1981): *Rural Society in South East India*, Cambridge University, Cambridge.

Grewal, S.S. and Sidhu, M.S. (1979): *A Study on Migrant Agricultural Labour in Punjab*, Dept. of Economics and Sociology, Punjab Agricultural University, Ludhiana.

Grewal, S.S. and Rangi, P.S. (1983): "An Analytical Study of Growth of Punjab Agriculture". *Indian Journal of Agricultural Economics*, Vol. 38, No. 4, pp. 509-519.

Guha, Sumit (2004): "Civilizations, Markets and Services: Village Servants in India from the 17th to the 20th Centuries". *Indian Economic and Social History Review*, Vol. 41, No. 1, pp. 79-101.

Gujarati, Damodar N. (1995): *Basic Econometrics (Third Edition)*, McGRAW-HILL Book Co., Singapore.

Hart, Gillian (1986): "Interlocking Transactions: Obstacles, Precursors or Instruments of Agrarian Capitalism". *Journal of Development Economics*, Vol. 23, No. 1, pp. 177-203.

Heady, Earl O. (1964): *Economics of Agricultural Production and Resource Use*, Prentice-Hall, Delhi

Hecht, J.Jean (1955): *The Domestic Servant Class in 18th Century England*, Routledge & Kegan Paul, London.

Hodson, D.F. (1973): "Problems and Constraints of Agricultural Workers' Organizations within Differing Continents and Agricultures". *Journal of Agricultural Economics*, Vol. 24, No. 1, pp. 125-139.

Jaynes, Gerald David (1982): "Production and Distribution in Agrarian Economies". *Oxford Economic Papers*, Vol. 34, No. 2, pp. 346-367.

Johl, S.S. (1975): "Gains of the Green Revolution: How They Have Been

Shared in Punjab". *Journal of Development Studies*, Vol. 11, No. 3, pp. 178-189.

Johl, S.S. (1975): *Gains of the Green Revolution: How They Have Been Shared in Punjab*, Department of Economics and Sociology, Punjab Agricultural University, Ludhiana.

Joll, C., Mckenna, C. and Mcnabb, R. (1983): *Developments in Labour Market Analysis*, George Allen and Unwin Ltd., London.

Keijiro, Otsuka, Chuma, Hiroyuki and Hayami,Yujiro (1992): "Land and Labour Contracts in Agrarian Economies: Theories and Facts". *Journal of Economic Literature*, Vol. 30, No. 4, pp. 1965-2018.

Kessinger, Tom G. (1974): *Vilyatpur: 1848-1968, Social and Economic Change in North Indian Village*, University of California Press, Berkeley.

Khurana, M.R. (1992): *Agricultural Development and Employment Patterns in India: A Comparative Analysis of Punjab and Bihar*, Concept Publishing Company, New Delhi.

Koshal, Manjulik, Koshal, Rajindar and Gupta, Ashok (2004): "Role of Education in Wage Determination in the Japanese Construction Sector". *Indian Journal of Labour Economics*, Vol. 47, No. 4, pp. 833-841.

Krishnamurthy, J. (1972): "The Growth of Agricultural Labour in India: A Note". *Indian Economic and Social History Review*, Vol. 9, No. 3, pp. 327-332.

Kumar, Dharma (1965): *Land and Caste in South India: Agricultural Labour in the Madras Presidency During the 19th Century*, Cambridge University Press, London.

Kussmaul, A.S. (1981): "The Ambiguous Mobility of Farm Servants". *The Economic History Review (New Series)*, Vol. 34, No. 2, pp. 222-235.

Laxminarayan, H. (1982): "The Impact of Agricultural Development on Employment: A Case Study of Punjab." *The Developing Economies*, Vol. 20, No. 1, pp. 40-51.

Leibeinsten, H.A. (1957): *Economic Backwardness and Economic Growth*, Wiley, New York.

Lenin, V.I. (1956): *The Development of Capitalism in Russia*, Progress Publishers, Moscow.

Lewis, W. Arthur (1954): "Economic Development with Unlimited Supplies of Labour". *The Manchester School of Economic and Social Studies*, Vol. 22, No. 2, pp. 139-91.

Lorenzo, A.M. (1947): *Agricultural Labour Conditions in Northern India*, New Book Company Ltd., Bombay.

Mann, Prem, S. and Kapoor, Bhushan Lal (1988): "Earnings Differentials Between Public, Private and Joint Sector in Punjab (India)." *Journal of Development Studies,* Vol. 25, No. 1, pp. 97-111.

Marx, Karl (1947): *Critique of the Gotha Programme,* Foreign Language Publishing House, Moscow.

Marx, Karl (1986): *Capital* (Vol. 1), Progress Publishers, Moscow.

Marx, Karl and Engels, Frederick (1976): *Selected Works (Vol. I),* Progress Publishers, Moscow.

Moses, Gary (1999): "Proletarian Labourers? East Riding Farm Servants." *Agriculture History Review,* Vol. 47, No. 1, pp. 78-94.

Mukherjee, Anindita and Ray, Debraj (1995): "Labour Tying". *Journal of Development Economics,* Vol. 47, No. 2, pp. 207-239.

Muro, Ross (1979): "The Problem of Success", *The Time,* May 28.

Muthiah, C. (1970): "The Agricultural Labour Problem in Thanjavur and the New Agricultural Strategy", *Indian Journal of Agricultural Economics,* Vol. 25, No. 3, pp. 15-23.

Naqvi, Nadeem and Wemhoner, Frederick (1995): "Power, Coercion, and the Games Landlords Play". *Journal of Development Economics,* Vol. 47, No. 2, pp. 191-205.

Newaj, K. and Rudra, Ashok (1975): "Agrarian Transformation in a District of West Bengal", *Economic and Political Weekly,* Vol. 10, No. 13, pp. A22-A23.

Oaxaca, R.L. (1973): "Male-Female Wage Differentials in Urban Labour Markets." *International Economic Review,* Vol. 14, No. 3, pp. 693-709.

Oberai, A.S. and Singh, H.K. Manmohan (1980): "Migration Flows in Punjab's Green Revolution Belt": *Economic and Political Weekly,* Vol. 15, No. 13, pp. A2-A12.

Olsen, Wendy: "Moral Political Economy and Moral Reasoning about Rural India: Four Theoretical Schools Compared". *Cambridge Journal of Economics,* Vol. 33, No. 5, pp. 875-902.

Omvedt, Gail (1981): "Capitalist Agriculture and Rural Classes in India". *Economic and Political Weekly,* Vol. 16, No. 52, pp. A140-A159.

Oomen, T.K. (1971): "Green Revolution and Agrarian conflict." *Economic and Political Weekly,* Vol. 6, No. 26, pp. A99-A103.

Osmani, S.R. (1990): "Wage Determination in Rural Labour Markets: The Theory of Implicit Cooperation". *Journal of Development Economics,* Vol. 34, Nos. 1&2, pp. 3-23.

Otsuka, Keijiro, Chuma, Hiroyuk and Hayami, Yujiro (1993): "Permanent Labour and Land Tenancy Contracts in Agrarian

Economies: An Integrated Analysis". *Economica,* Vol. 60, No. 237, pp. 57-77.

Pal, Sarmistha (1997): "An Analysis of Declining Incidence of Regular Labour Contracts in Rural India". *Journal of Development Studies,* Vol. 34, No. 2, pp. 133-155.

Pal, Sarmistha (1998):"A Limited Dependent Analysis of the Choice of Regular Labour Contract in Seasonal Agriculture". *Applied Economics,* Vol. 30, No. 10, pp. 1347-1359.

Pal, Sarmistha (1999): "Task Based Segmentation of Rural Labour Contracts: Theory and Evidence". *Bulletin of Economic Research,* Vol. 51, No. 1, pp. 67-94.

Papola, T.S. and Misra, V.N. (1980): "Labour Supply and Wage Determination in Rural Uttar Pradesh". *Indian Journal of Agricultural Economics,* Vol. 35, No. 1, pp. 106-120.

Patel, S.J. (1952): *Agricultural Labourers in Modern India and Pakistan,* Current Book House, Bombay.

Patnaik, Utsa (1983): "On the Evolution of the Class of Agricultural Labourers in India", *Social Scientist,* Vol. 11, No. 7, pp. 3-24.

Patnaik, Utsa (1987): *Peasant Class Differentiations: A Study in Method with Reference to Haryana,* Oxford University Press, Delhi.

Platteau, Jean-Philippe (1995): "A Frame Work for the Analysis of Evolving Patron-Client Ties in Agrarian Economies." *World Development,* Vol. 23, No. 5, pp. 705-879

Platteau, Jean-Philippe (1995): "An Indian Model of Aristocratic Patronage." *Oxford Economic Papers,* Vol. 47, No. 41, pp. 637-662.

Powell, Baden (1972): *Indian Village Community,* Cosmo Publications, Delhi.

Raj, K.N. (1985): *An Essays on the Commercialization of Indian Agriculture* (ed.), Oxford University Press, Delhi.

Rajaraman, Indira (1986): "Offered Wage and Recipient Attribute: Wage Functions for Rural Labour in India". *Journal of Development Economics,* Vol. 24, No. 1, pp. 179-195

Rajaraman, Indira (1987): "Contractual Aspects of Daily Hire: Rural Labour in India". *Journal of Developing Areas,* Vol. 21, No. 4, pp. 459-480.

Rajaraman, Indira (1987): "Labour Supply Functions with Incomplete Information". *Indian Economic Journal,* Vol. 34, No. 4, pp. 112-119.

Rangi, P.S., Sidhu, M.S. and Singh, Harjit (2001): "Casualisation of Agricultural Labour in Punjab". *Indian Journal of Labour Economics,* Vol. 44, No. 4, pp. 957-970.

Rao, V.K.R.V. (1962): *Agricultural Labour in India* (ed.), Asia Publishing House, New Delhi.

Ray, Raka and Quayum, Seemin (2010): *Cultures of Servitude: Modernity, Domesticity, and Class in India*, Oxford University Press, Delhi.

Reddy, M. Achi (1991): "Work and Leisure: Daily Working Hours of Agricultural Labourers, Nellore District (1860-1989)". *Indian Economic and Social History Review*, Vol. 28, No. 1, pp. 73-95.

Reddy, M. Atchi (1983): "Labour Relations in Andhra Pradesh Agriculture: 1881-1981." *Indian Journal of Labour Economics*, Vol. 26, No. 3, pp. 160-187.

Reimer, CW (1983): "Labour Market Discrimination Against Hispanic and Black Men." *The Review of Economics & Statistics*, Vol. 65, No. 4, pp. 570-579.

Reynolds, Lloyd, G. (1975): *Agriculture in Development Theory* (ed.), Yale University Press, New Haven, C.T.

Richard, Alan (1979): "The Political Economy of Gutswirtschaft: A Comparative Analysis of East Elbian Germany, Egypt and Chile". *Comparative Studies in Society and History*, Vol. 21, No. 4, pp. 483-518.

Rodgers, G.B. (1975). "Nutritionally Based Wage Determination in the Low Income Market". *Oxford Economic Papers*, Vol. 27, No. 1, pp. 61-81.

Rodgers, Gerry and Rodgers, Janine (1984): "Incomes and Work Among the Poor of Rural Bihar, 1971-1981". *Economic and Political Weekly*, Vol. 19, No. 13, pp. A17-A28.

Rogaly, Ben (1997): "Embedded Markets: Hired Labour Arrangements in West Bengal Agriculture." *Oxford Development Studies*, Vol. 25, No. 2, pp. 209-223.

Rosenzweig Mark R. (1980): "Neoclassical Theory and the Optimizing Peasant: An Econometric Anlaysis of Market Family Labour Supply in a Developing Country". *Quarterly Journal of Economics*, Vol. 94, No. 1, pp. 31-55,

Rosenzweig, Mark R. (1978): "Rural Wages, Labour supply and Land Reform: A Theoretical and Empirical Analysis". *American Economic Review*, Vol. 68, No. 5, pp. 847-861.

Rosenzweig, Mark R. (1988): "Risk Implicit Contracts and the Family in Rural Areas of Low Income Countries". *The Economic Journal*, Vol. 98, No. 393, pp. 1148-1170.

Roy, Shyamal and Blase, Melvin G. (1978): "Farm Tractorisation, Productivity and Labour Employment: A Case Study of Indian Punjab". *Journal of Development Studies*, Vol. 14, No. 2, pp. 193-209.

Roy, Tirthankar (2000): *The Economic History of India (1857-1947)*, Oxford University Press, Delhi.

Rudra, Ashok (1971): "Employment Patterns in Large Farms of Punjab". *Economic and Political Weekly*, Vol. 6, No. 26, pp. A89-A94.

Rudra, Ashok (1982): *Extra Economic Constraints on Agricultural Labour: Results of an Intensive Survey in Some Villages Near Santiniketan, West Bengal*, ILO-ARTEP, Bangkok.

Rudra, Ashok (1982): *Indian Agricultural Economics: Myths and Realities*, Allied Publishers, New Delhi.

Rupal, Gurcharan Singh (1979): "Punjab: Canada for Bhaias", *The Punjabi Tribune*, April 23.

Ryan, James G., 1980): *Wage Functions for Daily Labour Market Participants in Rural South India*, Mimeo, ICRISAT.

Sahn, David E. and Alderman, Harold (1988): "The Effects of Human Capital on Wages and the Determinants of Labour Supply in a Developing Country". *Journal of Development Economics*, Vol. 29, No. 2, pp. 157-83.

Sahota, Gian Singh (1978): "Theories of Personal Income Distribution: A Survey". *Journal of Economic Literature*, Vol. 16, No. 1, pp. 1-55.

Sanan, Manjula (1985): *Growth of Agricultural Labourers in India: An Empirical Investigation*, M.Phil. (Dissertation), Dept. of Economics, Panjab University, Chandigarh.

Sarkar, Suman (1986): "India's Agricultural Development: An Alternative Path". *Economic and Political Weekly*, Vol. 21, No. 19, pp. 825-836.

Schaffner, Julie Anderson (1993): "Rural Labour Legislation and Permanent Agricultural Employment in North Eastern Brazil". *World Development*, Vol. 21, No. 5, pp. 705-719.

Schaffner, Julie Anderson (1995): "Attached Farm Labour, Limited Horizons and Servility". *Journal of Development Economics*, Vol. 47, No. 2, pp. 241-270.

Schultz, Theodore, W. (1961): "Investment in Human Capital." *American Economic Review*, Vol. 51, No. 1, pp. 1-17.

Schultz, Theodore, W. (1964): *Transforming Traditional Agriculture*, New Haven, Yale University Press, New Haven.

Sen, Bhowani (1962): *Evolution of Agrarian Relations in India*, People's Publishing House, Delhi.

Sharma, Devinder (1986): "Migrant Flow Unabated", *The Indian Express*, April, 13.

Shergill, H.S. (1982): *Land Market Transactions and the Process of Growth and Decay of Peasant Farms: A Case Study of Sangrur District in Punjab*, Department of Economics, Panjab University, Chandigarh.

Shergill, H.S. (1987): "Impact of New Technology on the Employment of Share-Wage Annual Servants on Punjab Farms". *Indian Journal of Labour Economics,* Vol. 29, No. 4, pp. 72-81.

Sidhu, M.S, Joshi, A.S. and Kaur, Inderpreet (2007): *A Study on Migrant Agricultural Labour in Punjab,* Department of Economics and Sociology, Punjab Agricultural University, Ludhiana.

Sidhu, M.S. and Grewal, S.S. (1984): *A Study on Migrant Agricultural Labour in Punjab,* Department of Economics and Sociology, Punjab Agricultural University, Ludhiana.

Sidhu, M.S., Rangi, P.S. and Singh, Karam (1997): *A Study on Migrant Agricultural Labour in Punjab,* Department of Economics and Sociology, Punjab Agricultural University, Ludhiana.

Silverberg, James (1968): *Social Mobility in the Caste System in India* (ed.), Mourton Publishers, Hague.

Singh, Gurmukh and Singh, Nirmal (1978): "Patterns of Employment and Wage Structure of Annual Farm Servants in Different Regions of Punjab", *Agricultural Situation in India,* November, pp. 501-503.

Singh, Master Hari (1980): *Agricultural Workers' Struggle in Punjab,* People's Publishing House, New Delhi.

Singh, Pritam (1976): *Some Aspects of Labour Use in Punjab Agriculture: A Study of Ferozepur District from 1967-68 to 1969-70,* M.Phil. Dissertation, Centre for Political Studies, School of Social Sciences, Jawaharlal Nehru University, New Delhi.

Skoufias, Emmannuel (1993): "Seasonal Labour Utilization in Agriculture: Theory and Evidence from Agrarian Households in India". *American Journal of Agricultural Economics,* Vol. 75, No. 1, pp. 20-32.

Smith, L., Briggs, V.R. Brian and Smith, James. (1978): "Wage and Occupational Differences Between Black and White Men: Labour Market Discrimination in the Rural South", *Southern Economic Journal,* Vol. 45, No. 1, pp. 250-257.

Soni, R.N. (1970): "The Recent Agricultural Revolution and the Agricultural Labour". *Indian Journal of Agricultural Economics,* Vol. 25, No. 3, pp. 23-28.

Srinivasan, T.N. and Bardhan, P.K. (1988): *Rural Poverty in South Asia* (ed.), Oxford University Press, Delhi.

Stigler, G.J. (1962): "Information in the Labour Market". *Journal of Political Economy,* Vol. 70, No. 5 (Part 2), pp. 94-105.

Stigler, Georje J. (1946): *Domestic Servants in the United States: 1900-1940,* Occasional Paper No. 24, NBER, N.Y.

Stiglitz, J.E. (1976): "The Efficiency Wage Hypothesis Surplus Labour and Distribution of Income in LDCs". *Oxford Economic Papers,* Vol. 28, No. 2, pp. 185-207.

Sumner, Daniel, A. and Frazao, Elizabeth (1989): "Wage Rates in a Poor Rural Area with Emphasis on the Impact of Farm and Non-Farm Experience". *Economic Development and Cultural Change,* Vol. 37, No. 4, pp. 709-718.

Swaminathan, Madhura (1997): "The Determinants of Earnings Among Low Income Workers in Bombay: An Analysis of Panel Data." *Journal of Development Studies,* Vol. 33, No. 4, pp. 535-551.

Tandon, B.B. (1984): "Wage Differentials Between Scheduled Caste and Non-Scheduled Caste Agricultural Labour". *Indian Journal of Labour Economics,* Vol. 27, No. 3, pp. 119-137.

Taslim, M.A. (1989): "Supervision Problems and the Size Productivity Relations in Bangladesh Agriculture". *Oxford Bulletin of Economics & Statistics,* Vol. 51, No. 1, pp. 55-71.

Thorner, Daniel (1955): *The Agrarian Prospects in India,* Delhi University Press, Delhi.

Vaidyanathan, A. (1986): "Labour Use in Rural India: A Study of Temporal and Spatial Variations". *Economic and Political Weekly,* Vol. 21, No. 52, pp. A130-A146.

Vanackere, Martine (1988): "Conditions of Agricultural Day Labourers in Mexico". *International Labour Review,* Vol. 127, No. 1, pp. 91-110.

Wachtel, H. and Betsey, C. (1972): "Employment at Low Wages". *Review of Economics and Statistics,* Vol. 54, No. 2, pp. 121-129.

Weiss, L.W. (1966): "Concentration and Labour Earnings". *American Economic Review,* Vol. 56, Nos. 1&2, pp. 96-117.

Government Publications

Agricultural Labour Enquiry Report on Intensive Survey of Agricultural Labour, Vol. I, Ministry of Labour, Government of India, 1955.

Agricultural Labour Enquiry Report: Report on the Second Agricultural Labour Enquiry, Ministry of Labour, Government of India, 1956-57.

All India Rural Credit Survey (Districts Jullundur and Bathinda), RBI, 1959.

An Economic Survey of Village Bairampur (District Hoshiarpur), The Board of Economic Enquiry, 1922.

An Economic Survey of Village Kala Gaddi Thamman (District Lyallpur), The Board of Economic Enquiry (Government of Punjab),1932.

An Economic Survey of Village Suner (District Ferozepur), The Board of Economic Enquiry (Government of Punjab), 1936.

District Gazetteer Amritsar, 1914.

District Gazetteer, Amritsar, 1947.

District Gazetteer, Ferozepur, 1915.

District Gazetteer, Gurdaspur, 1912.
District Gazetteer, Gurdaspur, 1914.
District Gazetteer, Ludhiana, 1904.
District Gazetter, Jalandhar, 1883-1884.
District Gazetter, Jalandhar, 1904
Labour: Employment, Underemployment, Wages and Levels of Living (North West India), Vol. VII, Ministry of Labour, Government of India, 1955.
Occupations or Means of Livelihood (Table XV, Part II), Census of Punjab, 1901.
Punjab State Gazetteer, Faridkot State, 1907.
Report of the Indian Famine Commission (Reply to Inquiries of Commission), 1898.
*Report of the Royal Commission on Agriculture in India,*1928.
Resurvey of Village Chimna (District Ludhiana), The Board of Economic Enquiry (Government of Punjab),1961.
Resurvey of Village Gijhi (District Rohtak), The Board of Economic Enquiry (Government of Punjab),1960.
Resurvey of Village Tehong (District Jullundur), The Board of Economic Enquiry (Punjab), 1962.
Settlement Report, Tehsil Batala, 1909.
Some Aspects of Landholdings in Rural Areas, National Sample Survey (Seventh Round), 1961-1962.
Special Monograph on Birth Place Migration in India, Census of India, 1971.
Studies in the Economics of Farm Management in Punjab, Ministry of Agriculture (Government of India), 1954-55 and 1956-57.

Index